Palgrave Macmillan Studies in Banking and Financial Institutions

Series Editor: Professor Philip Molyneux

The Palgrave Macmillan Studies in Banking and Financial Institutions are international in orientation and include studies of banking within particular countries or regions, and studies of particular themes such as Corporate Banking, Risk Management, Mergers and Acquisition. The books' focus is on research and practice, and they include up-to-date and innovative studies on contemporary topics in banking that will have global impact and influence.

Titles include:

Bernardino Quattrociocchi
INTERNAL RATING SYSTEMS AND THE BANK-FIRM RELATIONSHIP
Valuing Company Networks

Miao Han
CENTRAL BANK REGULATION AND THE FINANCIAL CRISIS
A Comparative Analysis

Pierluigi Ciocca
STABILISING CAPITALISM
A Greater Role for Central Banks

Anabela Sérgio (*editor*)
BANKING IN PORTUGAL

Michele Modina
CREDIT RATING AND BANK-FIRM RELATIONSHIPS
New Models to Better Evaluate SMEs

Jes Villa
ETHICS IN BANKING
The Role of Moral Values and Judgements in Finance

Dimitrios D. Thomakos, Platon Monokroussos &
Konstantinos I. Nikolopoulos (*editors*)
A FINANCIAL CRISIS MANUAL
Reflections and the Road Ahead

Elena Beccalli and Federica Poli (*editors*)
BANK RISK, GOVERNANCE AND REGULATION
LENDING, INVESTMENTS AND THE FINANCIAL CRISIS

Domenico Siclari (*editor*)
ITALIAN BANKING AND FINANCIAL LAW
Supervisory Authorities and Supervision
Intermediaries and Markets
Crisis Management Procedures, Sanctions, Alternative Dispute Resolution
Systems and Tax Rules

Dr. Fayaz Ahmad Lone
ISLAMIC FINANCE
Its Objectives and Achievements

Valerio Lemma
THE SHADOW BANKING SYSTEM
Creating Transparency in the Financial Markets

Imad A. Moosa
GOOD REGULATION, BAD REGULATION

Elisa Menicucci
FAIR VALUE ACCOUNTING
Key Issues arising from the Financial Crisis

Anna Omarini
RETAIL BANKING
Business Transformation and Competitive Strategies For The Future

Yomi Makanjuola
BANKING REFORM IN NIGERIA FOLLOWING THE 2009 FINANCIAL CRISIS

Ted Lindblom, Stefan Sjogren and Magnus Willeson (*editors*)
GOVERNANCE, REGULATION AND BANK STABILITY
FINANCIAL SYSTEMS, MARKETS AND INSTITUTIONAL CHANGES

Vincenzo Formisano
NON-KNOWLEDGE RISK AND BANK-COMPANY MANAGEMENT
The Role of Intangibles in Rating Models

Palgrave Macmillan Studies in Banking and Financial Institutions
Series Standing Order ISBN: 978–1–403–94872–4
(*outside North America only*)

You can receive future titles in this series as they are published by placing a standing order. Please contact your bookseller or, in case of difficulty, write to us at the address below with your name and address, the title of the series and the ISBN quoted above.

Customer Services Department, Macmillan Distribution Ltd, Houndmills, Basingstoke, Hampshire RG21 6XS, England

Non-Knowledge Risk and Bank-Company Management

The Role of Intangibles in Rating Models

Vincenzo Formisano
Associate Professor of Business Economics and Management, University of Cassino, Italy

palgrave
macmillan

First published 2016 by
PALGRAVE MACMILLAN

Palgrave Macmillan in the UK is an imprint of Macmillan Publishers Limited, registered in England, company number 785998, of Houndmills, Basingstoke, Hampshire RG21 6XS.

Palgrave Macmillan in the US is a division of St Martin's Press LLC, 175 Fifth Avenue, New York, NY 10010.

Palgrave Macmillan is the global academic imprint of the above companies and has companies and representatives throughout the world.

Palgrave® and Macmillan® are registered trademarks in the United States, the United Kingdom, Europe and other countries.

ISBN 978–1–137–49712–3

This book is printed on paper suitable for recycling and made from fully managed and sustained forest sources. Logging, pulping and manufacturing processes are expected to conform to the environmental regulations of the country of origin.

A catalogue record for this book is available from the British Library.

Library of Congress Cataloging-in-Publication Data
Formisano, Vincenzo, 1963–
Non-knowledge risk and bank-company management : the role of intangibles in rating models / Vincenzo Formisano.
pages cm. — (Palgrave Macmillan studies in banking and financial institutions)
Includes bibliographical references.
ISBN 978–1–137–49712–3
1. Banks and banking—Risk management—Europe. 2. Bank management—Europe. 3. Financial institutions—Europe. I. Title.
HG2974.F67 2015
332.1068′1—dc23 2015023528

Contents

Tables and Figures

Tables

Figures

Preface

Structural changes in the financial system that have happened over the past decade, and are still occurring, have expanded the range of possible evolutionary trajectories of the organizations which operate in it. This has determined, at the same time, an improvement of the relationship between banks and businesses, with particular reference to the administration of the risks of the banking business.

Coherently with the viable system approach adopted in this work, the bank is a viable enterprise system, since it has the defining characteristics of this abstract category.

In this regard, using the basics of the above-mentioned approach, the goal to be pursued with this book is to analyze the risk of lack of knowledge in the management of banks, with particular reference to the role of intangibles in the assessment of creditworthiness.

The theoretical models of reference are the classic ones of management studies. The viewpoint from which the bank is studied, is that of a company that provides financial services to a client company – with conditions and pricing – just as happens in a normal customer–supplier relationship. Such an approach to the study of banking is innovative compared to traditional models of theories, typically treated as a part of the banking technique. Indeed, it shifts the focus from technical tools (such as loans, credit limits, and checking accounts) to the administration of risk with particular regard to the risk of credit and the role of intangible assets in the current rating models.

The logical path through which the present work articulates, is developed in six chapters.

Chapter 1 deals with the analysis of the context. In this area, starting from the definition of the systemic-life key of the financial system, the attention is focused on the governing body and the operational structure of such a system, with particular reference to the Italian reality. This is necessary to overcome some basic ambiguity and open the way to an interpretation of the banking system as a vital one. To all this we must add that, in an increasingly globalized context, all types of business, and therefore also banks, must have the ability to combine the objectives of creating both economic and social value, as effectively argued in studies of strategic management and emphasized in the Social Doctrine of the Church. In this context,the key role of the bank in creating values,and generating positive effects for the development of entire regions, becomes clear. In this sense, it is clear that cooperative banks and areas to which they belong co-evolve in search of competitive advantages, being resourceful for the development of both.

In this dialectic of mutual interdependencies, the culture of solidarity, along with the ethics matrix that historically characterizes the cooperative bank, as well as its structural and dimensional characteristics, play an important role. There will be important repercussions for the same development possibilities of the bank and its local social and institutional context.

From this perspective, the merging reality of forms of association on the territory promoted by smaller cooperative banks, here called local network of mutuality, are the result of adaptation processes to a social and institutional context that is changing. These networks, in turn, represent organizational forms able to exercise significant influences over the territories in which small banks operate, being able to represent a driving force for a healthy and more human development of more areas, more local communities, and more businesses.

In Chapter 2, the fundamental aspects behind the Basel Accords are analyzed. These aimed at strengthening the minimum assets of banks, and increasing risk management, thereby enhancing the efficiency, productivity, reliability, and solidity of the international financial system. In this context, the two methods the banks can adopt to evaluate credit risk are examined in depth: the standardized approach and the internal ratings-based (IRB) approach (which has two versions – foundation and advanced). The choice between the two methods – that differ in complexity, the nature of the assigned rating, and the number of computed variables – is essential, as it must be as coherent as possible with respect to the risk and the operational reality of the bank. The chapter ends with the highlighting of the weaknesses in Basel II which, after the international financial crisis, led the Basel Committee to supplement the existing Accord, thus strengthening it.

Chapter 3 is dedicated to the in-depth analysis of the conception of the bank as a viable system enterprise, since it has the defining characteristics of this abstract category. The bank is emerging, in fact, as a viable system of order L, consisting of a governing body and an operating structure, which operates within a financial system also composed of a governing body (ECB–Bank of Italy) and an operating structure in which the banking institutions represent a relevant component. The financial system exerts pressures and expectations, it imposes rules and constraints, and it aims at survival through the acquisition of competitive advantages needed to create value. The financial system is, therefore, composed of a set of elements, institutions, markets, and companies in connection with each other and with the components of other systems. From the practicality of this group of elements, responsible for the management of financial flows through the implementation of financial transactions, the financial system emerges, and is qualified as a supra-system of order L+1, compared to the banking viable system of order L, and is in a mediated way compared to other business organizations. The peculiarity of the banking business, and in particular the relationship with the ECB–Bank of Italy supra-system, forces the governing body, in its action, to respect rules, constraints, procedures, and comparisons with its own supervisory body. This makes binding its governance compared to other types of business. To all this, it must be added that the governing body not only acts on the operational structure of the bank, but it also has the task of managing banking risks. In fact, in recent years the Italian banking system has been undergoing a relevant transformation: among the elements of greatest innovation in banking management are the recent developments in the control and management of inherent risks in intermediation action.

Based on these considerations, in this chapter we will focus attention not only on the typical risks of credit intermediary activities, but also on those the viable system enterprise must deal with during its dynamic development. In the latter case, the reference is specifically directed to the unplanned and unknown risks. To protect themselves from unplanned risks, the company can transfer them outside the business – to insurance agencies, or by providing for specific funds internally to cover any possible losses. It can defend itself from the effects generated by the risks of not knowing by preparing a defense in charge of the property, which is called the allocated capital.

Chapter 4 focuses on the analysis of intra-systemic and inter-systemic relationships, with particular reference to both the bank–company relationship and its related risk/profit profile, and the bank–supervisory body relationship.

Chapter 5 deals with issues related to the analysis of intangibles of the company and their impact on the qualitative profile of their rating. The key questions are: What is the role of intangibles in the rating system? What qualitative information must the current models integrate? With the support of empirical research, this chapter attempts to identify a possible rating model in which the weight of intangible assets is completed by an algorithm that takes into account the local contexts in which the company operates.

In the final chapter, the credit scenario is analyzed at European, national, regional, and provincial levels. A sample survey has been carried out with the aim of examining in depth the main critical factors in the approach to the financial management of companies in the Italian province of Frosinone, and their relationship with the banking system with the entry into force of the Basel Accords.

All quotations from other publications have been translated by this author, unless stated otherwise.

1
The Context: The Financial System

1.1 The viable financial system

The functioning of the financial system, given the nature of the activity, takes place in a context of rules and controls. The raison d'être of the financial system is linked to the performance of certain functions that are critical, due to the way a modern economy of monetary exchange runs. These functions satisfy the specific needs of the economic system, thus allowing the development of production and distribution processes.

The financial system realizes, through the production and supply of financial services, three fundamental processes of the functioning of a modern economy:

1. Regulation of trade.
2. The accumulation of savings and investment financing.
3. Risk management.

A system which bases its functionality on the specialization and diversity of positions must have highly developed and efficient mechanisms for exchange and regulation of trade.

One of the factors behind the functionality of trade is the system of payments, and therefore the adequacy of monetary tools through which commercial transactions can be adjusted. One can understand the progress which has been possible, moving from a barter economy to a monetary one in which money is accepted as currency trading.

Currency trading is able to measure the value of goods traded and is widely accepted as a settlement of a transaction. The theme of this evolution has been the search for new means of payment that can reduce transaction costs and make balancing less risky.

The accumulation and allocation of savings constitute two fundamental aspects of the financial system. They assume that the system creates the most favorable conditions in order to make correct decisions (Barile, 2009b), pertaining to:

1. Saving (propensity to accumulation) on behalf of those with surplus income on consumption.
2. Investment of savings (choice of savings).
3. Financing of parties in deficit (forms of investment financing).

More favorable conditions mean, therefore, offering savers and end-users of the financial resources the strongest incentives, not only to maximize the volume of available resources, but also to activate forms and transfer circuits that make fundable, where possible, investments with higher expected profitability, given a certain level of risk.

The achievement of such a result falls within the concept of allocative efficiency. The financial system operates in order to make the process of transfer of resources functional and efficient in several ways: the definition of contractual forms, the development of markets as an organized meeting of parties with conflicting requirements, the production of price information, the presence of financial intermediaries able to perform integrative exchange market functions (ideal unassisted crossing of sellers and buyers) and to offer services that facilitate the circulation of financial tools.

The exceptional nature of the financial activity in general recalls a fundamental aspect which is the risk related to it; therefore the demand for mechanisms and operating procedures which favor the reduction of this risk will be compulsory.

Traditionally, capitalist economic systems are divided into two groups: first, the Anglo-Saxon model (UK and US) is a financial system focused on the market; the second model, formed especially in Germany and Japan, based its financial system on the prevailing role of intermediaries (Demirgüç-Kunt and Levine, 1999; Allen and Gale, 2000; Levine, 2002; Beck and Levine, 2004; Forestieri, 2011; Hardie and Howarth, 2013; Sawyer, 2014).

Schematically, we have the following models:

- Market-based model: characterized by the broad shareholder; relations between banks and companies are based on the short term; the number of listed companies is significant in relation to the industrial structure.

- Bank-based model: business ownership is highly concentrated and the relationship between banks and enterprises develops in the long term. The number of listed companies is relatively small. In these systems, banks play a significant role in the pattern of ownership of companies, constituting the main source of funding in the medium and long term (Golinelli, 2008).

The Anglo-Saxon model is characterized by trust in the complete autonomy of the market to ensure the most effective and efficient resource allocation. It is believed that the market, realizing the full competitiveness of the system and offering the same opportunities to each operator, is able to select investment opportunities for companies. This is achieved by allocating resources to investments that are judged to be more valid because they are the most profitable, and exerting an *ex post* control on the pursuit of such profitability through the monitoring of these activities.

A characteristic, however, of the countries with bank-based systems is that these systems were established, in terms of world economic development, at a later time than the Anglo-Saxon model. The decision to base their financial system on intermediaries was, for these countries, a result of a practical need to fill the gap of technology and industry more quickly than those countries where it would have been necessary to ensure a gradual development of the capital market, at that time still too limited, to fully support economic development.

For this reason, a financial system centered on the role of intermediaries, and in particular on the banking system that performs the dual role of lender and controller, lent its purpose effectively.

In an analysis of the differences between the two models, it is necessary to note the following. Those who favor the bank-based system argue that the dense network of relations that is established by intermediaries allows the creation of long-term oriented links. They are able to overcome the problem of asymmetric information and related distortions, known as adverse selection (Akerlof, 1970; Mirrlees, 1971; Stiglitz and Weiss, 1981; Myers and Majluf, 1984; Amit, Glosten, and Muller, 1990; Frank and Goyal, 2003; Brown et al., 2009; Scheuer, 2013); and moral hazard (Stiglitz and Weiss, 1983; Bizer and DeMarzo, 1992; Church, 1992; Bhattacharya and Thakor, 1993; Boot and Thakor, 1994; Ghosh, Mookherjee, and Ray, 1999; Laffont and Martimort, 2002; Berndt and Gupta, 2009).

At the same time, however, in those systems oriented towards intermediaries, and in particular towards banks, there is an underlying risk of a commingling of interests that are not compatible, allowing collusion between banks and businesses. The risk in this case is twofold. On the one hand, you configure the possibility that the close relationship of the company with the bank can be pathologically binding, assuming that this ratio appears uneconomic and that the management of the business can be unbalanced by excessive borrowing. On the other hand, situation of disequilibrium, both management and bank decisions may be binding and forced.

For the supporters of market-oriented systems, however, the supremacy of the market in the role of effective controller and timely indicator of capacity in financial businesses, makes it clear how it tends to be seen as a much more flexible tool, compared to a system of intermediaries, in responding promptly to real economic changes and needs. On the other hand, the opponents of the market-oriented system, have correctly pointed out that the market is subject to distortions that occur in the form of speculation and fluctuations due to financial or economic phenomena, and that these distortions manifest themselves in what is commonly called market failure (Scanagatta, 1995).

In fact, where certainty and complete information is lacking, the role of intermediaries regains its utility, allowing the economy to finance itself on better terms than in the case of their absence. On this aspect, Arcelli (1994) was very clear, stating that "it is rejected as unrealistic the hypothesis that if between the investor and the borrower there is a well-functioning market, the cost of intermediation is still an additional cost. Such view would confine banks and financial intermediaries in the category of rentiers intended to be swept away over time by increasingly efficient markets that would manage directly the allocation of resources."

On closer inspection, however, as stated by Golinelli (2000), the distinction between the two models seems to be gradually losing significance with the belief that the efficient allocation of financial resources is based on the interdependence of banks and markets.

For this reason, Golinelli concludes that:

> The existence of different categories of operators offering funds (institutional and individual investors) and demand for funds (small and large companies) causes comparative advantages for both models. This realization is setting in the convergence of the two models, market-based and bank-based, towards a structure of the financial system in which credit intermediaries and financial markets are in a balanced relationship of mutual complementarity. In this system, the burden related to the understanding of the indeterminacy shrinks

in relation to the possibility that the investment projects are continually examined jointly by – banks and markets – that operate with different timing and with different information.

1.2 Governing body of the European financial system

Taking into account the constitutive elements of the financial system, this, similarly to the business system, is considered as a viable system and is characterized by the presence of a governing body and an operational structure.

At a European level, the Maastricht Treaty represents the tool through which institutional innovations have been promoted (birth of the European Central Bank) and economic policies coordinated. Monetary policy, at European level, has been transferred to the European System of Central Banks (ESCB), which is composed of The European Central Bank (ECB) and the Central National Banks (CNBs) of the 15 countries of the European Union (EU).

The ESCB is a complex system, designed on the model of the other important "federal" monetary authorities, such as the Federal Reserve System and the Deutsche Bundes bank.

The complexity mainly arises from the fact that opposite needs have to coexist: the centralization of decisions in addition to the decentralization of analysis activities and implementation deals of the monetary policy.

The decision-making centralization is sought through the uniqueness of the ECB management system.

The main function of the governing body at a European level – the management of the monetary policy – is combined with other skills that, to some extent, are complementary to the execution of the first and main goal. The exchange rate policy and the official reserve management are relevant not only from a purely technical point of view, but also with regards to the target of price stability, which is fundamental to the management of monetary policy. The operation of payment systems has been historically included in the tasks of central banks, born as issuing banks and interested in monitoring the stability and efficiency of the money supply.

In such cases, the task of the governing body at European level has been to carry out an Automated Trans-European System of Real-time Gross Settlement (Target), a system which allows it to manage the liquidity positions of major participants, with arbitrage operations over the Euro area.

From the above-mentioned, and from a systemic viewpoint, we see that the purpose of survival is linked to the ability to create a single monetary policy whose primary goal is price stability (Golinelli, 2008). The preeminence of the aim of price stability has several explanations. Among the practical ones, the influence of the German model in the design of ESCB has to be pointed out (the Bundes bank has been historically linked to the aim of price stability), and the fact that the EMU project took shape in a period where the memory of the inflationary surges of the 1970s and 1980s still lingered.

With regard to the Italian experience, however, the governing body of the financial system consists in an organized set of institutions, designated to carry out the activities of planning, coordination, and control of the system. These functions of planning, coordination, and control on the operational structure, and in particular on the components – markets and credit intermediaries – are entrusted to the Bank of Italy and the governing body, CONSOB.

The decision-making functions of the governing body are divided into two major areas – *monetary policy* and the functions of *balancing and supervision*. The monetary policy function is included in the economic policy aims and relies on the decision-making functions in the field of monetary policy adopted by the governing body at the European level. The *operational management* of monetary policy is entrusted to the governing body of the financial system at the level of each individual EU country.

The *balancing and supervision* function is identified in a nutshell as the targets of *stability* and *efficiency* of the financial system. *Stability* serves to protect savers and the functionality of the payment system, and the governing body of the Bank of Italy carries this out jointly with the governing body at the European level (ECB).

Efficiency is understood in the double sense of *operational efficiency*, that is, the cost for the real economy of the financial activity, and *allocative efficiency*, which is the quality of the process of distribution of resources to alternative uses.

The targets of stability and efficiency are interdependent. In one aspect, it is a trade-off: maximizing results on the one involves increasing costs on the other. For instance, you can try to minimize the risk of instability; this involves a rigid balance, also from an administrative point of view, of the operation of the financial system.

Efficiency and stability, however, can also be seen in a complementary relationship. To some extent, this happens, for example, when the balance of information on the financial market ensures conditions for a proper and efficient operation of the same market, and it also limits the dangers of excessive price volatility that could result in a crisis of mistrust by investors. In the broadest sense, moving the reasoning beyond the short term, the reinforcement of the efficiency of financial intermediaries is a necessary condition to increase competitive capacity and, therefore, stability (as dependent on the success of competition).

As a body of protection of competition, the Bank of Italy has the task of supervising the market conduct of financial institutions, monitoring any potentially, or actually, harmful situations and behaviors of competition. In such a context, at an operational level, there is a close link with the supervisory actions; while at the institutional level, there is an integration with the activity of the Italian Competition Authority, exercising some of the general powers with regards to antitrust.

1.3 The operational structure: components, relations, and management processes with a particular regard to the Italian experience

The operational structure (area of management of the viable financial system) is based on two categories of components:

1. Markets.
2. Companies (financial intermediaries).

The functions of the financial markets may act in two main modes:

1. Means of transfer of resources within the economy between surplus units and deficit units.
2. Means of redistribution of the risk of real investment between employers and borrowers.

The combination of transfer and redistribution roles constitutes the main economic function of financial markets: the one which contributes to the efficient allocation of financial resources for the training of productive capital.

In an economic system, demand and supply of capital must tend to equilibrium and the capital investment has to be efficient in the sense that the marginal productivity of the different uses should be unvarying. Financial markets play a crucial economic role in making these two results achievable; the maximization of the aggregate return rate of productive capital and, ultimately, the performance of the entire economy, depend on them.

This is an economic function of the financial markets understood in a broad sense, that is, related to all types of tools, including credit ones.

More detailed consideration can be made, then, with regard to security markets.

With regards to the functions of security markets, there are aspects that qualify the activities of security markets that are strictly linked to the nature of negotiated tools and to the characteristics of the organizational form of the market.

These functions are:

- *Financing*: the issuance and placement of securities in the primary market (stocks, bonds) correspond to a supply of funds to the issuer.
- *Pricing*: of the negotiable securities and, implicitly, of the expected yield assessment for each security. As long as the yield expected by the investor represents the cost of capital for the issuer, there follows a direct effect on the demand for funds and thus an influence on the allocation process.
- *Liquidity of securities*: negotiable securities give rise to the secondary market, that is, an exchange system powered by the choices of investment/disinvestment of the participants. An efficient secondary market makes securities liquid regardless of their contract term; the liquidity perceived by investors is equivalent to a lower risk implying a rate of return/lower balance cost (it improves the financing of investments).
- *Reduction of transaction costs*: the operating costs of exchanges can be reduced if the exchanges themselves are concentrated in a structure with economic and organizational rationality (economies of scale, technical efficiency). The costs of information for investors, issuers, and intermediaries, in turn, are gradually more limited as the rules and procedures of the market reinforce the obligations of production and diffusion of information.
- *Transfer of the control*: of the joint-stock company (market for control) with a specific reference to the stock market; the negotiability of securities makes it possible to rebuild the shareholder structure of companies. This determines the possibility that the stock control moves from one shareholder to another, or among groups of shareholders. If the ownership is widespread enough, owner control is unstable. This creates an incentive for owners and management to

strengthen the company's position through improved performance and thus higher quotations. If this does not happen and the prices go down and the threat of *takeover* is possible. This game of conflicting interests represents, in a system of *public companies*, one of the mechanisms by which the market encourages improvement of business performance (thus of the economy).

The components of the market are divided into three levels: the subjects, tools, and procedures.

The subjects are summarized in three main categories: intermediaries (negotiators), managers of negotiation circuits, and control authorities. To these categories of the market, one must add those of the participants that use the market, or rather, the investors and issuers. The managers are responsible for the setting up and the operation of exchange and *pricing* circuits. For the controlling bodies, the growing role assumed by the authorities of self-regulation (management companies) has to be pointed out, with respect to what has been said concerning the supervisory bodies.

The little or no mutual visibility among the subjects of a system forces them to build organized meeting systems (markets) or to rely on intermediaries that facilitate contact. The difficulties in assessing the willingness and ability of those who take the funds to honor their commitments, has given rise to an endless variety of contractual tools aimed to protect the rights of lenders at different stages and in different forms. But the uncertainty that still remains on the outcome of such operations leads some to prefer the transfer to be carried out by specialized subjects (financial intermediaries) that are supposed to be the most gifted in both evaluating borrowers and in the diversification of risks.

The raison d'être of the financial intermediaries originates in the fact that they stand between the units in surplus and those in financial deficit, to break down the barriers that hinder direct transfer. They are, therefore, the ones who allow or facilitate transfer activities by eliminating or reducing the void of information that hinders the direct meeting of supply and demand. To do this, financial intermediaries assume certain roles, with the costs and consequent risks.

Financial intermediaries are not limited to letting the funds transit, as granted by the units in surplus (in those volumes, in those currencies, with the manner of determining rates), to units in deficit. To satisfy both parties, financial intermediaries, in fact, draw up two different contracts, in each of which the intermediary acts as counter party to one of the "home" contractors, managing the differences in their budgets. The transformation so performed may relate to: the deadline (they lend for a longer or shorter term than the expiry of the collection); the method of determining the rate (variable with respect to fixed, or vice versa); currency (collected in one way and loaned in another). They may finally provide the depositor with a lower degree of credit risk than the one the borrower offers them.

Such transformations represent, for financial intermediaries, some risks which could be managed in the specialization and in the numerosity of performed actions and then in diversification. It could be immediately noticed that, despite these changes, the brokerage activity is of a different nature compared to the one carried out by a pure mediator, who only puts in contact those who are willing to give money in exchange for financial assets, with whom he is willing to carry out the opposite operation.

A peculiarity of financial intermediaries is that they produce liabilities that are accepted as assets by the rest of the economy; that is, their ability to create their own tools to be placed on the market helps to extend the range of choices which can be experienced in the composition of portfolios of financial assets.[1] In other words, the role played by financial intermediaries is to make the choices of portfolio composition of the units in surplus compatible with the choices of indebtedness of the units in deficit (Onado, 1992). This depends on the ability of financial intermediaries to issue liabilities with the conditions of risk and liquidity as the units in surplus, in addition to acquiring business with the units in deficit. The latter can be short term and low risk, or have a longer deadline and higher risks. Based on all this, it is evident that financial intermediaries transform deadlines.[2] This is achieved by drawing up diverse contractual conditions with borrowers and with resource providers, as well as carrying out the function of risk transformation, meaning that the risk of the subscriber-buyer is less than the weighted average of the risks of the individual assets constituting the portfolio.

The existence of financial intermediaries is justified not only in satisfying different preferences in the composition of the portfolio and in indebtedness, but also in the canalization of savings formed through planned investment. The importance of their activities does not come, then, only from the need to reconcile changes of sign and amount in the financial balances of individuals and economic sectors, but also to adjust, little by little, the suitable volume of resources to the expansive process of investments in the economic system.

Financial intermediaries also perform a number of functions that are of great importance for the economic system as a whole. These functions are essentially related to the following:

- The transfer of financial balances, which consists in addressing resources from individuals and sectors in surplus to those in deficit, thus playing a role of specific support to the expansion of liabilities and financial assets in the context of the needs arising in the economic system. It is, therefore, a basic function of financial intermediation that allows you to combine different preferences, both in terms of supply and demand, and the conditions of risk, liquidity, and yield.
- Financial transformation, which consists in the trading activity (usually with a longer time constraint than that experienced over the corresponding liabilities) and, at the same time, in the modification of the respective attributes of the interest rate, liquidity, divisibility of the amounts, and repayment and risk techniques. In this function, what is important is not so much the mere transfer of funds from surplus areas to deficit areas, as the change in deadlines and in the overall attributes negotiated on liabilities and financial assets.
- Allocation of financial resources, which consists in the distribution of these resources between individuals and areas, selecting the most deserving initiatives and the most suitable technical forms, and, at the same time, varying the quantitative modes of loans to customers. The concrete manifestation of this function introduces discriminations between customer categories and sectors of the economy, creating a different degree of riskiness of the assets.
- Diversification of risk, which is the choice of the activities in the financial portfolio of individual intermediaries to optimize the risk/yield combination. With the same performance, the risk of financial assets can be reduced, or, with the same risk, the yield can be increased. It follows that, for the same yield linked to each activity, the risk can be lowered through their suitable composition, which is easily achievable by financial intermediaries for the containment and the saving they achieve in transaction costs.
- Production of information, which consists in the collection and processing of information and data for customer categories and economic sectors, which are used to make decisions on the investment policy. In this sense, financial intermediaries perform systematic

investigations on applicants to judge their degree of reliability and, therefore, on the same selection of investment initiatives. The mass of information so obtained is not recycled in the market, as it is intended for internal use only. The production function of information is affected by subjective factors related to the procedures followed in processing and analyzing data.

- Management of payment mechanisms, which is the creation of suitable instruments, by certain types of financial intermediaries, to be used to execute payments among different individuals. This function is essentially carried out by commercial banks, which are inserted into the payment system through the circulation of their debts. However, in more advanced systems, other financial intermediaries offer use of their own instruments for the balance of payments. This function has been improved through the use of technology, creating new instruments to facilitate the balance of payments; it also assumes considerable importance for trade facilitation, both internally within individual countries and internationally.
- Risk management, which consists in the careful selection and control of risk. The different financial intermediaries reveal a system of risks in their efficiency that must be carefully considered and evaluated, not to undermine the confidence of the public and of the holders of the liabilities of these risks. The different risks assume their proper identification through a process of composition of items in and out of the budget that involves elements of flexibility and balance.

It is easy to detect the existence of correlations and interdependencies between the functions taken into account and the previously considered ones, pointing out the importance of rational and consistent choices within a unitary scheme.

1.4 The purpose of the financial system: between efficiency and stability

The process of globalization of markets and the internationalization of the financial market, as well as the profound changes in the forms of trading and the appearance of new participants, led the governing body to change the types of participation in the system. This was necessary to stimulate a greater efficiency in the management of banks, in order to develop the brokerage business in terms of efficiency and stability and, therefore, to "prevent the systemic instability based on a careful assessment the elements of potential vulnerabilities in the financial system at the global level" (Golinelli, 2000).

The action of the governing body has taken on an even more important role concerning the systemic protection of the stability and efficiency of banks. The governing body has supported the traditional centrality of stability with the need to encourage the efficiency of intermediaries. Stability, efficiency, and therefore competitiveness of intermediaries, have become the goals to pursue for the financial system.

To achieve these aims, the governing body has gradually replaced instruments based on a *structural* supervision, able to directly affect the system, to *prudential* instruments, to the establishment of general rules of conduct, in principle not waived, where each intermediary could perform their own business independently.

With the transition to prudential supervision by the governing body, the preservation of the basic principles of system stability, which can prevent possible corporate crises, has not been neglected – although it cannot prevent the occurrence of individual failures.

Stability was put on an equal level with respect to the purposes of efficiency and competition. The pursuit of these last two aims is precisely instrumental to prevent the widespread inefficiency and inability to sustain the impact of competition that help to make the financial system less solid by exposing it more.

Among the purposes of the supervision of the governing body, the most widespread one within the various theoretical approaches remains, however, the overall stability of the financial system. The various theoretical approaches agree on considering the danger of instability as a characteristic element of finance; given the centrality of intermediation in allocating resources and in the process of accumulation, there is common concern about the possible consequences for labor and production markets. It follows that the maintenance of confidence in the financial system should be secured by ensuring the overall stability of the financial system. The possibility that an individual bank is declared insolvent is not excluded, therefore; in this case, the need for the stability of the system will require the governing body to take action to prevent a crisis of confidence.

All financial systems at European level have a governing body, which is given powers of direction, coordination, and control of the operational structure. Everywhere, these powers are wielded, more or less explicitly, in order to protect stability.

Less obvious is an indication of the purposes of efficiency and competitiveness of the financial system. In a very broad sense, efficiency refers to the ability to ensure that the transfer of financial resources, which the economic system needs, takes place at minimal costs (Lamanda, 1994); therefore, costs induced by supervision also have to be kept low. This means that the government body of the financial system, and in particular the Bank of Italy, needs to keep in mind, and to contain, the costs caused by its actions.

But efficiency signifies, even in its allocative dimension, the ability of intermediaries to direct financial resources to the most deserving uses.

This concept solicits the governing body to always keep in mind the compliance of the financial system with the needs of the real economy, its ability to support innovative processes and to constantly improve the quality of services offered (Aguiari and Di Nauta, 2012; Badinelli et al., 2012).

1.5 Globalization, crisis, and values in the Italian bank system: theoretical framework

The economic and financial crisis we are experiencing is not only the *cause* of the destruction of economic value, the collapse of investment, and misuse of finance; it is also the *result* of a lack of values reflected in the weakening of "the common sense of doing business" (Cafferata, 2009b), and almost in the loss of meaning that the institutions responsible for the protection of the common interest have suffered (Becchetti, 2005; Velo, 2009; Yang and Casali, 2009; Vargas and Vaca Acosta, 2009). The crisis in values and meaning has affected companies in the most advanced parts of the Western world. This is demonstrated by the serious recent and past dysfunctions that affected large, worldwide enterprises, highlighting some important issues of transparency and accountability, as well as of balance of business.

On this subject, the Church's Social Doctrine has repeatedly made fundamental contributions. In the wake of the *Centesimus Annus* Encyclical, the *Caritasin Veritate* (§7) makes its specific contribution, which is based on the principle of solidarity, which means "taking care, on the one hand, and relying on the other, on that complex of institutions that give structure to the social life juridically, civilly, politically, and culturally, which in such way, takes the form of the polis, the city."

There is a high level of convergence in the Italian business management culture of the possibility of both business and consumers acting based not only on simple economic-utilitarian reasons but also on ethical and accountability ones, towards its *stakeholders* and towards future generations.

Testimony to this is the growth, and the high speculative level, of reflections on the social responsibility of the company (Matacena, 1984; Coda, 1985; Caselli, 1997; Sciarelli, 2007; Cafferata, 2009a); and, more recently, on the social responsibility of the consumer (Caselli, 2003; Velo, 2003; Pepe, 2007); as well as the considerable field research carried out in this regard (Molteni and Lucchini, 2004; Golinelli, 2009).

To all those companies that want to last over time, a new consciousness and a more careful ability to combine the creation of economic and social value is required, as effectively argued in studies of strategic management (Porter and Kramer, 2007) and emphasized in the Social Doctrine of the Church (CV §40).

This is also applied to the bank business and more generally to finance (Antonucci, 2007; Golinelli, 2008), especially in our time. You cannot, in fact, forget that the purpose of operating a bank, as well as any other business, is to produce and meet the needs of the community to which it is referring (Cafferata, 2009b).

In this context, the key role of new forms of bank business in creating value, being generators of positive effects for the development of entire regions, is affirmed. In *Caritas in Veritate* (§45), these new forms are recognized, encouraged, and made explicit when referring to "banks offering accounts and investment funds, so-called 'ethical'." Development of an "ethical finance" system is achieved in certain circumstances through microcredit and, more generally, through microfinance.

These processes are praiseworthy and deserve a large amount of support. *Caritas in Veritate* (CV §38) also emphasizes the richness of the interaction among companies that pursue different institutional goals, stating that, "Next to the private profit-oriented company, and to the various types of public enterprise, productive organizations, which pursue mutual and social goals, must be able to root and express themselves. It is from their reciprocal encounter in the market that we can expect some sort of hybridization behaviour, and hence an attentiveness to the civilizing of the economy."

The above-mentioned principles are applied particularly in the cooperative banking sector. The purpose of a mutual cooperative bank is registered in the statute and in "articles of incorporation," and its pursuit necessarily involves an integration, in its management of "shareholders" with "stakeholders," of economic and social goals. This integration involves beliefs and values and requires fairness, sharing, and creativity but also the ability to produce profit, which remains important (CA §35), also for the *community of reference* (CV §40).

Between the local bank and its reference area, there is a *co-evolutionary relationship*, which requires ongoing attention to the dynamic coherence between the company and the local community, as well as the cultural synchronization with the evolution of the institutional context of reference (March, 1991; Lewin et al., 1999; Paniccia, 1999, 2002; Volberda and Lewin, 2003; Paniccia in Cafferata, 2004; Cafferata, 2009b).

In its dialectical co-evolutionary comparison with the local context, the bank must also demonstrate that it is able to transmit stimuli that are understandable outside, and to cause changes in the behavior rules of the entities in relation with it, primarily investors participating as co-stars in their system of value (CV §65).

To develop these abilities, cooperative banks, especially smaller ones, seem to meet fewer difficulties than large cooperative banks and banking groups in Italy. The local bank, in fact, with its local structuring, its mutualistic purpose, and microcredit activity that mostly characterizes it, is naturally integrated in the reference area and has an important role in the development of local social capital. It is structured and restructured according to the dynamics and characteristics of the territory of which it is a basic part. Moreover, thanks to the above features, it is by vocation, traditionally, the bearer of cultural values of solidarity and of an ethics matrix on which it leverages not only to thrive but also to engage in fruitful interaction with the territory of reference.

In this sense, the *local network of mutuality* is the result of processes of adaptation to changes taking place in the social and institutional context. Such networks in turn represent organizational forms able to exercise significant influence on the territories in which individual banks operate (Polese et al., 2009).

In conclusion, when discussing the *value* and *values*, with regard to the bank-business relationship and the environment, it is clear that economic value is important. However, we want to acknowledge here the value of people, who then become the value of the projects, but also cultural, ethical, and moral values, which are the *foundation of assurance* on which it is possible to create any healthy business development project, agreed with the political-institutional world as well.

1.6 Recent changes in the Italian bank system

The business economics and legal literature has overviewed the criticality and opportunities both of strategic choices made by banks and of regulation expected by the Consolidated Law on Banking, Legislative

Decree n. 385/93 (TUB), highlighting certain weaknesses of the regulatory mechanisms with consequences also for cooperative banks.[3]

In Italy, the banking system in the late 1980s appeared to be very much segmented, mainly controlled by the public and substantially impervious to foreign competition.[4] The 1990s were marked by profound changes that affected even the ownership structure. The main causes of the change were attributable to the privatization of the banking system, the liberalization of the credit market, the increasing integration of markets, technological and financial innovation, and internationalization.

A few large banking groups of significant size emerged (Onado, 1992), in which the culture of solidarity and the ethics matrix have not managed to survive, or have a low incidence. Despite their construction, they have often made an important contribution to savings banks and cooperative banks that are traditionally bearers of such values (Cesarini, 2003).

Consequently, an intense and generalized phase of owner reallocation was initiated in the banking system,[5] which led to the acquisition of local banks,[6] especially in the South,[7] by banking entities external to the territorial area of reference.

Against the above-mentioned deep structural changes, a broad and articulated debate started. The basic matter of this is synthesized by Giordano and Lopes (2008), who claim that the current structure of the Italian bank system is: "actually able to achieve those efficiency gains that inspired it or whether the future scenario will not impose the problem of the availability of credit to the thick Italian production or the one, more generally, of the absence of a virtuous model of bank–company relationships can work, as an agent of development of the Italian economy."[8] A summary of the debate leads us to point out the contribution of Brighi (2008), who compares the different types of banks, with their strengths and weaknesses, summarized in Table 1.1.

Field studies show conflicting results on the consequent effects of the aforementioned changes. Table 1.2 lists some of the most significant ones.

As we have seen, there are many people who believe that the local banks of a mutualistic nature are more effective in assisting small- and medium-sized enterprises (SMEs). In reference to the Italian case, the credit cooperative banks and cooperative banks are created and develop with a mutual vocation to support small productive activities within the local network of mutuality, revealing a predisposition to this effect even

Table 1.1 Different types of banks with their strengths and weaknesses

	Strong points	Weak points
National bank	Economies of scale and varieties Existence of more developed financial centers Quality of the available human capital	Lack of consolidated customer relationships on a local level Excessive standardization of financial services
Regional bank	Consolidated customer relationships Big enough to offer some financial services autonomously	Partial outsourcing of some advanced financial services
Small local bank	Consolidated customer relationships in the management of the so-called "ordinary" stages of an enterprise's life Competitive advantages in terms of interest rates and favorable optional conditions More flexibility in personalized services and counselling	Lack of economies of scale and purpose High costs in the qualification of the personnel with an outsourcing of the most advanced financial services to consortia and service desks, or as alternative group agreements or company agreements

Source: Author's elaboration on Brighi (2008).

more pronounced than the other local banks, such as the former savings banks (De Bruyn and Ferri, 2005).

1.7 Evolution in the segment of cooperative banks and related system of corporate governance

The cooperative credit bank is not an Italian peculiarity; on the contrary, it is present throughout continental Europe,[9] and, albeit to a lesser extent, also in the Anglo-Saxon nations.

Within the limits of a summary reading of regulations on cooperative banks, it can be said that most of the atypical nature of such banks in Italian banking is a direct consequence of their legislative framework.

Currently, cooperative banks in Italy continue to be an intermediate reality between cooperatives and corporations. Indeed, as cooperative

Table 1.2 Overview of the effects of the changes in the Italian banking system

Berger et. al. (1998) and **Bonaccorsi di Patti and Gobbi (2001)** point out that after mergers and acquisitions, even after increasing the average size of banks and reducing the numbers of local lending institutions, loans to the SMEs tend to be taken out at least in the short term.
Ferri (1997) and **Berger and Udell (2002)** claim that the consequences can be attributed also to other factors, such as the distance between the central management and the associated managements of the bank, as well as the management of the processes relating to *decision-making*, in addition to the role played by the bank in the acquisition (buyer or acquiree).
Sapienza (2002) shows that the acquisition increases the probability that the bank will cancel credit relationships, especially with the SMEs previously entrusted by the acquired bank.
Bonaccorsi di Patti and Gobbi (2003) do not point out any increase in the probability of rationing for the SMEs entrusted by the bank.
Panetta (2003) argues that the reorganization of the banking system in the south wouldn't have actually determined any negative consequences for the access to credit of the SMEs.
Ferri and Inzerillo (2002) conducted a search among SMEs and they came to the conclusion that in the south the credit rationing was perceived as a serious problem, and also that there was a related belief that, at least in part, the proprietary reorganization of southern banks played a role in this.
Brighi (2008) argues that the Italian consolidation process did not happen at the expense of the local banking system; but that, on the contrary, it emerged rather strengthened by it. The research conducted on aggregated data derived from the "Bollettino Statistico Banca d'Italia" points out a net result in favor of the smaller banks (medium, small, and minor). In particular, between 1997 and 2007, the percentage share of medium bank deposits of the total shows an increase of 8.55 percentage points, that of small and minor banks of 4.99 percentage points, while that of big and major banks decreases by 11.61 percentage points. This result was also confirmed when analyzing the shares of bank loans on the total: over the same period they showed an increase of 3.77 percentage points for medium banks, an increase of 7.86 percentage points for small and minor banks, while showing a decrease of 13.57 percentage points for big and major banks.
Bonaccorsi di Patti et al. (2005) point out that the consolidation process in Italy seems to have produced beneficial effects in terms of major credit granted by the local banks to the SMEs.
Amel et al. (2004) point out some advantages associated with the better screening of customers, and consequently they reveal more favorable economic conditions for good quality companies.

Source: Author's elaboration.

Table 1.3 Summary of main legislative evolutions in cooperative banks in Italy

Birth in the 19th century of the Luigi Luzzatti initiative. The absence of *specific* legislation meant that these institutions were entered into a particular branch of the joint-stock company, with two major limitations:

1. The shares could be held only by members of the cooperative (and affiliation was granted only to *desirable* individuals).
2. The vote was per capita.

The first limitation was later abandoned.

The Banking Act of 1936 continued to promote this corporate form without changing the frame of reference.

Legislative Decree n. 105/48 allowed cooperative banks for the first time to wholly distribute profits and asset liquidation to members, thereby placing them at odds with the **Basevi Law of 1947**, according to which the cooperative companies were instead indivisible.

L. n. 59/92 separated the regulation of cooperative banks from that of cooperative companies.

L. n. 207/92 established the transferability of the shares of cooperative banks, and in particular the transmissibility of the property rights if the buyer has not been admitted as a member.

Legislative Decree N. 481/92 (for reasons of capital strengthening and general interest of creditors) enabled cooperatives to transform into joint-stock companies or to implement mergers from which joint-stock companies arose (Art. 41, par. 2).

The **Consolidated Law on Banking (TUB) Legislative Decree n. 385/93** was the first comprehensive reform after the Banking Act of 1936. Not even the TUB, however, contained information on the operations of cooperatives (unlike what happened in the case of cooperative credit banks, for which Art. 35, par. 1 states that "they exercise credit predominantly to the members.").

Source: Author's elaboration.

banks, they are characterized, in accordance with the Consolidated Law on Banking, by the peculiarities highlighted in Table 1.4.

To confirm this, it is shown that the company law reform of Legislative Decree n. 6/2003 excludes banks. It follows that the corporate governance of the same keeps the typical setting of a cooperative with a *corporate governance* that should cover in its scope the mechanisms that regulate the *principal–agent* relationship and the *firm–stakeholder* relationship (Marris, 1964; Fama, 1980; Shleifer and Vishny, 1997), as well as the set of "relationships between a company's managements, its board of directors, its members and shareholders and other stakeholders" (OECD, 1999).

Table 1.4 The main peculiarities of the cooperative bank in the current Italian system

Vote per capita: each member has one vote, regardless of the number of shares held (Art. 30, par. 1).
Shareholding limit: no member may hold shares in excess of 0.5 per cent of the share capital (Art. 30, par. 2).
Minimum size of the shareholders: the minimum number of members cannot be less than 200 (Art. 30, par. 4).
Approval clause: the admission of an applicant as a member happens through a resolution of the board of directors (Art. 30, par. 5).
Variable capital: in accordance with the principle of "open door," the variations in the number of members to whom changes in share capital correspond are not subject to the formalities related to the change in capital assets, such as the amendment of the deed of incorporation.
10 per cent of profits to be compulsorily allocated to the legal reserve, that they may distribute profits to shareholders (Art. 32, par. 2).
They do not necessarily have to address service to members (there are no provisions on the efficiency of the bank).
Free transferability of shares (the full enjoyment of property rights) is not inhibited by the approval clause.

Source: Author's elaboration.

Such considerations also apply to cooperative banks, whose administrator members perform the difficult task of reconciling the integration of the various *shareholders* and *stakeholders*.[10] The failure to achieve this objective has a negative impact on the profitability of cooperative banks in the medium to long term.[11] Finally, some empirical research studies (Ferri et al., 2001; Pittaluga et al., 2005; Bongini and Ferri, 2007; Hesse and Čihák, 2007) have shown that, in the current context, cooperative banks, compared to limited banks, are characterized by a greater stability of directors and profits, and better financial strength.

1.8 The role of cooperative banks in the development of local networks of mutuality

The perception of the importance of the local bank for the development of the Italian economy, traditionally focused on SMEs enterprises, has its roots in the history of Italian credit policy, as highlighted in Table 1.5.

In the words of Menichella, there is therefore the intuition that the competitive advantage of local banks must be based on the combination

Table 1.5 Importance of the local bank for the development of the Italian economy

In the 1950s, the Bank of Italy, led by Donato Menichella, vigorously pursued the development of local banking. In order to increase the available credit in all areas of the country, Menichella relied on the expansion of local banks, rather than the enlargement of the branch network of larger ones, in the belief that local banks produced greater allocative efficiency, thanks to a better knowledge of entrepreneurship. Menichella stated that the capital "will be mainly provided by small and peripheral institutions, living next to each smallholder... for those who are far and not able to appreciate the nature and seriousness of the need." (Amatori and Barca, 1997). Moreover, he believed that local banks were better able to protect savings: "Every day you play with your name, your honor, your reputation, the reputation of your families in places where you carry out the onerous task of collecting savings."

Source: Author's elaboration.

of information and reputation; precisely that combination which, in recent years, has been theorized and formalized by the literature on information asymmetries that, in his view, are reduced in the case of small and local banks, but organized on a mutual basis in the credit cooperative banks and cooperative banks .

In fact, in cooperative banks the principle of *relationship banking* is stated,[12] which, along with its smaller size, allows the reduction of information asymmetries between the bank and customer.

Another thing that stands out is the relationship of trust that is established between the member and the bank, enabling it to generate social capital. Indeed, it may be noted that a member of a cooperative bank invests in it not only to obtain financial advantage, but for the prospect of also receiving social benefits (Hanifan, 1916; Coleman, 1988; Putman, 1993).[13]

The main elements of the competitive advantage of cooperative banks are outlined in Table 1.6.

Cooperative banks represent, for these reasons, an ideal substrate for the creation of social capital (Valentinov, 2004). The principles inherent to the system of governance of cooperative banks contribute, in fact, to increasing the share capital of a territory in all major dimensions: participation, association, and capital relationship; specific and generalized trust, civic and moral norms (see Table 1.7).

With this premise, one question is how small-size intermediaries can survive the existence of big banks if the function of the credit company, as proposed by Diamon (1984), is as a diversified intermediary

Table 1.6 The higher specificity of the competitive advantage of cooperative banks

The cooperative bank is a "spontaneous city institution" (Pipitone, 2008).
The local dimension of the bank; its ability to adhere to the economic fabric of the respective settlement area is universally recognized (Murè, 1989).
Relationship banking represents all the relationships between banks and customers that go beyond the performance of simple and aseptic financial transactions (Ongena and Smith, 1998).
The long-term interaction, from which it would depend on the ties within the community, allowing the cooperative bank to impose punishments for deviant behavior – from social sanctions to ostracism (Banerjee et al., 1994).
Peer monitoring, the reciprocal control among the members of a local community or association, tends to mitigate the information and incentive problems that are typical of SME financing (Hoff and Stiglitz, 1990; Stiglitz, 1990).
The existence of repeated interactions over time among the members of a group, which activate reputation mechanisms able to sustain cooperative balances (Banerjee et al., 1994).
The cooperative form tends to give stability to top management. Stability in top management can be a good thing or a bad thing.[14] It is bad if it fails to sanction management inefficiencies. However, it is a good thing when, without prejudice for management efficiency, it allows the bank to keep corporate strategies on target with long-term objectives: it can promote the accumulation of *soft information* about customers (see Berger and Miller et al., 2002; Scott, 2000) and, therefore, permit the pursuit of organizational strategies that benefit the function of lending to SMEs (Hart and Moore, 1998).
The principle of limited liability and the characteristics of the shares of cooperative banks make a dimensional growth easier for these banks.
"The cooperative company is an expression of a cultural model that borrows from political democracy, the criterion of participation to the company" (Zoppini, 2006).

Source: Author's elaboration.

that plays the role of delegated monitor in an environment characterized by adverse selection problems that leads to economies of scale and efficiency.

The overcoming of any inefficiencies, due to the size of the smaller cooperative banks, is therefore strategic to achieving management efficiency and survival. Local banks may exceed their size limitations by joining a network that was set up through the establishment of CABEL (a multi-purpose center for local banks).[15]

Table 1.7 Cooperative banks and incidence of share capital

Share capital produced according to the size of the shareholdings, associations, and relational capital:

- Availability of some members to perform unpaid work for the organization.
- Availability of members to finance social and cultural activities for the organization.
- Creation of social relationships through membership of the organization.
- Creation of social relationships through the work environment.
- Cooperation with other cooperatives.
- Socio-cultural initiatives.
- Donations.
- Involvement of stakeholders in decision-making processes.[16]
- Democratic control of the government of the company through the vote per capita.
- Extension of the corporate base, understood as a voluntary membership to the share capital of a company.

Share capital produced according to the generalized and specific trust:

- Satisfaction with level of information on issues relating to the territory.
- Contacts with businesses and owners.
- Contacts with others from the local community (suppliers, customers).
- Duration of the credit report.
- Duration of the bank–customer relationship (loyalty: average age of the customers/users).
- Growth of the relationship with respect to the variety of products and services offered.
- Exclusive relationships.
- Mutual trust between banks and businesses.
- Development of the ability to work in groups, and sensitivity towards other people's problems.
- Quality of customer/user experience (measured by customer satisfaction surveys).

Share capital produced according to social norms and civic sense:

- Initiatives, training, and information inside the enterprise.
- Initiatives, training, and information external to the enterprise.
- Training scholarships.

Source: Author's adjustment on Marchello and Michetti, 2010.

Joining this network allowed cooperative banks to: address environmental complexity (Richardson, 1972; Hakansson and Ostberg, 1975; Golinelli, 2008, 2009; Barile 2009b); focus on their *core competencies*; bridge the gap of specific knowledge; combine the advantages of small size with those of large structured organizations (Barabási, 2002), with a consequent impact on economic performance, resource allocation (Frels et al., 2003) and collaborative advantage. This highlights the role and the importance of alliances and cooperative strategies (Castells, 1996; Gulati, 1998; Capra, 2002) and contributes to the conceptualization of the *service value network* (Allee, 2000).

In conclusion, in the cooperative bank model, the activities related to the social sphere are the result of compliance with business rules dictated by the same statute (an integral part of the memorandum). In this sense, the concept of social responsibility in this banking model is implicitly defined and refers to the set of policies and strategies for sustainability, implemented for the interests of the company and the community as a whole.

The vision of corporate social responsibility is made explicit by Cafferata (2009a), who states: "companies operate not only to decide on the fate of the world – and not all are able to do so or are successful – but also and above all to produce goods or services, possibly doing it well."

The model of local cooperative banks favors the development of relations among members, companies, and institutions linked together by their territorial bond. So, starting from Cafferta's assumption that the companies operate to produce goods or services, possibly doing it well, it can be said that the local cooperative bank, by promoting microcredit,

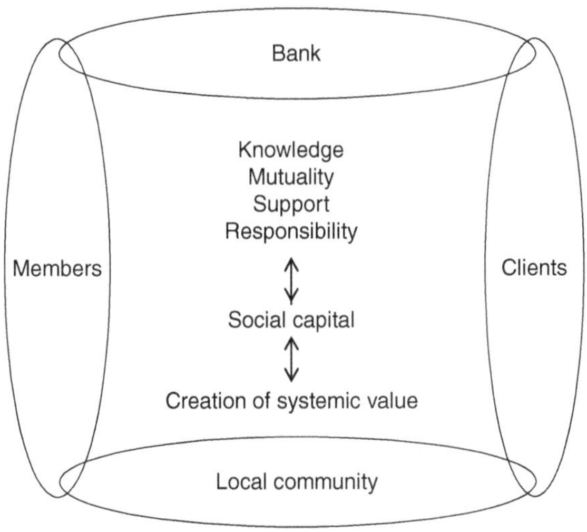

Figure 1.1 Business, social capital, and contest relationship
Source: Author's elaboration.

by investing in SMEs enterprises and in families, combines the principles of risk spreading (sound and prudent management) with the ones of supporting the most vulnerable and needy parts of society, in accordance with the principles of mutuality, solidarity, and subsidiarity, as highlighted by the Social Doctrine of the Church.

Therefore, the local cooperative bank – favoring a virtuous circle of members, clients, and territory – stimulates the creation of share capital of a local network of mutuality (Figure 1.1), which can be defined as follows: network of institutions, entrepreneurs, families, and individuals belonging to the same territory, united not only by economic goals, but by cultural, social, and ethical values.

2
The Evolution of Prudential Regulation

2.1 Examination of the essential points of the Basel Accords

The Basel Committee on Banking Supervision was established in 1974, under the auspices of the Bank for International Settlements, by the Governors of the Central Banks of the most industrialized countries (G-10), following a default in a German credit institution which had determined negative effects in many countries. This body does not have legislative autonomy in finance and it is not a supranational supervisory authority.

The documents it produced, however, represent guidelines and recommendations that individual national authorities of participant member countries are required to transpose into their own systems.

The primary purpose that this body intended to pursue was to consolidate the minimum assets of banks, and to strengthen risk management, thus enhancing the efficiency, productivity, reliability, and robustness of the international financial system.

On the basis of such assumptions, in July 1988 the "International Agreement on Asset Valuation and Capital Accord" was issued, which indicated, among other things, a system of measures as to the minimum capital base of credit institutes, adequate to cover the risks assumed in connection with efficiency.

The regulatory capital, which must be reported monthly by each bank to the Bank of Italy, is divided into three components: core capital, supplementary capital, and capital deductions.

The core capital (see Figure 2.1) consists in positive and negative elements, which cover the general business risk, representative of the joint participation in risks by the shareholders.

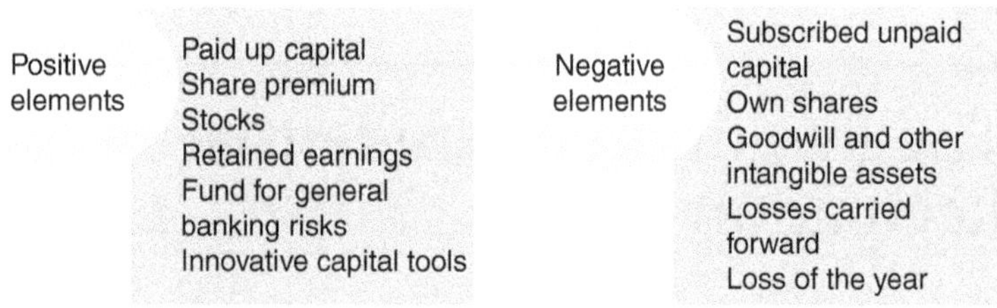

Figure 2.1 The core capital (Tier 1)
Source: Author's elaboration.

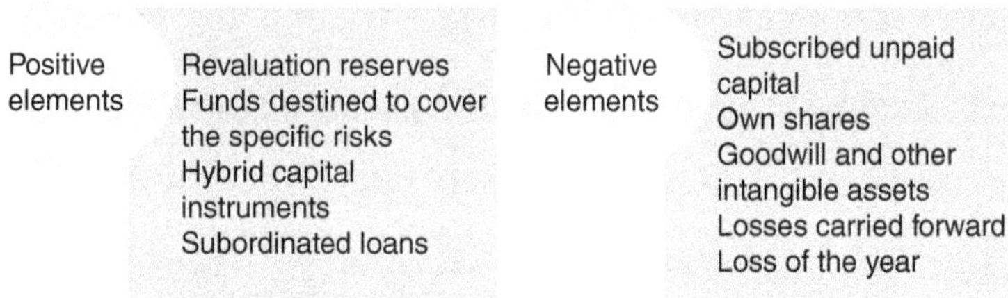

Figure 2.2 Supplementary capital (Tier 2)
Source: Author's elaboration.

Supplementary capital (see Figure 2.2) includes positive and negative elements that are not strictly of a patrimonial nature, subjected to quantitative and qualitative limits, such as: the revaluation reserves, funds destined to cover specific risks, hybrid capital instruments, and subordinated loans.

Finally, capital deductions are the mandatory adjustments that are made to the total of the core capital and supplementary capital, such as investments in credit and financial institutions.

With these capital regulations, they wanted to avoid, or at least prevent, any exposure of banks to the risk of default that would create such consequences as to generate the so-called "domino effect," with serious repercussions on the national and even on the international economy (see the recent case of Lehman Brothers).

A further objective, that was supposed to be achieved, concerned the harmonization of rules relating to capital requirements, which the banks had to standardize, so as to avoid speculation aimed at harming competition.

The quantification of the minimum requirement for each position to be held for a prudential aim, at least equal to 8 per cent, had to be calculated according to a standard methodology, as the percentage relationship between the "regulatory capital" of the intermediary and the total of credit and market "risk-weighted asset" (RWA), shown in the balance sheet of the intermediary itself at a certain date, that had to be evaluated using some different coefficients which estimated the implicit risk of the counterparties.

This ruling was applicable equally to all non-financial companies, regardless of their size, their geographic location, and by the perception that the market had on the credit risk of the individual borrower (Bianconi, 2004).

Banking activities were divided into categories depending on the liquidity, the nature of the borrowers, and the countries of residence (see Table 2.1).

It is possible to express the same size using the Total Capital Ratio (TCR).

In this formula, the total capital ratio is given by

$$TCR = \text{Regulatory Capital}/(RWA + 12.5 * Rm) >= 8\%$$

where

RWA = Value of weighted activities for credit risk
Rm = Market risk

The coefficient of "solvency," being bound to the capital, should not be used in any activity in order to preserve the strength and reputation of the credit system.

Table 2.1 Risk weights expected by Basel I

Risk weights	Assets entered into balance sheet
0%	Cash and similar items; credits of central banks in OECD countries; treasury stocks issued by the governments of OECD countries.
20%	Credits of multilateral development banks and loans guaranteed by such institutions or securities issued by the latter; securities issued by American local government.
50%	Fully guaranteed mortgages secured on residential real estates, which are – or will be – occupied by the borrower or let out.
100%	Credits of private companies; shareholdings in private companies; credits of banks and governments of non-OECD countries.

Source: Author's elaboration.

The capital allocated to manage the risks generates, thus, an opportunity cost for the credit institute that, not being able to use it in alternative investments, loses the opportunity to increase revenues.

The Agreement while representing a paradigm of undisputed value, showed over time a number of limitations and critical situations:

- Opacity in the actual capital base of credit institutes.
- Lack of consideration of the actual counterparty risk, not taking into consideration the maturity of loans or the peculiarities of the borrower.
- Standardized application of weighting factors of risk.
- It did not examine the operational risk but only the credit risk and market risk.
- It did not consider the diversification of the loan portfolio.
- It did not foresee the use of instruments of risk mitigation.
- It offered the opportunity to create forms of arbitrage on the assets that worsened the capital structure of banks. It also led to a situation of under-capitalization of the companies that have benefited from a total amount of credit which is not commensurate with their economic situation (Gambel, 2006).

This regulation was in force until the enactment of the New Capital Accord on Assets defined as Basel II, transposed this with Directives 2006/48 / CE and 2006/49 / CE of 14 June 2006.

This renewed discipline has revolutionized the criteria for assessing credit risk by encouraging banks to develop "internal methods," to modify those related to the calculation of market risk and impose an allocation of regulatory capital that addresses the operational risk arising from their *core*. Basel II is characterized, therefore, as having stimulated a dynamic evolution of the banking system, aimed at strengthening the methodologies used for calculating regulatory capital, also because of the possible capital savings, in addition accentuating the reputation of such a system at the international level, through the introduction of two new *pillars* (see Figure 2.3).

This tripartite division manifests the scientific approach of government acting in the financial system that reflects a number of more articulate constraints and incentives that integrate and complement each other (Proietti, 2012).

The innovated regulation does reward quality and value of companies in the estimation phase of regulatory capital, to be held for the risks assumed and to provide greater transparency in the measurement and management of these risks.

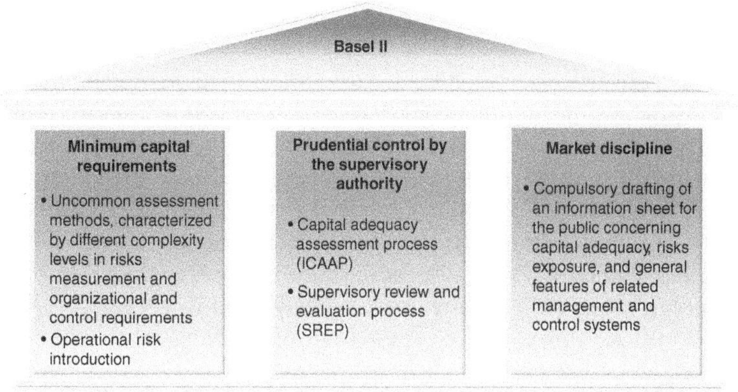

Figure 2.3 The three pillars of Basel II
Source: Author's elaboration on Bank of Italy source, 2006.

However, the revolutionary change concerns the attribution of "creditworthiness," also called "rating," in the selection, investigation, and subsequent monitoring of the counterparties.

This constant observation of customers, aims to identify, quickly, any deterioration in the creditworthiness of the borrower, which determines the renegotiation of the terms of the loan.

In practice, the capacity of credit and the solvency of unit in deficit are estimated, on which depends the amount of absorbed capital and consequently the pricing to be applied to ensure an adequate return.

In fact, the rating, the measuring the creditworthiness, that is, the probability that a person who contracts a debt is likely to repay it at its maturity, is expressed as a probability of default (PD) and is associated with a given timeline. It has a very clear scientific origin which is the basis of all formulations of corporate finance: the cost of credit has to be variant according to the risk that the lender assumes,[1] therefore, and it lets the person who generates the cost of risk pay directly the same cost (Formisano and Russo, 2012).

With regards the cost of financing, the following have to be considered:

- The costs related to the so-called "funding," that is, the interest that banks charge depositors to allocate funds.
- Internal costs of management.
- Other assessments of a commercial nature.
- The cost of the expected loss.
- The cost of unexpected loss.

However, the terms offered by banks are not a unique function of the rating. Although this assumes an undoubted importance,[2] ways of mitigating credit risk are also considered,[3] and in particular guarantees, as well as analysis of a commercial, strategic, and relational nature, related to the development of the relationship with the customer.

An in-depth study presupposes the existence of a high degree of consonance among the parties, expressed in terms of mutual trust, transparent communication tools, and assessments aimed at creating shared value (De Laurentis, 2011). In these cases, the *risk*, highlighted in the evaluation phase of the rating, may be overlooked.

In addition, the strategic-competitive positioning of the bank, in a geographic area or in a customer segment, plays a crucial role in determining the *pricing*, especially in terms of diversification of the portfolio.

The crisis, which has affected the world economy since 2007, has, however, highlighted a critical factor in the bank–company relationship, accentuated by the application of rating systems: the problem of pro-cyclicality.[4] This phenomenon generates an amplification of the fluctuations of the business cycle,[5] which, under bad economic conditions, means that the banks, to abide by the regulation in Basel II, can reduce inputs or increase the cost of money in order to dominate the growing level of risk.

In this way, there is a negative impact on the evolutionary dynamics of companies, contributing to a further escalation of the crisis.

In such situations, the rating systems underline a critical period for the company, because of, for instance, the decline in the volume of business that creates less operating income and/or enrollment of some entries of the assets in the balance sheet at the *fair value*, as required by accounting standards.

This is due to the fact that many of these systems are mainly based (as will be shown) on the quantitative component and on performance trend.[6] However, over the years, the need to give greater weight to the qualitative component in the assessment of creditworthiness has been reported by many.[7] Through these more sophisticated rating systems, the unexpressed value of the company could be captured.

The transposition of Basel II and the subsequent evaluation of creditworthiness established, in many cases, that banks apply the rating systems in a "hard" way, leading to a condition of dissonance with businesses.

The rating, in fact, is mainly perceived by SMEs as a threat to their survival.

When a company addresses a bank for a loan, it is in possession of more information than the bank itself. This is called information asymmetry. But in the bank–company relationship, a poor level of data/information, instead of encouraging dialogue, makes it more complicated.

To avoid this, a company must explain the reasons that led it to make such a request, specifying the destination of the capital borrowed, illustrating the projects which are deemed to create or enhance corporate value by entering new markets, in new strategic business areas that will help to achieve competitive advantages,[8] or because assets have to be covered.

The quality of the output of the rating systems depends, therefore, on the information flow of input that allows a company to strengthen and improve the judgment the bank has to make as to the allocation of funds and the conditions of the loan. If the bank makes capital savings, they will transfer them to the customer. Then the customer must acquire a certain rating "culture," so that it can act on the levers that allow it to improve its creditworthiness. Some indications to that effect derive from a document,[9] drawn up in Europe, dedicated to the activities to be pursued in order to improve the rating of businesses.

The six basic rules that SMEs can apply in order to better manage the process of obtaining bank credit in the changed financial scenario are:

- **Rule 1: Ask the bank for information** on the documentation that it has possibly prepared with reference to Basel II and the new rating systems.
- **Rule 2: Provide clear, complete, up to date, and accurate documentation**, which is the starting point of the rating systems. If it is not possible to provide precise figures, it is important to indicate that these are estimates and it is necessary to provide the related fields of variation. The late submission of any requested information may result in the definition of "problematic loan" being assigned, with negative repercussions for valuation purposes.
- **Rule 3: Check the price of the loan and other contract terms.** As the conditions of the loan depend on the assessment of creditworthiness, the company has the right to obtain information from the bank about the areas of information leading to the rating. On this point, the Bank of Italy has called on intermediaries to provide clarity on the rating systems and certainly they haven't revealed the calculation algorithm, which is a sort of "trade secret," in the sense that, if they had the information areas that produce

a rating system in the public domain, the difference between one system and another would determine the model that makes the information areas of the scoring. This does not allow banks to derogate from their obligation to document for the customer the areas of information used for the allocation of creditworthiness, upon which their decisions are based. Until the implementation of Basel II, in 2006, there was a strong opacity in rating systems. The Bank of Italy called for full transparency on the information areas and the impact that these areas have on the composition of creditworthiness.

- **Rule 4: Manage your rating actively**, through participation in meetings on the subject, organized by banks to illustrate the factors calculated in order to measure credit and to what aspects of business management special attention should be paid. Some banks also offer more evolved consulting services on ratings, since they propose solid measures and not financial ones, designed to improve the rating of the counterparty. They try to support and help the loan customers in the growth. But this is an additional cost for the bank that is "flipped" on *pricing* to customers.
- **Rule 5: Be sure to be able to keep the loan.** As part of their ongoing monitoring of outstanding loans, banks observe the evolution of the situation of each entrusted company. In accordance with the formulation of the contract, they can intervene if problems arise concerning the "health" of the enterprise. The banks, as mentioned above, assess the creditworthiness of the customer not only in the initial evaluation of the counterparty, but throughout the life span of the relationship. The rating, in fact, constitutes a dynamic variable, in accordance with the economic and financial environment in which the company is evaluated.[10]
- **Rule 6: Consider the alternatives.** Although bank credit is traditionally the most common form of financing, there are also other operational solutions. In finding the best financial conditions it is better to be aware of all the currently available alternatives such as:

    - "Mezzanine" financing, a hybrid form of loan that combines elements of both participation and loan.
    - Financing by companies of private shareholdings or risk capital that in exchange for their capital contribution acquire share holdings in the company.
    - Public sources of funding or subsidized financing.

2.2 Standardized approach and the internal ratings-based approach

For the determination of minimum capital requirements, the Basel Agreement provides that banks can adopt two different and alternative approaches for assessing credit risk,[11] characterized by an increasing sensitivity to risk: the standardized approach and the internal ratings-based (IRB) approach, the latter with its two foundation and advanced versions in relation to the risk parameters to be estimated. This is done through the evaluation by the bank, for each position, of some parameters, the value of which is then inserted into a calculation formula, the so-called regulatory function, which returns a capital requirement expressed as a percentage of exposure (Manzelli, 2009).

The choice between the two methods, which vary in complexity in the nature of the rating and number of computed variables, should be as consistent as possible with respect to the risk and the actual operations of the bank.

The standard approach, provides that, to determine the weights banks can use the assessments of creditworthiness provided by external evaluation, ECAI (External Credit Assessment Institution),[12] or ECA (Export Credit Agency).[13]

The list of recognized ECAIs is published on the website of the Bank of Italy, along with its *mapping*, which is the association of the ratings made by the ECAI to the classes of risk weights, provided by the supervisory provisions. Reviews are encoded using alphanumeric characters, each of which corresponds to a judgment on the debtor's ability to meet the expectations of the financial supra-system.

This approach was intended for those banks, especially smaller ones, that do not have the financial resources and human capital, or the interest, to develop their own internal rating system.

The recognition of the ECAI by the Bank of Italy is intended to allow credit institutions to use external ratings for the determination of risk weights to calculate the capital requirement for credit risk. This recognition is based on the verification of requirements that relate to the "methodology" used for the definition of the ratings, in terms of:[14]

- Objectivity.
- Independence.
- Periodic review.
- Market reputation.

- Transparency of the methodology and judgments.
- The eventual adoption by the agency of a code of conduct in line with the best practice internationally.

The Bank of Italy also highlights the following exposure classes:[15]

- Central governments and central banks.
- Supervised.
- Local authorities.
- Non-profit organizations and public sector entities.
- Multilateral development banks.
- International organizations.
- Businesses and other sujects.
- Retail exposures.
- Short-term exposures to corporates.
- Undertakings for collective investment (UCI).
- Securitization positions.
- Exposures secured by intangible assets.
- Exposures in the form of bonds.
- Past due exposures.
- Exposures belonging to high-risk categories for regulatory purposes.
- Other exposures.

For each regulatory exposure class, as mentioned above, the supervisory regulations provide, in cases in which ECAI assessments are used, the application of different weightings according to the rating on the creditworthiness of the counterparty.

This association is fixed by the Bank of Italy, on the basis of the methodology proposed by the Basel Committee, considering both quantitative and qualitative factors. The supervisory authority, in addition, supervises its operating structure in order to avoid the opportunistic phenomena called cherry picking, aiming to consider, for each exposure, the judgment that results in a lower capital requirement.

Currently, the recognized ECAI entities are: Fitch Ratings,[16] Moody's Investors Service,[17] DBRS Ratings Limited,[18] and Standard & Poor's Rating Services.[19] These provide solicited assessments, except in the "public finance" area (central governments and central banks, public sector entities, territorial sector entities, multilateral development banks), for which unsolicited ratings and the Cerved Group,[20] making unsolicited valuations for the sector "companies in other subjects," are recognized.

In international practice, in fact, recognition may be required for one of the following rating categories: *solicited* or *unsolicited* ones.[21]

In the first case, it is the same rated entity that is required to provide a series of accounting and *extra-accounting* information that integrates into the investigation at the base of the release of the *rating*, at request, for a consideration, a judgment of reliability that is a certification of its borrowing capacity.

In the second case, the rating is at the request of a third party, usually a bank, despite the absence of an explicit request of the rated entity. The assessment is based on a set of information that is substantially similar to the cases of *solicited rating*, but it follows operational and organizational processes which are different in some parts. In the formulation of unsolicited ratings, there is not a requirement to disclose the opinion expressed by the agency, to the rated subject.

Only in very particular cases do the agents act spontaneously to evaluate a subject or a release; this policy is pursued mainly by Moody's and Standard & Poor's, who justify it as a fulfillment of the information investors need. Smaller agencies, however, criticize and oppose this practice, considering it just a way to increase market share, thanks to a virtual tax assessment.

The differences between the two categories have led, in recent years, to a bitter dispute at the level of regulatory bodies (European Commission, CEBS, CESR, IOSCO, and national supervisory authorities) about the opportunity or not to use these ratings within the framework set by Basel II.

Banks need to communicate, to the Bank of Italy, and systematically update the list of ECAI/ECA they use, where valuations are to be used without the opportunity of continuity for all exposures belonging to the class (regulatory) of reference to avoid opportunistic choices.

In presence of evaluations by the following:

- ECAI/ECA: the one to which corresponds the highest weighted factor is chosen – if the ratings are more than two, the two combined to the lowest weighted factors are chosen and the higher of the two is applied.
- More *solicited and unsolicited* ECAIs: these can only be used in the absence of the former. If a broker does not use ratings submitted by ECAI, or rather the chosen ECAIs, they do not assign a rating to the debtor, they apply alternatively.
- Different weightings on the basis of the scores assigned by the SACE Ltd or other ECA recognized by the regulatory authorities of other

member states of the European Union, if the financial intermediary has declared that it intends to use such scores.
- A risk weight of 100 per cent.

As for business loans, the opportunity to refer to external ratings allows for the application of a more appropriate weighting to the real risk of the position.

The standard method provides for the possibility to further reduce the weights using risk-mitigation techniques, such as:

- Financial guarantees (such as securities, gold, deposits, and cash).
- Personal guarantees (with several limitations) and credit derivatives.
- The possibility of resorting to compensation.

With the method based on internal ratings (IRB), which constitutes the main news of Basel II, along with the evaluation of operational risk, the bank gives, through its analytical models validated by the Bank of Italy, a credit to the company, taking into account all the available information, including that acquired by direct contact with the customer.

The Basel Committee has determined that banks, in order to use the IRB, should adopt them and use them for at least three years;[22] for this already in 2003, some of them, in order to take advantage of the potentiality of new assessment techniques, established and launched the first internal evaluation methods.

The IRB approach,[23] unlike the standard approach, provides that the minimum capital requirements are not calculated on the basis of predetermined coefficients, but through specific functions of risk weights.

The risk factors are estimated internally by the banks using their analytical models, which contain methods and procedures for determining the credit risk of the counterparty, after the validation by the Bank of Italy of a set of organizational and quantitative requirements. The first ones concern: corporate governance,[24] internal organization,[25] internal validation,[26] the use of the rating system in business management, the process of assigning ratings, and information systems. The main minimum quantities requirements relate to:

- The structure of the rating systems, such as the large number of minimum rating classes: seven for non-defaulting debtors and one class for those in default.
- Assigning to a pool of retail credit exposures.

- Quantification of risk parameters, such as the minimum content of the data files, the length of the time series, the estimation of LGD suitable for an economic downturn.
- Use in specific areas of operation: from the models acquired from outside suppliers to the completion of internally developed rating systems.

Banks authorized to use internal methods for the calculation of capital requirements for credit risks or operational ones, are obliged to publish periodically "the info to the audience – Pillar 3."[27]

This document is also the necessary condition for the recognition for prudential purposes of the methods and techniques mentioned above, whose legislation provides that the qualitative information is disseminated at least every six months and that those of a quantitative nature, relative to regulatory capital adequacy and sheet, are published quarterly, although with different criteria and procedures.

For the purposes of IRB, activities in the banking portfolio are divided into the following classes:[28] exposures to central governments and central banks, exposures to supervised, exposures to corporates, retail credit exposures, exposures of capital tools, securitization positions, and other activities.

The internal rating systems that represent an evolution of *credit scoring systems*,[29] offer the possibility for banks to exploit extensive information assets, strictly confidential and used for internal purposes only, acquired in their relationship with customers.

Since the rating system is not only a tool for the calculation of capital requirements but must play an important role in management, banks may be authorized to adopt the method based on internal ratings for the calculation of capital requirements only if the system of rating plays a key role in approving loans, risk management, internal capital allocation, and governance functions of the bank.

IRB models predict that each exposure is not multiplied by a single weighting factor but for a weighting function related to the probability of default (PD), the loss given default (LGD), exposure at default (EAD), and the expiration of the exposure (maturity), in order to obtain risk-weighted assets that fully reflect the real risk of the portfolio.

With the methods based on internal ratings, each bank can decide for themselves to use the foundation method or the *advanced* one, depending on the number of risk factors that it is called to estimate.

With the foundation method, we estimate the probability of default of the debtor, while the value of the other risk factors is a function of

Table 2.2 Example of external ratings issued by the specialized agencies

AAA	Represents the highest rating evaluation. It denotes an excellent quality of the entity responsible for payment and a remarkable ability to pay interest and repay the capital lent.
AA	Indicates a high ability of the company to pay interest and repay the capital lent. This capacity is not significantly affected by foreseeable events.
A	The company has a strong capacity to pay interest and repay the capital lent, but it is partially sensitive to adverse economic conditions or unfavorable economic circumstances.
BBB	The repayment capacity of the unit in deficit is still enough to make consonant the relationship with the banking system. However, adverse economic conditions or changing circumstances could affect this attitude to a greater extent.
BB	The company, while still proving to possess the ability to meet financial commitments in the short term, cannot be expected to maintain the same condition over time, in case of any situation, economic and cyclical conditions, and adverse policies.
B	The debtor is even more vulnerable in the event of adverse economic conditions, even if in the immediate term they are able to meet their financial commitments.
CCC	The company is highly vulnerable in deficit; insolvency is a real possibility and its ability to meet its financial commitments depends on economic and cyclic factors, and external politicians.
CC	The company is, at the time of evaluation, vulnerable.
C	A bankruptcy petition against the undertaking was presented, but the commitments expressed in terms of payment of interest and repayment of principal are currently honored.
RD	The company has not complied with the payment of only some financial commitments, but continues to honor other obligations.
D	The company is in a bankrupt state and is therefore insolvent. The probabilities of repayment of financial commitments are virtually nil.

Source: Author's elaboration on ABI (Italian Bank Association) source, 2005.

the regulation values set by the Bank of Italy. This methodology was designed for banks that have limited experience in ratings.

The *advanced* method, however, quantifies autonomously all risk factors required by the regulations (probability of insolvency of the debtor, the expected loss in the event of default, exposure at default and, where applicable, remaining life of the debt) only if it respects more stringent standards than those contained in the basic method.

The latter method is reserved for those who are able to demonstrate to the Central Bank that they have developed refined and reliable instruments of credit control.

With the advanced method of internal ratings, the bank enjoys maximum autonomy in developing their own criteria and models related to the quantification of credit risk; it can act in such a way as to minimize the absorption of capital.

The two methods, therefore, differ in complexity, the nature of the rating and number of calculated variables.

The weighting factor,[30] under the two IRB approaches, is calculated differently (see Table 2.3).

The banks and financial institutions that have chosen to adopt the IRB models for risk assessment have developed the appropriate analytical tools that include the "best practices" of the banking industry in the field of measurement and management of credit risk, with a relevant impact on internal organizational processes.

Table 2.3 Methods of calculation of the weighting factor according to the two IRB approaches

Risk parameters	**IRB foundation**	**IRB advanced**
PD – Probability of default	Estimated by the bank	Estimated by the bank
LGD – Loss given default	Estimated by the supervisory authority, the Bank of Italy, on the basis of technical forms and real guarantees	Estimated by the bank
EAD – Exposure at default	Estimated by the supervisory authority – the Bank of Italy	Estimated by the bank
M – Maturity	Estimated by the supervisory authority – the Bank of Italy	Estimated by the bank

Source: Author's elaboration.

If this on the one hand led to higher costs and difficulty of implementation, on the other hand it has produced substantial benefits and alternative uses that can lead to the reduction of capital requirements, thus decreasing the cost of capital and the determining of competitive advantages.

Firstly, on equal terms, in the banks that adopt internal ratings, credit to SMEs generates capital absorption 50 per cent lower than the credit granted to large enterprises. Secondly, even the banks that use the standard models (more punitive than the first) are eligible for capital requirements for companies with revenues of less than 5 million euros and have an advantage of 25 per cent compared to fixed assets required by lending to large businesses. However, as regards the measurement of credit risk, banks should, therefore, over time, switch from the standard system to that of the foundation internal ratings system and, subsequently, to the advanced internal ratings system, acquiring ever more advanced instruments and skills for the measuring and managing of risk.[31]

As for alternative uses, through the use of internal ratings, banks, as well as assessing the creditworthiness of a counterparty, are able to:

- Improve the adequacy of the monitoring mode of borrowers.
- Refine the methods of quantification of pricing applied to customers, depending on the actual risk.
- Encourage the use of portfolio models for the government's credit risk.
- Facilitate the calculation of provisions in defense of expected losses.
- Respond effectively to the complexity of the new regulatory environment.

The use of an internal rating system provides a succession of stages:

- Identification of a statistical model to estimate the probability of default and the recovery rate attributable to each counterparty and entrusted to each operation.
- Selection of types of transfer of the assessments made by the experts of the trust to the statistical model.
- Identification of the parties to which is entrusted the responsibility of integrating statistical methods with the valuation of intangible assets of the debtor.
- Selection of customers that have certain characteristics that allow only the application of statistical methods.

To give stability to the rating and the subsequent relationship with the customer, it is important for banks to assess the characteristics of "structural" models, especially with regard to the time line; that is, whether to classify the counterparties based on their current condition or their prospective condition.

Let us first consider the "Point in Time" methodology, since the rating changes with the varying of the condition of the borrower during its economic "annual" cycle. This methodology assesses the repayment ability of the company based on the current economic situation, neglecting the effects of possible changes in macroeconomic variables. This is the technique used by banks.

In a second methodology, called "Through the Cycle," the evaluation is based on an analysis during the course of an entire business cycle, generally five to seven years, depending on the industry in which it operates. PD estimation takes place not only in the presence of favorable economic cycles, but also in scenarios where conditions are worse. This implies that the rating tends to remain unchanged during the entire period and therefore is less sensitive to the volatility of the economic situation compared to "Point in Time" methodology.

In particular, the counterparty rating may change at any time in the economic cycle due to unforeseen events, both exogenous (cycle duration unexpected, strong financial market turbulence, etc.) and endogenous (changes in the strategy implemented by management or corporate economic variables).

The choice of an internal rating system should be consistent with the work done by the bank in terms of customer segment considered, information sources used, specific qualities and characteristics of the data. The assessment criteria chosen must be applied consistently in all territorial structures of the credit institution.

Instructions for the treatment of qualitative information and specific guidelines regarding *override*, to prevent disparities in interpretation by analysts, will therefore be prepared.

The adequacy of such guidelines is also checked through regular analysis of the causes of registered variances, compared to automatic scoring to assess ongoing compliance with the requirement of homogeneity.

As regards, in particular, the credit lines granted to units in deficit, within the same bank the quantification of risk must be made using internal rating models distinguished by the segment of the counterparty, which has certain specific features, as well as the quantity and quality of the data, actually usable for each segment.

The internal methods are distinguished according to the importance accorded to automatic judgments and those of the experts working in the banking sector in:

- *Statistical models.* The opinions expressed are characterized by a high efficiency and objectivity of evaluations, both in terms of cost and time taken, being able to take advantage of forms of operational standardization. This is the preferred model for the analysis of the portfolio consisting primarily of small customers who have and mainly supply accounting data. The rating assignment is done by entering the data of the individual counterparty into a predefined formula that does not allow the use of any *overrides* by analysts.
- *Judgmental models.* These are based on subjective-discretionary assessments made by analysts (*expert judgment*), whose expertise and direct knowledge of the counterparty allow them to change the opinion expressed by the statistical model, taking into account the elements of nature which are not strictly quantitative. These are applied only in the case of concentrated portfolios, for the presence of very few counterparts exhibited against the credit institution, which present a wealth of available information, strongly differentiated from the point of view of quantity and quality.

  It is important to determine in advance the proportion between quantitative and qualitative elements, in order to homogenize the opinions expressed by different operators of the same bank, since this approach suffers, as accurate and structured as it is, the risk of inequality in the allocation of ratings to individuals with similar characteristics.
- *Hybrid models,* which blend together the characteristics of the two types above, with a prevalence of qualitative information.

When choosing the type, the bank must take into account the dimensional characteristics, the operational specificities, organizational structures, and the concerned portfolio segments (large corporate, corporate, retail). Indeed, for the retail segment, quantitative and standardized information are necessary, while for the "corporate" and "large corporate" segments, which present greater complexity in the evaluation, the totality of the business project should be taken into account, as should its strategic-competitive prospects and intangible elements.

The internal rating system was one of the "largest investments in knowledge, processes and procedures in recent years, whose role has expanded over the past five years," according to De Laurentis and Maino (2010),[32] in terms of:

- Reliance on time (transaction).
- Trade policy.
- Customer strategy and long-term relationship.
- Monitoring of the portfolio: prioritization of intervention (Early Warning/Watch list).
- Risk control and reporting, RAPM, incentives and objectives, budget.
- Provisioning policies for expected losses.
- Economic capital and management/hedging portfolio.
- Regulatory capital (supervisory formula, Pillar 1 floor).
- Calculation of capital adequacy in accordance with Pillar 2.
- Transparency and market disclosure (Pillar 3).

In the formulation of internal ratings, each bank can choose the information sources used, synthesizing them with weights that may differ significantly between banks.

This justifies the different marks awarded to the same company by credit institutes, which are different according to their typology and size.

The Italian best practice is to use four information areas jointly:

1. Statistical/quantitative analysis. Through an analysis of data from financial statements or other financial reports, the ability to generate positive cash flows is determined, of a company that presents a balance and financial structure and has the ability to create value over time. The evaluation is based on a statistical model of multiple regression applied to financial ratios and reports provided by the company itself as the following:

    - Index of strength: determining the relationship of debt compared to equity – it is the "weakest point" of many Italian SMEs.
    - Profitability index: assesses the ability to create value.
    - Index of the financial cycle.
    - Liquidity index: measures the existence and strength of the economic-financial balance.
    - Incidence and evaluation of financial charges.
    - Budget.
    - Business plan.
    - Significant events and outstanding issues after the closing of the financial statements, such as mergers, divestitures, increases or decreases in the share capital, the starting and/or repayment of loans of considerable amount, and so on.

2. Trend analysis. This evaluates how the customer has behaved with the bank and the banking system in general. It analyzes the dynamics

of the relationship in general (if the company is not a new applicant), acquired through internal statistics and data provided by the SIC (Credit Information System),[33] such as:

- Frequency and severity of trespassing.
- Number of bank counterparties.
- Regularity of the portfolio effects (nature, number of defaults, etc.).
- Procedures and the evolution in the use of credit lines, their structure and duration.

3. Information regarding the production sector resulting from the data,[34] relationships,[35] research reports and statistical institutes that are external market leaders and specialized in risk analysis sector, Istat (National Institute for Statistics), Cerved, Prometeia, and so on, such as:

   - Geographic size of the market: local, national, international.
   - Local and national sectorial indexes.
   - Sector positioning against benchmarks.
   - Forecasts on the trend of the sector.

4. Qualitative analysis, which consists in measuring the ability to make corporate strategic choices coherent with the evolution of the reference context. The assessment is based on judgments and estimates made by the banking analyst, which are derived from a cognitive process of interpretation of the company reality.

To aggregate and synthesize the different information, banks use rather complex methodologies, such as mathematical-statistical multivariate models, which synthesize in a single numeric value the different counterpart information. The models used can be classified into four main categories: linear discriminant analysis, logit/probit analysis, neural networks, and expert systems.

The combination of the results of the four areas of analysis determine the rating class of the counterparty, which is associated with the probability of default.

In a context like the current one, in which we are experiencing the most severe economic and financial crisis since the war for its breadth and depth, it becomes crucial to overcome the paradigms of standardized computing of credit that attach substantial weight to the quantitative and trend component, compared to the real added value of the companies that is inherent in qualitative factors.

The over-reliance on information derived from a set of fiscal indicators, and the lack of attention to those of a qualitative nature, accumulated through long-term customer relationships, constitutes a distortion of the spirit of Basel,[36] which aims to assign a rating in which both objectively quantifiable variables and also qualitative ones are weighed. This is confirmed by Sabatini (2010), who argued that "in a situation like the current one, the opinion on the reliability of the company expressed by the rating can not only be the result of a quantitative analysis, but must be the combined result of the company's ability to represent and enhance the qualitative information that characterizes it and the bank's ability to best use this information through an open and constructive relationship which increases their mutual trust."[37]

The studies[38] carried out in the international literature (Berger and Udell, 2002; Bugera et al., 2002; Jens et al., 2002; Lehmann, 2003; Godbillon-Camus and Godlewski, 2005; Grunert et al., 2005) have shown that the combination of qualitative variables and financial data provides a more accurate prediction of the risk of default by counterparties. The mere reading of the financial statements, as claimed by Formisano et al. (2012), may be detrimental, failing to fully reach the real factors of excellence or criticality of companies, such as:

- The fact that financial statements are based on a *backward-looking* logic, compared to one in which the business is located at the time of applying for finance.
- It is a type of assessment that assumes the existence of historical data, while in the case of start-ups, it is based solely on prospective data, which would occur only after the disbursement of the loan.
- It does not consider the non-accounting data that allows you to refine customer segment segmentation.
- It examines data aggregates that are often unable to analyze the dynamics of flows in detail.

However, it is essential that the balance sheets of corporate borrowers are transparent and able to represent the real business conditions in terms of income, balance sheet, and finance.

Inadequate and incomplete information results in a gap of knowledge between units in surplus and those in deficit, with adverse consequences, including the rationing of financial resources for companies with good *business fundamentals*, the incorrect *pricing* of loans, an increase in suffering for SMEs and the non-optimal allocation to the balance sheet by banks for credit risk.

2.3 Transaction towards Basel III

The Basel II Agreement, even if it was reputed by many, recklessly, to be a major contributor to the great crisis that erupted in 2007,[39] presented incontrovertible weaknesses (Tutino et al., 2011):

- In several cases, the capital held by banks, while respecting prudential regulation, proved inadequate both in terms of quantity and quality, also due to the inability of analysts in making the measurements.
- The methods of risk assessment were deficient in representing the real world.
- Despite the emerging of obvious flaws in the methods of assessment and management of different risk profiles, what turned out to be absolutely underestimated was the liquidity profile.
- Abuses have occurred in the margins of discretion applied by some national systems that have generated an uneven application of the law, thus generating competitive distortions. In some cases, a large proportion of regulatory capital was formed by placing on the market "hybrid" instruments, which increased in a fictitious way the capital ratio at the expense of the Core Tier 1.
- The pro-cyclical aspect of the regulatory paradigm also induced extensive recourse for management and prudential purposes of "Point in Time" methodologies of credit assessment.[40]

The Basel Committee, in order to overcome these problems and prevent recurrence of the global spread of the financial crisis, has provided new supervisory regulations for banking regulation to strengthen the solvency and liquidity of the banking system.

The proposals contained in Basel III provide a new system of micro and macro prudential supervision of credit institutions.

The elements that characterize the new regulatory framework, which after a long transition period will come into force in 2018, have a higher level of quality and quantity of capital put in place for unexpected losses.

The assets must be increased by resorting to *Common Equity Tier 1* (CET1), or rather the issue of ordinary shares, using surplus funds and the share premium account. Furthermore, more selective criteria for the computability of other capital instruments were provided. The regulation deductions may be applied only to the base assets, so that the banks exhibit ratios coherent with the net equity base.

The composition of regulatory capital was revised, foreseeing that Tier 1 must have the capacity to absorb losses in terms of business continuity (*going concern*), and Tier 2 in the crisis of the intermediary (*gone concern*).

From a quantitative viewpoint the new regulations involve the following:

- The minimum requirement remains unchanged at 8 per cent of risk-weighted assets, although it will have to be made up of 4.5 per cent *common equity* (Basel II quantifies it as 2 per cent).
- A broader coverage of risks with respect to market risk and counter-party on derivatives, to securitization and off-balance sheet transactions.
- The degree of leverage will be more restrained. The maximum size is fixed at 3 per cent, calculated as the relationship of Tier 1 and the non-weighted assets, including the off-balance sheet.
- Strengthening of the requirements on liquidity (which will be examined later).
- The introduction of an anti-cyclical buffer which is aimed at dealing with periods of high financial stress. In the event that the banks should reserve an amount of capital of an insufficient amount than the one provided by the Agreement, the regulation imposes limits on the distribution of profits and in the allocation of bonuses, which will be much more stringent as more buffer is reduced.
- Encouragement towards further harmonization among the laws applied in individual local contexts, in order to simplify competitive comparisons.

The combination of these factors is intended to curb the probability of contagion of systemic risk through greater ability of credit institutes to deal with any economic-financial shocks (Modina, 2012a).

3
The Banking Business: The Governing Body and the Operational Structure

3.1 The bank as a viable system enterprise

Systemic thought and its formalization in a general systems theory had a significant influence in all disciplines, and therefore also does so in the one that has the banking business as the object of investigation. It has been decided to associate with the company the qualification of system in relation to the following conditions:

a) The presence of multiple components, both of tangible or intangible nature.
b) The interdependence and communication among these components (the principle of interdependence and communication).
c) The start-up of the relations in order to achieve the goals and objectives of the system (the principle of communion towards a purpose).

In Italy, the systemic approach in business phenomena is commonly traced back to the fundamental studies of Gino Zappa, considered to be the founder of business economics.

With regard to business events, Zappa (1956) noted that:

> The company is not a dissociated mass, it is not a *holding*, it is not a combination of temporary factors and disjoint phenomena. That is not enough to illustrate the so-called elements of the company staff body and its heritage, and then bring the notion of business to that of its factors, to reveal the essential circumstance or characteristic condition that makes the phenomena of a company like ordered and ongoing units.

> Instead the banking company represents a working reality: it is becoming day by day, *it is continuously assembling in its structures*, it is always renewing and it always fulfills; in the dynamic implemented processes, it always changes and openly shows itself as the changing circumstances, to which the company has to adapt.

Conceiving the company as an economic coordination, whose phenomena are not likely to be investigated separately from each other, due to the constraints of space and time that characterize the unified management of the company, Zappa tends to embrace a vision of the company which, with hindsight, could be defined as holistic.

With a closer look, however, the theoretical and cultural context of Zappa's thought does not lend itself to be consciously oriented towards a systemic approach; however, the current interpretation of his work allows itself to get closer to the systemic viewpoint. In line with the new ways of approaching the study of phenomena resulting from the spread and evolution of systemic thought, and simultaneously with what has happened internationally, the consideration of the company as a system, begins to assert itself fully even in our doctrine around the 1950s.

The banking business, as noted, is a system since it represents "a set or a grouping that our mind can conceive in a unitary and ordered way by virtue of connections and interdependencies that directly, link all parts or separate components, forming an ensemble."

A more fitting viewpoint on the assumptions of systemic thinking in the process of formalization is to be found in the works of other scholars, for which the company is considered an open, dynamic, planned, governed, and controlled system. It is seen as a system with a socio-economic dimension, whose self-regulation activity is strongly influenced by the governing body, with a view to achieving more important outliving possibilities of the system.

Starting from the 1960s, especially after the motivation of systemic studies coming from overseas, the doctrine was mainly oriented to define the possible systemic qualifications of the company, taking advantage of the progresses made in several disciplines.

The first metaphorical associations – business as a mechanical system, an organic system, ora mechanical-organic system – introduced by the analogic procedure that represented the company as a cybernetic system, as a self-poietic system, as a cognitive system, and so on.

Among these approaches, the one that qualifies the banking business "as a cognitive system, able to operate on the basis of its knowledge and able to continuously feed the knowledge that it is provided with, deserves special attention"(Vicari, 2008).

Coherently with the approach that the main available asset in a company is the knowledge of an undertaking, it is still confirmed that "the company generates differential value – compared to competitors – mobilizing the assets of specific knowledge inherited from its history or acquired outside to design, build and sell products, processes and relationships that incorporate its knowledge and make it usable by the customers who have been served" (Rullani, 2003).

The different approaches and preparations behind the study of entrepreneurial phenomena, along with the need to build the closest links with other disciplines, push the proliferation of systemic qualifications attributed to the company.

Although, in fact, there are strong reasons to put together these management and organization doctrines in a single set, in an attempt to establish a unified science of economic administration of companies (or Business Economics), the different profiles of observation of the entrepreneurial phenomena have originated diverse points of view, each of them with its own privileged perspective of observation, reaching particular systems of understanding. From these approaches, according to the adopted viewpoint, the company could be considered, according to different interpretations, as a system focused on, for example:

- Operations or exchanges.
- Accounting value.
- Structures and social dynamics.
- Static and dynamic variables of the organization.
- Management operations.
- Risks.
- Decisions.

None of the above-mentioned interpretations is unfounded. Indeed, the company can be seen from different points of view and can actually be represented as a system, because of the different listed foci.

Each observer, thus depending on their characteristics, inclinations, opportunities, and so on, is brought to privilege the aspect that is more coherent with their research objectives, choosing a research perspective among many that the systemic approach allows. This wealth and variety of perspectives precisely testifies, after all, to the validity of the systemic approach to the study of the company.

In response to the proposals of conceptualization of the company in a systemic viewpoint, over time, several representations have also been developed through the use of an analogical or metaphorical approach. This was necessary in an attempt to transpose the survey on the structure and behavior of entrepreneurial organizations, and relevant conclusions emerged in specific disciplines.

For this, the benefit of analogies and metaphors to the understanding of phenomena and complex realities such as companies cannot be denied. However, the systems approach to the study of entrepreneurial organizations, although it represents a shared reality which is no longer discussed, has also known criticisms in the past, aimed at bringing its validity into question.

These criticisms are derived, in many cases, just by excessive use of metaphors and from an analogic application that has tried to transpose properties and laws of operation, typical of other categories of systems, to the company system.

In this regard, it is necessary to introduce the notion that the metaphor, through the inversion of a term with a figurative one, allows us to understand a particular experience with reference to another one. The idea of the company as a body, for instance, highlights the features and elements which equate it to living organisms, such as flexibility and adaptation to the environment, organ functionality with respect to outliving, learning, and so on.

The analogy, instead, aims to extend special knowledge obtained in one particular subject area to another, through the application of models derived from the first, allowing you to develop new and more realistic ones. Conceiving the company as an autopoietic system, for example, means to use developed skills with reference to living organisms and apply them to the company in order to explain their behavior.

Moreover, it appears clear that the shift from metaphor to analogy can be made with ease. The idea of the company as a machine (metaphor), as well as pointing out the parallels from a structural point of view, also brings some assimilations (similarities) in terms of systemic behavior.

In the following pages, we will review some of the most significant systemic conceptualizations adopted in the systemic definition of the company, resulting from metaphorical and analogical applications. Among these, in addition to the benefits for the understanding of the entrepreneurial phenomena, interesting from the view of the governing body, the risks resulting from an excessive emphasis on such proceedings will be pointed out.

The concepts presented below will be useful when the presuppositions for the subsequent classification of the company as a viable system will be established.

3.2 The area of government decisions and the area of management deals

To reach a specific definition of the viable system enterprise through an isomorphic representation of viable systems, we proceed with the identification of the type of adjustments that, in line with the historical-evolutionary course expressed by the company, make a coherent representation to provide an interpretation consistent with the perspective of investigation adopted here, which allows us to:

1. Attribute to it the typical conceptual elaborations of the company economy.
2. Normalize the perspective of the company, typically that of the governing body, tending to start and direct the system towards the achievement of its goals and objectives. This is accomplished through activities and processes carried out by a structure with implicit knowledge and a respectful autonomy for routine decisions.
3. Put the emphasis on the concept of business as an open system, surviving in the changing environment, dynamically upgrading its organizational scheme and its structure, and exchanging resources by virtue of interactions with other systems.

It seems redundant to specify the motivations on the base of the first point, which are easily understood, considering the purpose of such work.

With the second point, however, it is considered appropriate to focus on the need to express a consideration where exploring the behavior of entrepreneurial organizations.

It is therefore necessary to consider that in an entrepreneurial activity the two relevant moments are traditionally separated, the one of government and the one of management, designed to qualify a typical dichotomy of the company. The representation of the company as a viable system reflects such dichotomy, by characterizing the viewpoint of the person in charge of the government, who processes and plans the strategic direction, using an operational structure committed to the implementation of the agreed strategic approach.

From this step, with the third point there is the need to distinguish the area of those decisions aimed at ensuring the company has a flexible and functional organizational scheme, as well as purposes, such as the objectives to be pursued.

It has previously been stated that a system, in order to be qualified viable, must be able to survive in a context, implementing learning processes, able to allow adaptation to the context itself or, under certain conditions, its modification. However, not until now, has it been clarified how the system manages to do so and how the necessary decisions for this purpose are considered and then transformed into activities to be performed.

It is therefore necessary to show how, through the modification of the set of reports identifying the structure, it is just up to a specific subject of decision, the governing body, to decide, as appropriate, to adapt, transform, or restructure the business system, to ensure the continuation of the trend to the purpose.

The hypothesis that follows concerns a new representation able to explain how the organizational scheme, translated into an extended structure and, therefore, with implicit knowledge integrated into the routine (decision-arranged replies), through the specific activity carried out by the governing body, might be connected to the environmental context.

Connection activity requires the governing body to change the environmental context in organizations, which ranges from the configuration and monetary structure to the qualification of a viable suprasystem. The governing body, on the basis of their knowledge, must make presumptions from the environmental context, opportunities, and external relational rules.

Imagining, then, being faced with the whole details of all the decisioning areas of a viable system, it is assumed that it is the identification of the subset of decisions and its extrapolation from the above-mentioned area that characterizes the action of government.

From the extrapolation of these decisions, obviously, the set of management decisions appears evident. Therefore, it is supposed, again, that the remaining set of management decisions is added to the area of operations, forming a new aggregate called operating structure; this, containing both the management and the real operating time, comes to coincide with the area of management.

3.3 Government of the bank firm

The government of the banking business is an ongoing process of identification and selection of development alternatives in short and longer term. From a systemic viewpoint, the bank system consists in changing the corporate structure in an evolutionary sense. This is achieved through the design and implementation of a process of structural development that includes an increasing capacity to raise the levels of economic efficiency.

This means not only the rejection of invariance with respect to time of the company structure, but the company awareness of the need to guide its evolution. In this way, the several specific structures that happen in time are characterized by an increasing capacity of government and efficiency. The development of the company that must be achieved through an ongoing sequence of modifications of its overall structure, such as to ensure economic efficiency increases, with a permanent nucleus enriched with governmental capacity.

These structural changes are intended to implement the chances of survival of the bank as a viable system enterprise, through the achievement of adequate levels of consonance with the reference supra-systems. Considering the banking business at time T, characterized by its specific structure ST, the bank system is expressed in the identification of the most appropriate line of development, in relation to ST, the opportunities and constraints of the market – so in the design and construction of a new appropriate specific structure to the chosen strategy.

The magnitude of the changes to be made to the technical-productive, marketing, financial, organizational, components, and so on of the structure, in harmony with the chosen development line, requires, in relation to the business characteristics and the market environment, more or less long periods of time.

Important structural changes, environmentally unfavorable to the change, will take a long time; structural changes that affect only the most temporary and more mutable components, in favorable environmental conditions, can also be implemented in the short term. A distinction, in the context of structural changes, including adjustments and transformations, emerges (Golinelli, 2009).

The "adjustments" are those modifications of the structure, affecting only the components for their nature and/or more easily modified situations of environment, that can be achieved in limited time intervals. The "transformations" are those modifications of the structure that affect also more permanent components; for their nature and/or more difficult environmental situations to modify, implementation may require longer periods of time.

For a better understanding, we will follow the company engaged in the action of development. If we consider the short term, this action is concretely shown when expressing the budget for the year. Considering the company at time T(T < Tn) with its specific structure ST; it properly, faces the time T, and then in advance with respect to Tn, end time of year n, the preparation of the plan for the year n + 1.

This involves the choice among different alternatives in relation to the abilities and skills of ST and the situation and prospects of the market environment and then the provision of the necessary capacities for the implementation of the chosen line of development. Ultimately, the design and implementation of the new specific structure STn will determine the behavior of the company in the year n + 1, the structure that will be the result of a more or less wide complex of adjustments made in ST. But at time T, the company, as part of the governing body's longer term, may need to design and initiate the implementation of structural broader reach changes.

Therefore, adjustments and transformations are concrete manifestations of the ongoing entrepreneurial government action aimed at the research, design, and implementation of short- and longer-term development lines. The specific structure STn is therefore the result of both adjustments (made in time Tn – T) and turned-on transformations, to be implemented in a more extended period of time; this complex of adaptations and transformations gives the structure an ongoing variability in time.

Therefore, we reflect that:

- The higher the entrepreneurial dynamism and the higher the rates of development taken as targets, the more relevant entities and intensity of structural change there will be. This leads to rising research costs, design, testing activities, and thus the amount of funding needed to cover the investment programs that result from development activities themselves.
- The amount of available funding depends largely on the income flows accumulated in earlier periods and flows that spring simultaneously with the implementation of structural changes.

The interconnection between "adaptations" and "transformation" is clear; the first is more content and secure, and still crucial to avoid lack of funds and/or the increased cost of capital that makes the latter one less attractive or impossible. Adjustments and transformations are developed over time, sometimes overlapping, causing the succession in time of specific structures (Golinelli, 2011a).

These, more or less different, must generally satisfy the condition of ensuring an income flow that, for intensity and trend is able to allow –

through self-financing, the increase of creditworthiness, and the possibility of increases in capital – the cover for financial requirements relating to adjustments and, above all, to structural changes.

The peculiarity of the banking business and in particular its relationship with the supra-system of the Bank of Italy and ECB, obliges the governing body, in its action, to comply with rules, constraints, procedures, and comparisons with the supervising organ. This definitely makes the governance activity of the same more binding, compared to other sorts of business. Moreover, the governing body, in addition to acting on the operational structure of the bank, is responsible for managing banking risks.

In fact, for some years the Italian banking system has been undergoing a profound transformation: among the elements of greatest innovation in bank management must be considered the evolution that occurred in the control and management of credit risk systems. The reasons that led to intervention in this area of bank management are known and can be traced to:

- The relevance of losses on receivables as an element that has a significant impact on the financial results of the intermediaries operating in Italy.
- The fact that the supervisory authority has always controlled credit risk: recently, this has found more organic regulation as a result of regulatory actions regarding the internal control systems and the modification proposals in the "Basel Accord on Capital Requirements."
- The growing interest of investors in the economic performance, capital stability, and performance levels of credit and financial intermediaries.
- The change in attitude of the directors and the management, who are more sensitive to incorporating, in an integrated manner, the issues of management control and risks, as part of the organizational processes for the bank system.

The afore-mentioned elements have focused the attention of scholars and practitioners on the development of systems of credit risk management (CRM) (Borghesi, 1985; Borghesi, 1994; Crockford, 1986; Beaver and Parker, 1995; Carter and Crockford, 1999; Harrington and Niehaus, 1999; Smullen, 2000; Crouhy et al., 2001; Culp, 2001, 2002; Doherty, 2003; Godbillon-Camus and Godlewski, 2005; Jorion, 2007; Felisari, 2008; Bessis, 2011; Hull, 2012). According to the author, a CRM system is the set of integrated models and measurement tools that allows, along with the existence of appropriate organizational procedures, a settled and optimal management of the credit risk.

Therefore, the elements characterizing a CRM system, and that set it apart from all those instruments and procedures that have always been used by all credit intermediaries, are the following:

- The clear, unambiguous, and shared identification of objectives to be pursued.
- The precise definition of the object of the test system and the fundamental characteristics that it must own, not only in the short term but above all in the medium term.
- Innovative approaches followed for the creation and management of the system, as well as those underlying the definition and choice of models, indicators, and instruments adopted for risk measurement.
- The fundamental importance of all organizational elements (procedures and processes) that allow the measurement model to be operational for management purposes, and that such a model will be designed and then implemented.

Finally, when we refer to CRM, the appeal to the term "system" assumes that all activities conforming to the management of credit risk are seen in an integrated manner; that all projects of intervention in measurement and management systems are coordinated in a strategic and operational viewpoint, by people who are able to perceive fully the scope and its realization, and that they are, at the same time, provided with a particular sensitivity to the formalization and communication aspects of the entire corporate structure.

From what has been said, it is clear that interventions leading to the development of CRM systems in the bank can be seen, from a reductive viewpoint, as a set of more or less exhaustive changes of the control systems in use, or can be interpreted, following a much broader view, as "epochal" changes in the approach to the management of credit risk. These can only be organized according to a planning logic that includes a medium- to long-term deadline and that adopts a modular approach.

In order to find effective solutions for the above-mentioned problems of credit intermediaries, it is necessary to overcome, in terms of motivation, a regulatory approach. The development of control systems of risk and management should not be seen as a formal fulfillment of requests coming from external control bodies, but as a real need for the development of the modes of government that can also affect the reputation of the bank (Gabbi and Patarnello, 2010).

Another critical element concerns professional skills. In many situations, the development projects for CRM systems, and the solution of the problems related to them, are delegated to specialists in the credit sector that tend to intervene on the procedures and tools according to a bottom-up approach. This leads to the strengthening of structures of lines of control on operational processes that, not always, is combined with the actual existence of organizational autonomous units responsible for the auditing of the risk and ensuring sometimes, on the one hand, the existence of an appropriate information flow addressed to senior management and, on the other hand, the integration with other models and monitoring tools in use in the rest of the bank. Let us consider, for instance, the problems related to the measurement of credit risk arising from efficiency of the financial area on traditional or innovative tools.

An evolutionary approach to credit risk management (Resti and Sironi, 2008; Duffie and Singleton, 2012), requires that the adoption of models of analysis of exposures be understood and managed in an appropriate way; actuarial statistical knowledge, which does not always form part of the cultural baggage of those traditionally responsible for the auditing. Furthermore, expert subjects of models for quantitative analysis should also be included in the structure, presupposing, however, that the definition of the most important variables for the prediction of defaults and the identification of their possible availability in the information bank system cannot be done without the input of experts in management of operational processes. The latter are the main recipients of the outputs of the models for measuring risk and should actively contribute to their implementation.

Therefore, it is critical to adopt approaches that rely on expert subjects in management and control of market risks, and also the management and control of credit risks, assuming that they can operate within the area of credits by borrowing the same solutions as the finance area.

With regard to the measurement models of credit risk, it should be noted that among the operators, sometimes there is a lack of awareness of the main concepts, also due to the lack of homogeneity of vocabulary which is found in the various contributions present in doctrine. In practice, there are synonyms, and the concepts of scoring[1] (Bailey, 2001; Frame et al., 2001; Altman, 2002; Thomas et al., 2002; Anderson, 2007; DeYoung et al., 2008; Udell, 2008; Avery et al., 2009; Ferreira et al., 2013) and rating are very often confused (European Commission, 2007; Campanella, 2014). However, in particular, the internal rating systems represent an evolution of credit scoring systems,[2] giving banks the possibility to exploit these extensive information assets, strictly confidential and used for internal purposes only, acquired in the relationship with customers.

The attention that is given to the definition of an internal rating system leads some to overlook the differences that exist between the probability of default rating (which requires a clear and unambiguous definition of default event) and systems that assign scores on the basis of mere fiscal indicators. In some cases, it is believed that the transition from scoring in the rating assignment, is entailed in the mere consideration of subjective elements that are added, in a more or less controlled way to the automatic evaluation of the system with the risk of tainting, on balance, the results.

The goal of building a system of internal ratings (De Laurentis and Caselli, 2004; Felisari, 2008; Cuneo and Maino, 2010; De Laurentis and Maino, 2010; Formisano et al., 2014), leads us to consider the quality of customer classification processes based on the allocation of objective scores (scoring) as a marginal problem, that can be overcome by purchasing classifications developed by others on the basis of analysis models that often are not known and, sometimes, even demanded by users or disclosed by those who attribute the rating.

Following this path, you may risk adopting analysis models that are not compatible with the composition of the portfolio of the intermediary and do not always reflect the evolution of the dynamic assumed by the credit risk with respect to the operating environment of the bank; especially, in doing so, there is a permanent dependence condition on the external environment.

In other cases, we are seeing a tendency to overcome the limits of a customer classification based on the probability of default, to reach the calculation of capital absorption related to the estimate of the unexpected losses, the amount of which is independent from the approach and from the algorithm adopted for the calculation. Looking ahead, the determination of the VaR (value at risk) of credits is an objective to be pursued in the medium to long term and represents one of the elements that characterizes an evolved CRM system. But this evolution should not be regarded as a goal to be achieved at any cost in a short time, even at the expense of the steps that precede it (scoring and rating), which must necessarily be completed in the best conditions and tested for the necessary amount of time.

Whoever writes a CRM system must, above all, provide, in the measurement phase, a quantification of the expected loss on the individual positions; This should certainly take into account both statistical data related to the probability of default of the debtor, considered individually or as belonging to a homogeneous class, and be immediately attributed to the individual relationship that is to be established between the bank and the entrusted party, evaluated from a quality point of view.

Indeed, to ensure a correlation between aspects of measurement and operational management of the credit report, a check of the risk/return profile of the same must be done, already in the preliminary analysis of the cost effectiveness of the operation. The above requires that models of risk analysis that insist on the different phases of receivables management (analysis, monitoring, and review) are integrated with each other, to the point of being seen as part of a single complex model that, depending on the stage of the process of credit management and the available set of data, information elements are provided specifically to it, although based on predefined algorithms.

The output generated by these, must also be perfectly integrated with the control procedures of the management and performance analysis, in order to ensure the effective analysis of the risk-adjusted return that is, today, a basic element of strategic and operational bank management.

Regarding the flows of externally-produced information, we report how the development of CRM systems of and classification systems should see the adoption of more rigorous approaches, to the quantification of expected losses and to administrative and accounting management of funds adjustment of exposures in the budget and in reports. Indeed, given also the requirements imposed by the supervisory authorities for the description of the qualitative aspects of CRM systems in the financial statements of banks, it is not considered that an advanced system of control and management of credit risk can coexist with evaluative approaches that consider little or, sometimes, a single class of customers on which is implemented a lump-sum depreciation, based on a single percentage expressing the expected losses related to loans granted.

A further observation concerns the relationship between CRM systems and auditing activities in banks. In fact, from a different viewpoint, the CRM system must be able to be used by the audit function, while being directed primarily to the achievement of the purposes of granting operational and risk control.

In particular, the use of the CRM can facilitate the activity of the revision of credit, proposing analysis grids that, on the basis of a predefined series of anomalies, allow an activity of remote control based on the logic of exception to be carried out; but this must also be verifiable by an internal or external subject. To this end, it becomes essential that the elements related to the definition of the analysis model, the performance of the planned retrospective tests to verify the correctness of the results of the model, and the effective use of information elements generated by the system, are properly formalized in appropriate documentation which is continuously updated and made available to all interested parties.

The problems that banks have been facing for a long time, and that are derived from a still inadequate integration of business information systems, are well-known (Calcagnini, 2009); However, this problem is a push to keep on innovating systems towards a redefinition of the processes of data and production creation and distribution of information flows, which can only lead to the logic of creating a data warehouse of credit, rather than being used as a justification for not changing risk control systems and support systems for the governance of the bank.

3.4 The re-engineering of the credit process

The observation of the process of credit between financial intermediaries of international standing and structures that are already "credit risk oriented" shows how they are the result of an important transformation of the credit process, induced both by a rapid change in the business itself and by economic reasons and management motivations.

According to a recent survey by the Associazione Bancaria Italiana (2015), the business of lending in Italy continues to generate very low yields. The phenomenon of lower margins requires the transformation of the same philosophy of credit from simple activities of position to dynamic management of business segments, where the biggest challenge will be focused on policies of capital allocation and on pricing of credit linked to the different levels of risk. This means that the outlined transformation of the credit process absolutely will not eliminate credit risk but, more likely, will help to segment it better and to develop an interest rate policy more in tune with the different levels of risk that the management will decide to accept.

In addition to economic reasons, there are also management reasons; these lead to a necessary change of perspective of the credit process. In this regard, it is interesting to note that the current productive structures of the business of lending can be a source of inefficiency when it is considered that in the inquiry stage, in the passage of information/authorizations between general management and branches, it is possible to recover at least 40 per cent of the processing times (checks, requests for data and information, etc.) for the assumption of credit risk.

A further element of reflection is represented by the concrete manifestation of the signs of pathology of the credit report. According to a recent survey, only 3 per cent of such signals emerge during the revision of the loans. Other considerations lead, then, to a rethink of the credit process for the obvious advantages induced, such as: support for the pricing policy; improving the management of litigation; a prediction *ex ante* of probability of losses; the improvement of the monitoring phase of credit risk.

It is clear that the transition to a credit oriented risk structure requires, first and foremost a cultural transformation for the management of the bank, because of their traditional way of making credit changes. The re-engineering of the credit process tends to the objective of reducing costs also through simplification, customer segmentation, and the creation of new professional figures oriented to the management of the customer relationship (relationship managers).

The transition to a credit risk oriented structure involves, among other things, the overcoming of the approach to traditional credit analysis, exclusively localized on the assessment of the individual counterparty based on strong aspects of subjectivity. The definition of a rating system facilitates the overall government of credit risk and leads to more in tune trade policies with the risk/return profile.

The shift from a classic process of credit to a credit risk oriented process involves significant organizational impact. This change is, at the same time, one of the main risks (if not the largest) in the introduction of an internal model for the measurement and management of credit risks.

The risk is linked to the fact that the creation of an internal rating system is sometimes perceived as a problem of algorithms and organizational tools. The broader perspective of risk management holds that the issue is only partly a matter of choice and tuning of tools. In this regard, it is possible to say that the problem mainly lies with organizational and operational procedures at all levels.

3.5 Main risks in the implementation of a CRM system

Hereinafter, are outlined those risks (the list is not exhaustive) that can be considered the main risks in the creation of a rating system:

- Organizational: this is the risk of not considering the organizational impact resulting from the transition to a credit risk oriented structure.

In this type of risk, the attention of the vertices of the bank is focused primarily on issues related to data, algorithms, and hardware, without making a preliminary analysis of impacts and relative changes in the organizational structure of the entire credit process. This risk results in the underestimation of the overwhelming organizational impact.

- Objectives: the relative risk to the objectives is to consider a CRM system as a simple method of measuring the credit risk. To sum up, the CRM model should be considered almost as an end in itself and is instrumental to the introduction of an internal model of capital allocation.
- Credit cultures: it is not possible to imagine the installation of a sophisticated system of credit risk management without acting preventively on corporate credit cultures. Clarification of value objectives, a new philosophy for the credit process, relations between the network and general management, and organizational implications will constitute many future challenges to achieving the proposed goals. Acting on the culture means, among other things, to sterilize the negative effects of a top-down approach, avoiding the spreading of "team orders" that are not metabolized by the structure. It should be taken into account that the shortcomings of credit culture and of process can undermine the rating system as a whole; it is not possible to start up only with policies and well-written procedures to address the shortcomings of credit cultures.
- Temporal coherence: once "in place" the process of credit risk management has to be made coherent over time, to avoid the fact that it is a static factor to the evolution of the company and the market. One of the possible interventions is a periodic recalibration that is independent of the CRM system, aimed at its maintenance over time from a dynamic and not static viewpoint.

Apart from the problem of the size of credit intermediaries, which nonetheless has significant implications on the choices of an organizational nature, it is possible to imagine some relationships and reports that will arise in the future among new functions (and/or functions transformed into their purposes) in addition to its implications on the structure of internal audit. In this area are included:

- The relationship between the risk management function and the credit committee. The observation of the organizational models of credit groups in the Anglo-Saxon model provides, in certain cases, a function of "group risk manager" who is allocated the responsibility of the management of credit risks, and market and operational risks. The function itself is divided into several subareas to which a different risk manager is assigned (credit risk manager, market risk manager, etc.). The risk management function and/or credit risk manager, in dealing with the credit committee, has at least two main aspects: advisory and evaluation of creditworthiness in relation to the absorption of capital. On the one hand, the risk management function plays an advisory and supporting role in favor of the credit committee in the deliberative activity; on the other hand, it checks the contribution of the operation to the venture capital or, in other words, the potential extent of absorption of capital.

- The structure of credit risk management. The philosophy of CRM should be promoted and sponsored by the management also through the provision of a credit risk policy, in which the risk appetite of the bank should be defined and which should be approved by the management board. Other considerations are then carried out with regard to the credit approval process and the CRM team that has the responsibility of monitoring the credit risk and offering advice to the management and/or the credit committee of the bank in a proactive perspective and then to anticipate criticality. Structure of credit risk management means, therefore, not only providing consulting to the management and monitoring the risk, but mostly involves a radical spread and dynamic time for corporate credit culture as a new competitive factor.
- Evolutionary connotations and the role of the internal audit function. The transition to a credit risk oriented structure can affect the role of the internal audit function. The observation of the internal audit function within credit institutions that are already strongly credit risk oriented, leads us to extrapolate new connotations of systemic control. This means moving the focus from the detailed evaluation (examination of the degree of risk in bank lending for individual end borrowers) to a different level that goes beyond operation of the machine and the internal control system. The transformation of the methods of internal audit analysis, in a credit risk oriented structure, lead us to imagine that they are more focused on the review of the organization (credit risk management organization), and of internal procedures and limitations, as well as the flows of relative information reporting to senior management. It is important to note that recently, in US banks at the organizational level, loan review units play a second level control on the activity of lending; their purpose is to maintain the integrity of the whole

system of company rating from a methodological viewpoint. These units report to the chief auditor or chief credit officer of the bank.

In conclusion, we can observe that the approach to the issue of CRM is a journey in stages, in which different variables are needed, such as the preliminary strategic analysis, the assessment of the organizational impact, and so on, with the final goal of reaching a total risk integration (credit, market, and operational risks).

3.6 The activity of control on bank risk management

The lack of consideration of all the different components of a CRM project and/or the emphasis only on some of them (such as aspects related to the tools and/or data) is reflected not only in the lack of understanding of the scope and the constructive complexity but, above all, in a low probability of success of the whole intervention. It is therefore necessary to imagine a training project, in complete harmony with the features of the company, in which all the possible variables are put in a systems perspective (risk integration).

In recent years, bank attention to organizational structures has grown considerably; in particular, to the control of typical risks of intermediation. This evolution has been driven by a growing emphasis on organizational processes that enable the bank's top management to make decisions with a greater awareness of the potential risks and also by a new regulatory framework of reference that promotes internal restructuring.

The operations of the supervisory authorities in the field of control and risk management have been firstly focused on the organizational structures designed to cope with the various banking risk categories. To this end, already in October 1998, new supervisory instructions on the systems of internal controls were issued.

Among the general principles of internal controls, the regulation emphasizes how the control activity on risk management should be organizationally allocated in the bank in structures other than those of production and internal audit (Bessis, 2011). This indication has encouraged the start-up of a significant number of organizational restructures in banks, aimed at making the placement of the risk management function in the structure more rational. The reason why the risk management function should be disconnected from the area of the production units is intuitive: the autonomy of the control function is in fact an indispensable element in order to effectively perform its own role in the bank. Even the differentiation with respect to the internal audit function is also recommended, and for banks with more complex operational structures is crucial, because, while risk management performs ongoing controls, a review unit operates only at a later time, in order to verify the correctness of the procedures adopted by both the production units and the risk management itself.

As a part of risk management, the internal control system must cover all types of risks: credit, interest rate, market, liquidity, operational, settlement, fraud and infidelity, legal, reputation, and so on. Also, the Istruzioni di Vigilanza state that for quantifiable risks "banks must have systems able to identify, measure and control exposure to individual types of risk, as well as manage the overall exposure, even taking into account the possible correlations among the different risk factors."[3]

With regard to the management of credit risk, in particular, the supervisory regulations indicate that the whole process concerning the granting of credit, should be incorporated into the internal regulations of the bank and must be periodically tested. Furthermore, it emphasizes the need that "banks have at all times a correct perception of their exposure to each customer or group of customers, in order to proceed, if appropriate, in a timely revision of the credit lines. This requires an ongoing updated information base from which the identification data of customers, legal and economic connections with other customers, the overall exposure of a single borrower and group of related customers, the technical forms from which the exposure comes from, the updated value of collateral are present" (Bank of Italy, 2000).

Despite being a regulatory framework of principles, the attention of the supervisory authority is clear, because banks should establish appropriate organizational structures and because risk management should possess the necessary tools, including quantitative ones, in order to perform its role effectively.

Going into more detail, it can also be seen that for the management of individual risk factors, the actions of the supervisory authority are based on a comprehensive approach to integrated management and awareness of the risks in the risk management functions of banks. This is verified, for example, in the prudential regulations for market risk, defined as the risk that can be produced by an adverse movement in prices and of market prices.

Although the management of market risk is only the first stage of an integrated process of management and of control of the risk exposure of banking intermediation, the choices made in this field are a good indication for the function of risk management, and also for the management of other types of risk. In fact, the next step, and most important one, concerns the management and control of credit risk; a further study, only recently analyzed by the banking industry, lies in operational risk management.

The need for banks to control exposures incurred on the trading portfolio resulted in the dissemination of models of management of market risks, based on statistical techniques such as VaR. These models are designed, firstly, to provide the bank management with knowledge of the bank's degree of risk exposure and all the intermediate directions, with a precise indication on the maximum risk assumed by individual traders. Secondly, such models, following a recognition by the supervisory authority, may be used to calculate capital requirements, replacing the standardized requirements defined exogenously by the same authority.

In fact, also in January 1996, the Basel Committee on Banking Supervision issued an update to Capital Accord of July 1988, in order to take into account market risks, where the validity of the internal models that banks use for the management of risks arising from unexpected changes in market prices was recognized, and also for the calculation of the minimum regulatory requirements. The same legislation was enacted in the EU (EU Directive 98/31of 22 June 1998) and, finally, was transposed into Italian regulations.

The recognition of internal models for prudential purposes acquires a particular importance, not only because it represents a profound innovation in the methodology of supervision, as the supervised entities collaborate in person in determining capital requirements, but also because it is based on a typical instrument of internal risk management. In fact, the supervisory instructions clearly state that the internal model is established "essentially for the function of risk management" and that its use for regulatory purposes is only a by-product of the model itself. Moreover, the qualitative and quantitative characteristics that the model must have in order to be recognized as valid by the authorities are such as to emphasize its integrated use in the organization; a knowledge at least by senior management of its general characteristics, its pervasiveness in the structure of the bank, at least in those segments exposed to possible market risks.

As it is known, the supervisory regulations on credit risk (solvency ratio) of the Capital Accord of July 1988, provided for a standardized system based on the weighting of the subject given on the basis of its riskiness. Nevertheless, the lack of accuracy of regulation (only four weights were initially planned) has produced over the years relevant phenomena of regulatory arbitrage that led the Basel Committee to revise the Accord.

Moreover, it is possible to see how risk management models are taking a central role also in the approach of supervision of credit risk management: the consultation paper on the reform of the Capital Accord, published by the Basel Committee in June 1999, already made explicit reference to the possibility of using the feedback (rating) of domestic banks on the solvency of the debtors and, ultimately, even on internal models of the portfolio for the calculation of capital requirements for credit risk. Even for operational risks, with the introduction of Basel II, the use of systems of internal evaluation has been provided for.

In the management of inherent risk, it is evident how the use of internal evaluation systems by banks could lead to a better allocation both of economic capital and of regulatory capital. With regard to the first, in fact, a careful perception of credit risk associated with the individual borrower is essential in order to allocate the capital for homogeneous groups of debtors in an efficient way. The efficient allocation of capital, indeed, allocates more where the risks of default are higher, and vice versa.

Similarly, in terms of regulatory capital, the evolution of the Basel Agreement resulted in a saving of capital for banks able to assess, in a satisfactorily and rigorous way, the solvency of individual borrowers; banks that, in the absence of such criteria of internal evaluation, are forced to apply the standard capital requirements set by supervisors.

Furthermore, the use of internal ratings is an operational tool that can positively influence the sound and prudent management of the bank in the various stages of custody, the pricing of products, the monitoring of positions, the process of capital allocation, and performance evaluations.

In light of the trends in regulation, the risk management function is called to focus much more attention on ratings. Traditional CRM techniques, in fact, must be supported by an increased use of quantitative models able to estimate, for each debtor, default probabilities and recovery rates in the event of insolvency. In addition, a new organizational structure should be prepared, based on the consistency of the lending process and management of credit risk with the results of the rating process. The development and growth of internal rating models increase the importance of risk management functions and give greater emphasis to the results of the processes of measuring credit risk.

A further aspect of such measures by the authorities, and inherent to the credit risk, concerns the tools that the market provides to make management easier. On this point, apart from any possible evolution of international regulations, measures that have governed the treatment of supervision of the securitization of loans and credit derivatives have to be considered. With the above-mentioned measures, prudential safeguards for the use of the tools have been defined by which an evolved function of risk management can better manage its exposure to credit risk. Both criticization and credit derivatives are tools for managing this risk, emphasizing the aspect of liquidity in the market, in order to be exchanged among individuals who want to reduce their exposure and willing subjects (of course with a suitable remuneration) who want to increase it. A more careful perception of their exposure and an aware assessment of the strategies to be pursued will therefore induce risk management to consider the opportunity that the bank is active in these new markets and rapidly evolving as an entity that wants to purchase or sell the credit risk referred to a particular subject or a plurality of subjects (Gabbi, 2012).

The ownership structure of banks is also itself the subject of regulation, since it affects their decision-making processes and performance (Zazzaro, 2004; Forestieri, 2011; Sarcinelli, 2014). According to the nature of the subject owner, the types of existing banks are public banks, owned by the state; Industrial Bank, owned by non-financial companies, and independent banks, owned by financial firms.

In all these cases, it is assumed implicitly that the owner holds full control (absolute control). This is exercised due to the possession of the absolute majority of votes.

The state and non-public bank is owned by the state. As sole shareholder, it has the responsibility to exercise corporate governance through the appointment of managers. From this, the bank with state participation must be kept separate then, where the state holds a capital share, whether majority or minority. The public bank, however, is owned by a public body, through a direct or less emanation of the public administration, and it is managed and controlled by it. This type of bank can be divided into two diverse categories: those with social purposes objectives and those with private purposes objectives.

The first category includes those institutions that have the goal of distributing credit to certain sectors of economic activity that would be penalized if funded by institutions that follow the logic of profit maximization.

The second category, however, includes those banks with state ownership, but which have no function of a social nature.

One of the criticisms made of state ownership comes from the separation of ownership and control. The managers, guided in allocation decisions by the state, may have goals other than profit maximization.

Where the choice of management is based on political criteria, rather than on an economic assessment, managers can pursue political objectives, which can interfere with management decisions, producing worse results (Bianchi et al., 1998).

If, however, the bank does not have value maximization as its objective function, it is very unlikely that it will impose this on financed companies and that it will use this policy as a tool of credit allocation (Forestieri and Onado, 1998; Scannella, 2011). The existence of a market in which shares of the banking company are listed, can, however, correct the tendency of management to deviate. The market, as for all listed companies, may signal the deviant behavior, with a drop in stock value; this could allow takeovers to replace the management.

A study on the levels of efficiency in state banks (Conti and Fabbri, 1996) concluded that non-state banks, in the surveyed countries (Italy, Germany, France, and Spain), attain"average" performance levels above those of the state banks; and in particular in the Italian banking system, where private banks appear consistently more efficient than public ones. All other sorts of banks are private ones, in which the regulation can affect the share ownership by providing different rules and informational constraints that are more stringent than those that most of the firms apply.

In this category, first of all, there are the industrial banks and independent banks. The bank–company relationship in these cases provides the possibility for companies to hold shares in the capital of banks. Firstly, industrial enterprises belong to different categories of financial companies (insurance, *merchant banks*, leasing companies, etc.). Secondly, the industrial bank and the independent bank represent advantages linked to the contribution of managerial skills, especially useful in a time when the banking sector is undergoing a radical transformation process and internationalization (Porta, 1997).

Other effects are related to economies of diversification that might occur if the participation of an industrial company could bring some mix of services offered by the bank.

Also some negative effects are connected with the presence of industry in bank capital. It gives rise to situations of conflict of interest that may lead to the granting of credit by the bank to the company industry, which is present in its capital, without a careful consideration of the returns and risks, in this case of financial instability. These behaviors, even if they cannot lead to instability, are harmful in terms of allocative efficiency, as they may end up favoring some destinations with credit instead of others that are perhaps more productive from an economic point of view (Porta, 1997).

The *public company bank*, another type of private bank, is, however, organized in corporate form and the capital is distributed among a very large number of members. In this case, the property is spread among a very high number of shareholders so as to ensure that none of them is influential in terms of control of the bank. In this case, this determines a marked separation between ownership and control, creating the possibility of a subordination of the objective function, with respect to the objective function of the shareholder, compared to the autonomous and potentially conflicting function.

Here we are referring to the expense preference theory of Williamson (1964), which suggests that managers who control the company maximize their own utility function, which does not include profit among its determinants. In fact, managers can show preference to expand items such as their prestige, salary, technical equipment of their staff, and so on (Sciarelli, 2007).

The conflict of interest that emerges between owners and managers may resolve, on the one hand, according to the expense preference theory, in the search for higher dimensional structures than the optimal ones, with risky investments, and, on the other hand, different actions from those now assumed. In particular, it can happen that managers maximize their utility functions by implementing less risky investment projects than those that would result from the pursuit of a profit maximization hypothesis.

In an authoritative study, in fact, Saunders, Strock, and Travols (1990), have confirmed the hypothesis that the portfolio of assets is more risky for banks whose shareholders have a strong control over managers.

The ownership structure is considerably different when considering a bank organized as a cooperative. The distinctive feature of the cooperative is that the members have a very different relationship with the banking institution from that which exists in the normal banking company. In the latter, members are exclusively bearers of capital resources (financial partners); in some cooperatives, members are characterized by the fact that they work in the employ of the cooperative itself (working members), other shareholders are receiving the services offered by the bank (shareholder users).

Another aspect of fundamental importance is the norm of the vote "per capita," according to which each member is entitled to one vote at the meeting, regardless the value of their holding. The cooperative banking company has some similarities with the public company, because the capital is divided among many members, and each of them can have a significant influence over the management of the company. So, in the cooperative society, it is possible to have the same problems that arise from the separation between ownership and control as in the public company.

In the capital of cooperative banks also other companies, as users of the services of the bank, participate. If a business group managed to acquire control, then the cooperative bank would present the same problems as in the industrial bank.

Finally, the presence of users as shareholders might present the cooperative bank with a further problem of conflict of interest between these two categories of members.

3.7 The operational structure

The ability of the business system to achieve adequate levels of consonance and, where appropriate, resonance with supra-systems of reference does not depend entirely on the quality of the decisions of government. It is also the result of a series of activities and processes carried out by a specially designed and built apparatus, so that these decisions might be implemented in practice. The aforementioned apparatus is qualified for its particular property, the operational structure, characterized by a plurality of components and the relative relationships of connection.

The interactions among the components of the operational structure, and between them and the external environment, show a behavior of that system that the governing body perceives as a systemic one. In addition, through the reading of the referred variables that express the different states, it is particularly suitable to represent the evolutionary dynamics of the business system in its unity.

From the point of view of the viable system enterprise, the operational apparatus must be more correctly understood, as the logical component devoted to the execution of activities and operational processes, in search of consonance and, on the assumption of this, of the resonance with the supra-systems. In the following paragraphs, characters qualifying the operational structure and the conditions that enable it to perform, in terms of efficiency, activities, and processes necessary to fulfill the systemic purpose, are analyzed in more detail.

The assumption made in the approach is that the governing body significantly contributes to the definition of these characteristics and conditions, both in the first design of the operational structure and in the dynamic phase, when the reflection of government decisions on that structure and the resulting performance of the management processes, allow the implementation/emergence of the business system. Through the design and modification of the operational structure, therefore, the governing body preorders the evolutionary dynamics of the business system, facilitating the entry, the combination and the development of suitable skills in order to achieve the set of objectives and the general purpose of the system.

The operational structure is thus seen as the unitary object of government decisions, in search of the most suitable structural coupling (consonance) with supra-systems, which is the condition for resonance. The attention paid to the design, development processes, and stabilization of the operational structure will then appreciate the difficulties and, sometimes, the complexity (Barile, 2009b; Cravera, 2009; Barile and Saviano, 2010; Barile and Saviano, 2011; Dominique, 2011) of the problems that the ultimate decision-making body of the company is facing with regard to the ability to:

- Guide the processes of change, adaptation, and stabilization of the structure.
- Counter the resistance that this opposes to such processes.
- Address the pressures arising from self-organizational structural components.
- Direct the emerging system towards obtaining consistent results with the objectives set in the drafting of the strategic guidelines.

Within the conceptual premises that have been identified in the viable system company, the premise-based perspective of investigation and entrepreneurial phenomena adopted in this chapter, various meanings of structure have been proposed, distinguishing finally, within these, the operational structure. To properly investigate the theme of the operational structure, however, a few assumptions are required. The different conceptions of the structure identified in business studies and their variously attributed characters, then, will allow us to come to a proposal of the qualification of a more consistent operational structure with the perspective of the present work.

In business studies, the direct or indirect recall to the concept of structure is very frequent. This is the result, as noted above, of the general acceptance of the systemic view of the company, seen as a complex of human elements, technical and financial resources, appropriately combined according to their defined relationships.

These elements and relationships come together to form, in general business studies, the structure of the business system.

However, the systemic typical analysis of each subject area, concerning entrepreneurial phenomena as the subject of study, has generated different modes of representation of the structure which, by virtue of the identified variables to express it, have led to a partial vision of the same, summarized as follows:

a) Technical structure: this refers to the characteristics of the production-marketing apparatus, which are essentially a nucleus of capacity incorporated in the complex of the elements, interconnected by technical constraints (such as production coefficients, time codes) as a function of the nature of the activities to be performed, the technologies used, the processes of creation, and placement of the product.
b) Financial structure and balance sheet: from this perspective, the concept structure is brought back to the quantities derived from accounting and related reports. The latter refers to the relationships that can be established with certain categories of jobs and financial sources, identified in order to understand the existence of conditions that, in the historical-optical viewpoint, ensure the company's ability to operate in balance sheet situations
c) Organizational structure: in the organizational literature, the concept of structure is understood with reference to the manner in which, in a more or less formalized way, the division of labor among individuals, groups, and organizational units has been implemented, as well as the breakdown of hierarchical authority and connected responsibilities. Overall, the organizational aspect of the structure is a manifestation of the relationships between the different components and the interactions that they have to realize, so that individuals and social groups are able to produce as a systemic behavior oriented to the achievement of the aims and objectives of the company. As part of this presentation, the so-called social structure is also important, as a complex of roles, positions, and tasks that, in their articulation, combine to determine and address the so-called social dynamics that take place in the company.

Importantly, all of the above modes of representation of the structure assume importance in the perspective of governance. The need is felt, therefore, to reach a unified vision of the concept of structure, so that the governing body can properly understand the logic of design and modification. A unitary conception of the concept of structure could be found in the significant works of those scholars who have focused their research on the concept of "corporate structure."

It should, therefore, start from this concept, as it is more consistent with the perspective of the governing body here adopted.

More specifically, thanks to Fazzi, we have the conception of the corporate structure as a complex character and quantitative relations and pro-tempore constant acts to specify the mode of being (nature) the company itself. He, in fact, introducing the concepts of "ways of enterprise" and economic variables such as relevant and complementary aspects covered by the world of business ideas, says: "permanently adopted ways, relative processes of operations and of the most significant economic variables of the system, are then the components of the corporate structure, seen from the summit as a logical model; they result ina simplified representation of reality; a logical model to enterprise level, but also a scientific model, a tool of mental importance for our studies, as it provides a framework for the best conceptual approach of the great strategic processes, based precisely on the government of the company structure through which the company pursues its research and economic continuity" (Fazzi, 1982).

From these considerations an idea follows about the structure as a significant representational model of government, where the governing body is able to represent the company as a whole with executive power, becoming its innovative action and development. It is, therefore, the unit of decisions, which implies a propulsive address, divided into targets and pathways that could then become the subject of partial decisions and not contradictory ones, just because they are coordinated and linked by a common unitary design.

The construction of the conceptual notion of corporate structure allows, therefore, to outline the essential characteristics of the government of the entrepreneur, who sees the company as a "structure," as a "system of quality–quantity"; that is, as "a complex system of qualitative and quantitative traits" on which they, innovator of economic combinations, intend to exercise modifying and renewing actions. The company structure, in other words, gives specific connotations to the company system, contributing significantly to predetermine the possible evolutionary stages.

It is with reference to the intended corporate structure, characterized, in relation to the incorporated capacities, by margins of action that find their expressions in degrees of more or less wide elasticity, that the company system finds its reason for being and is able, over time, to express its potential. The government of the company consists in, therefore, the government of the evolution of the structure through the study, the setting, and implementation of organic plans of business decisions intended to change the corporate structure in an evolutionary sense. Corporate structure, again, that, in its character and quantitative expression, for each company, conceives as a dynamic system its specific character and helps to determine the laws of the state changes.

The set of qualitative and quantitative characters, with their mutual articulated composing, originates the distinctive features of the company structure. Thus, for example, the catalog of products, technologies, and operating cycles adopted to obtain them, the apparatus of diversified production capacity, used in a repetitive manner, equipped with labor force more or less qualified and ranked according to the stage or in specialized departments lines or chains of production and assembly, are all elements that characterize the corporate structure. The flows of procurement, production, sales, and related inventory levels and loads ordering, while assuming the changing of trends in short time intervals, ranges from one period to another according to the regularity of fact or by an application of constant criteria for the regulation and control, also shaping part of the structure in the sense defined above.

The dynamic environment, the ongoing development of company–market relations, necessitates a constant modifying action and renewal of the company structure. It follows that the notion of corporate structure is a conceptual tool of great importance for the analysis of the processes of government and regulation of the company from a systemic viewpoint.

From the recently expressed considerations, referring to a conception of the corporate structure as a unitary object of the decisions of the governing body, the different perspectives of observation and representation of the structure described in the previous paragraph come together in a single view.

From such a conception of corporate structure it is possible to obtain, in relation to the principal purposes of this chapter, the concept of operational structure, intended as a necessary logic to translate the strategic decisions of the governing body into actions and operations, to achieve levels of consonance with the environment and, in this way, achieve a high degree of resonance with the supra-systems of reference.

Taking as a basic perspective of this work the one of the governing body, it is possible to notice, from the above as with the latter, especially with regard to the design and modification of the operating structure, that it should be able to master a wide range of variables. This ability can only derive from an integrated view of the different perspectives of analysis and observation previously mentioned.

It is preferred, therefore, to consider the different modes of representation of the operating structure in relation to the different dimensions on which it is articulated. Considering it of such dimensions, it is possible to see the mutual interdependencies and as the same may, individually and as a whole, influence the development path along which the enterprise system searches for the most suitable conditions to exert its potential.

These dimensions may, therefore, be considered as:

a) Real. Significantly, this determines the structural aspect, in relation to the quality and quantity of capacity built into the human and technical elements of the structure. Flows of cost and revenue, resulting from the processes of production and sales, are manifestations of the validity of technical and technological structure itself, quantifying and qualifying, in terms of earning capacity, successive states of equilibrium of the business system. These aspects may constitute constraints for correct operation of the business system or, on the contrary, highlight the appropriate margins of elasticity that are more or less wide on the adequacy of the technical and technological needs of the expectations raised by the supra-systems of reference.
b) Financial and balance sheet. This occurs primarily in the entity and the composition of cash and financial characterizing of the structural setting, with consequent impact on the ability of the company to modify them, in relation to their quantity and quality, through the introduction of new media from the outside. The varied composing of monetary and financial flows related to the business, combined with new contributions of means different from the conditioned management, within the range of possible evolutionary paths of the system to those actually prosecuted. Then the financial configuration deeply characterizes the dynamic character of the equilibrium states of the system; this in the sense that it can accommodate or make the passage of the structure difficult, from one state to another, even if characterized by a higher level of economic balance. From a strictly balance sheet viewpoint, aspects related to the level of capitalization of the company also become important with regard to the need to put in place an adequate degree of resonance with the over-financial systems and property. In this context, the establishment of an appropriate balance between the allocated capital and venture

capital favors the above resonance, constituting a significant aspect of the government.

c) Social. Observed with reference to the variables concerning the organization of work, this reflects a particular attention to the definition of roles, positions, and duties; these depend on the network of relationships and social exchanges that are determined by the interaction between individuals and groups operating in the enterprise and among them and the company itself. It is in this sense that the business system is characterized as a social system, in which the satisfaction of individuals and groups that work play a key role in the achievement of the goals and objectives. In this respect, it also highlights how the action of government, in the design and modification of the operating structure, should carefully consider the conditions that lead to the formation of an adequate socio-relational climate to ensure that the activities and processes are characterized by very skilled contributions that, however, must be consistent with adequate remuneration of an economic and moral order.
d) Cognitive. This refers to the wealth of knowledge that is present in the facility at any time. It is the result of knowledge gained through experience and learning. It is a fundamental aspect in the current economic environment, directing the evolutionary dynamics of the business system to pathways to obtain positions of competitive advantage. Therefore, it is the duty of the governing body to maintain and possibly increase the cognitive assets, admitting adequate capacity combination and recombination of built knowledge, in the operational structure, favoring relations with which it can be transferred from one component to another, or acquired by other entities and business systems.
e) Temporal. This takes place in the so-called structure of the times. This expression means the complex interdependencies and interrelationships among multiple and different times (chosen and imposed) that will inevitably affect the relationships and interactions between all the elements and components of the operating structure, and among them and the external environment.

These dimensions are closely interconnected and interdependent. It is possible to note, in fact, as, in a systemic viewpoint, a planning and modification action affecting the decision variables, relating to one of them and involving a repositioning of the expression of the remaining variables.

The need to reconcile the different dimensions in a unified vision has important consequences for the governing body, which must be equipped with the necessary skills to:

1. Assess them as a single task.
2. Synthesize them in an appropriate model to represent the different explanatory variables, which can be used in decision-making levels of government for raising the chances of survival of the business system.

In this way, the governing body may be able to dominate the complexity involved in the operational structure, reducing the level of complication.

The efficiency of the operating structure is derived from the degree of consistency with which it uses its own internal means in relation to the objectives, strategy, and guidelines adopted. These, in turn, must be consistent with the environment and the banking system in order to minimize the impact of the structure on the earning capacity of the bank (this structure affects proportionally the relationship between the cost and size of the cash management and that of services).

The improvement of the conditions of operation and productivity of organizational structures, coherent with the strategies and the institutional variables and market, elevates the allocative efficiency globally expressed by the brokerage system. It improves also the effectiveness of interventions in terms of adherence to the satisfaction of the needs individually and/or collectively expressed by operators in surplus, as well as those in deficit, representing the latest polarizations of financial flows.

As part of a banking company, financial efficiency must be distinguished from operational efficiency.

The first can be expressed by the "profitability of money management" indicator, which assesses the ability of the company to make money from the profitably invested capital in its business (all investments and productive uses). The profitability of money management is obtained by subtracting the average return on capital coverage rate of money management. This is the return that the invested capital must generate to cover the cost of funding and expected losses on lending.

Operational efficiency can be estimated by the indicator "percentage of the structure," which identifies the conditions of productivity of the organizational structure of the bank. The latter affects the income capacity, depending on the relationship among the total amount of the costs inherent in it and the size of the money management and that of services.

The incidence of the structure is expressed by the following relations:

- Structure costs/capital employed: this is the relationship between the volume of the costs incurred in the management of the structure intended for the performance of the business and the potential operational management of money, expressed in the form of capital invested.
- Cost structure/income contribution of service management/cost structure: indicates how the proceeds from services are able to absorb the costs of the company structure.

An overall concept of efficiency is expressed by the indicator "operating profitability." It represents the bank's ability to tightly manage the resources available in an economically profitable way, both in the form of capital investment and in factors of production. "Management profitability" is obtained by subtracting from the "profitability of money management," the incidence of the structure as defined above, and is expressed as the ratio between the gross operating result and the average capital invested.

The study of the relationship between financial efficiency and operational efficiency is relatively new when referring to the case of banks. For a long time, the need to consider the operational and organizational efficiency beside the financial one was not felt or was probably underestimated. Of course it was essential, but not limited to capture the profiles of the structure and productivity of resources, especially not directly financial ones; it should be only considered that financial efficiency is primarily influenced by the price and the effect amount of capital invested. So, indirectly, by the determinants that affect the quantities and prices, in relation to particular contexts of monetary and financial policy.

This may lead to the achievement of highly positive results, but is insufficient to express how the overall earnings capacity drawn from the bank is attributable to exogenous factors (interest level of balance of the system, any administrative, fiscal policies, etc.) and to endogenous factors, related to discretionary decisions pertaining to the duties of cost containment in capital spending, the most efficient combination of human factors and technology, in addition to specific choices and combinations of the portfolio.

In addition, referring mainly to assessments of financial efficiency leads us to underestimate the fact that they are managed from organizational functions, and therefore most of the results and the factors that determine the overall business efficiency largely depend on them: the number of employees, and wage systems levels, areas and levels of professionalism, choices of mechanization and procedures, rationalization of decentralized decision-making and executive functions of the dependencies, and so on.

The observation of the experience leads us to point out that, even in the past, the results achieved in the context of organizational evolution were highlighted by each bank, referring almost exclusively to that of a technical-structural or technological one, to be read in function of policy of real growth or objective and oriented development, above all, to quantitatively optimize the function of production and therefore the profitability.

The references to other functions that characterize the organizational system of enterprise remained few or none: to adapt to external changes, the preservation of the structural model, and the integration function of the individuals in the organization, was usually delegated to technicians or intermediate managers, if not a company or external institutions.

4 The Bank–Company Relationship

4.1 The relevance of inter-systemic relationships

The understanding of a phenomenon by an observing subject assumes the activation of a cognitive process that, thanks to the identification, consolidation and use of conceptual schemes, leads to complication and so to creation of a model, out of what previously would have appeared as a blur and a number of indeterminate events.

What is important is that there is no objective reality, but a reality as a result of a process of perception which presupposes the simultaneous presence of the following elements:

1. An observing subject.
2. One or more purposes of investigation.
3. A specific context.
4. A time period relating to the investigation.

The change, also only relative to the perspective of the observing subject and the change of the purposes of investigation, has significant implications for the conclusions where the analysis of a specific phenomenon could arrive and, in the case of a specific context, in a given time. To illustrate this, it is assumed that the observed object is a specific company operating in Italy.

The different entities that may be interested in the survival of the company, although for different purposes, represent, for this interest, partial and several observation points from which it is possible to understand the evolutionary dynamics of the viable system.

In addition to the subject, either directly or indirectly involved in the survival of the company (we should think of the entrepreneur or manager, or the supplier or customer, or also the employee), there are other categories of subjects who may have reason to observe the structure and the behavioral dynamics of the viable system enterprise, for documentary research, statistical, or scientific purposes.

It is evident, therefore, that the observation and study of any area or phenomenon connected with the company investigated, does not concern only the choice or the delimitation of the research field, but it requires qualification/justification of the specific observation point, or of the perspective of the researcher involved in the survey.

This implies a relativization of the search result in terms of the different conclusions to which it is possible to come. Having assumed that the object to be observed is a specific environment in our case, the survey may reach different conclusions if it is performed from two different vantage points with their different purposes: considering, for instance, the opinion of the researcher and of that of the governing body.

In the case of the scholar, the purpose of the investigation is to be as faithful as possible to the representation of the entities, in the context and of relationships intervening among them, in order to draw conclusions about the logical behavioral and evolutionary dynamics of the business taken into consideration.

Of course, as it has been said, the cultural matrix to which the student belongs, induces different perspectives on the conduct and results of the study. It is possible to verify that the student of political economy analyzes the main macroeconomic variables, and among these companies as well, in order to arrive at the general direction of economic policy; the student of industrial economics observes companies in order to determine the laws of operation, the trends at the macro level and in relation to specific sectors.

Finally, the student of business administration tries to learn the laws of operation of companies at the micro level in order to determine the conditions for survival in a specific context.

According to the perspective adopted here, that of the governing body, however, the survey effort is justified by the purpose of collecting a set of information – both quantitatively and qualitatively significant– that may merge into a model of representation of the context useful for the functional decisions necessary to the survival of the governed system. A proper representation and analysis of the context is, in fact, the necessary condition, since the evolutionary dynamic of the business system can take place in conditions of consonance and, at the limit of resonance with the context, thus implementing their own probabilities of survival.

Choosing the governing body as an observer subject comes from conceiving the company as a viable system. It is therefore necessary to recall some conceptual categories, suitable for the representation and interpretation of the environment in view of the viable system.

The qualification of the company as a viable system is important not only in order to understand the internal dynamics of the system, but also and above all the relationship between the enterprise system and the systemic entities and non-systemic entities that surround it. The vitality of a system, indeed, is directly related to its stage of perception of environmental changes and its ability to make decisions of government and management such as to recover, maintain, and improve conditions for survival.

It follows that a system is viable when it is able to survive in a particular environment, pursuing its own purposes and joining to it the achieving of objectives by virtue of coexistence with third party systems, defined supra-systems and sub-systems, from which and to which respectively it draws and provides guidelines and rules.

Following this logic, the role played by the governing body becomes crucial in perceiving, describing, and interpreting the aims and expectations expressed by the entities that surround it. This, in order to define and implement development paths of consonants and, ultimately, resonant companies with the context.

The achievement of such purposes for a specific viable system company is therefore closely linked to the capacity of the governing body to set a rational process of description and interpretation of the context, configuring, in the first place, a representative map of the entities which characterize the same context and secondly, reconstructing for each of the possible entities the behavioral dynamics.

The realization of such map, can be the result of an attitude, an involuntary predisposition to the schematization, or it can arise from the application of an almost complete methodology of analysis. But the impossibility of an observation that could lead to objective opposable results to any observer, involves that the identification of a methodology having a general validity and universal applicability, is at least pretentious.

However, it seems appropriate to seek to consolidate an already set conceptual matrix, treating the concepts related to the viable system and complexity, in view of reaching as rational an approach as possible that addresses the formalization of complete models that have a temporary and contextualized worth (Golinelli, 2008; Barile, 2008; 2011; Barile and Saviano, 2011). The realization of this goal requires that some of the basic concepts of general systems theory and viable systems are cited.

In this sense, indeed, any study and analysis of the context, requirements for the planning and implementation of a decision-making process able to generate value and thus ensure the survival of the company, cannot be separated from the assumption of an observation point, from the need for contextualization of the research and from the awareness of a subsequent subjectivism of the cognitive path.

4.2 The evolution of the bank–company relationship

Considering the bank-company relationship in general terms, without contextualizing both subjects, is a mistake, since the specificities of each of them are not taken into account, and therefore the different nuances that the relationship itself can have in function of both on the corporate conduct and environmental circumstances, are not well focused on.

To analyze the phenomenon it is, therefore, necessary to give some examples, trying to adopt a scheme of description of the relationship that considers the non-financial company as a customer, which expresses a need for financial products and services, and a bank as a provider, offering solutions for the satisfaction of that need.[1] For the analysis of the application, the relevant variables are:

- The type of entrepreneurial formula underlying the company, which is defined as simple or complex along the descriptive dimension.[2]
- The area of the application of the rapport, which is defined descriptively as ordinary or extraordinary,[3] according to the size.

For a simple company, the needs resulting in the necessity to meet financial expectations, are related to the size of operative activity, primarily commercial, and, possibly, to the request for a storing of elasticity to follow the cyclical demand, which is often not formalized and results in an achieved over-reliance through the practice of multiple trusts and the possibility of trespass for short periods.Occasionally there are requests for funding related to investments made to support the development of the enterprise. Buyers over time are rare unless evolutionary pressures intervene in the industry of reference, which would alter the existing competitive structure. The offer is commonly perceived in an undifferentiated way, that is, banks are recognized as providers of a commodity and not as strategic suppliers.

The extraordinary problem is delegated to a professional/accountant that directly communicates with the lenders. In this context, the variable price plays a strong difference as an element of choice in the purchasing process. Lately, this has been outlined by an involvement of SMEs in service components, whose price, however, continues to be confused with that of the products.

This is a problem mostly connected to the low level of financial literacy of Italian SMEs.[4] As regards the nature of the relationship with the bank, it is of a transactional nature in ordinary finance. Even in extraordinary operations, the character is transactional because the relationship is generally handled by a professional external to the company.

For a complex enterprise, the area of the needs is characterized by a financial requirement that is, in turn, characterized by the size and the characters of operational activity that go beyond a commercial nature. Indeed, it has a high level of sophistication (multi-currency treasury, coverage of economic risks, issuance of financial instruments for the funding on the capital market, etc.) Often the complex company also expresses extraordinary financial needs, which happens with a medium frequency.

In this context, the management team is able to segment the offer of the banking sector and to recognize in it the presence of the service component. There is, therefore, a progressive rationalization of the number of banks and an orientation to the choice of the few banks that become strategic partners of the company. As part of the competition, in the face of a greater push towards the variable price given by its greater bargaining power, there is still the ability to recognize an independent value/price from the service, also because of the importance that the financial function is taking in its own value chain.

In the ordinary area, the bank is called to meet encoded and financial needs in some predefined schemes (overdraft subject to clearance, mortgage, etc.). The selection of solutions to the expressed needs is based mainly on the sale of products, while the level of the offered service is usually low and oriented to develop a general understanding of the financial needs of enterprise. The level of competition is high and mainly based on the price (expressed in the form of both rates and commissions).

This is due both to the low defensibility of banking products, in terms of protective barriers to entry,[5] which makes the product itself easily imitated by competitors, and to the number of competitors in a fragmented market, this represents the model of perfect competition.[6] The consequence of this situation is a strong push to internalize all the activities of the value chain of the bank in order to capture the entire margin, to be able to withstand the pressure on prices. The nature of the relationship in the ordinary area is therefore of a transactional nature and related to a typical agency relationship, regulated by contract.

In the extraordinary area, are the complex financial needs that the bank is required to meet; difficult requirements to classify within standardized schemes. Their solution requires an offer distinguished by high professionalism and a character of confidentiality. The service component is prevalent in respect to any offered products and the competition is essentially based on the level of product differentiation as well as on a high level of service offered to customers.

The actors in this market segment compete, then, to a medium-low level and hardly ever on price. The consequence of this is the ability to outsource part of the activities of the value chain without having a relevant impact on the level of the margins achieved. In this case, the orientation is to keep in the company only activities generating competitive advantage.

As part of the relationship, the status of the relationship is of a relational nature in the case of family businesses and is based on the recognition by the company's ownership, of material authority, mutual interest, and sharing of values with the financial partner, often with the mediated recognition and influence of external consultants. In the case of companies with widespread/managerialized property, however, it is transactional and it is based on the recognition of a material authority by the ruling group in respect of the financial partner.

The relationship between banks and SMEs has been traditionally identified as the relationship between a bank that operates in the ordinary area and a simple company from a management perspective. In this type of relationship some phenomena that characterize it well are associated. The first of them is the multiple bank, which is the practice followed by banks and shared by companies to split the company's total bank debt on multiple credit lines granted by different banks, each with a limited amount of the total.

On the supply side, there are the following factors that have led to the development of the practice of multiple banks:

- The conditioning of the Banking Act of 1936/38, which imposed the time specialization.
- The company size of the Italian banking system, which consists of banks not able to provide the entire finance required by the customer company, even for reasons related to the minimum ratios, required by the regulation, including the amounts of individual credit exposures and their capital.
- Simplification of the production function during allocation of capital; the bank prefers to abdicate its function of efficient allocation

of resources through analytical methods for the selection and monitoring of investment proposals/financing, so the bank can reduce its operating costs.
- The lack of stratification of the Italian financial system, which has evolved along a horizontal dimension (large number of companies carrying on the same activities) and has not thus encouraged the development of specialized operators able to establish an exclusive relationship with companies.

On the demand side, other factors that have encouraged the practice of multiple bank relationships may be referred to as:

- The choice of under capitalization of Italian SMEs.
- The disproportionate demand for debt, distributed among a plurality of banks, is functional to a two-fold objective: to compensate the weak point of the low capitalization and manage the risk, often more theoretical than actual, of the revocation of confidence by one or some banks.

In Italy, there are many causes that led over time to a preference for debt over equity. Surely, the conditioning exercised by the tax law has influenced this; it considers borrowing costs as deductible matter in determining taxable income of enterprises, with the consequent saving of taxes rather than the alternative of financing with venture capital, but it should also be considered a conscious choice that keeps intact over time the ownership of the company.

To all this, must be added the desire to maintain the information of the company for purposes that go beyond the financial area such as, for example, the opportunity to resort to practices of avoidance and tax evasion to reduce the taxes already paid.

Certainly the practice of multi-reliance makes the bank–company relationship very weak and of a transactional nature, underlining in this way some disadvantageous aspects for both parties.

The disadvantages for SMEs are summarized as follows:

- High cost, both in relative and absolute terms, of debt. This occurs because the company is thought to be incorporated by the bank as very risky because of the high leverage ratios, the high rate of observable sufferings in the sector of custody, of opacity of information found in the financial and corporate communications. The high rates

depress self-financing and help to keep the firm undercapitalized and with a rigid financial structure, leaving little margin to maneuver.
- The ongoing demand for collateral guarantees, especially of a real nature, which represents a form of coverage of risk by the bank every time it must make up for a client company's lack of information.

For the bank, the phenomenon determines:

- Greater investment risk, as fragmentation in the average size of loans disbursed by each bank reduces its ability to regulate the conduct of the company in line with the overall volume of its credit facilities.
- Inefficient cash management at both banking system and individual bank level.
- Trivialization of the role of the bank.
- Difficulty in managing financial crisis situations with regards to the position of the company.

Ultimately, the practice of multi-reliance has created advantages and disadvantages in the bank–company relationship, but obviously since its spread, the advantages will prevail over the disadvantages, as long as the scenery on which that relationship was built remains.

For some years the characteristics of the relationship between banks and SMEs, as defined in Table 4.1, have been subject to strong pressure for change – from both the supply side and the demand side. In particular for banks, these pressures are attributable to:

- The increasing stratification and specialization of the financial system. This is the result of a greater maturity of the same, which is pushing many intermediaries to specialize in niche activities. This

Table 4.1 The evolution of the bank–SMEs relationship

	Company		
	Simple	**Complex**	
	I From the bank–company relationship	II ...relations with compicated contents	**Ordinary**
Areas	III	IV ...relationship with extraordinary	**Extraordinary**

Source: Author's elaboration.

makes it necessary for them to implement retention strategies that enable them to penetrate the client vertically, and abandon development policies along horizontal lines that are sometimes only to expand the number of customers served.

- The evolution of tax banking law that eliminated the principle of time specialization and has incorporated in it the principles of competition and business activity also in the banking sector. One consequence of this is that the strategies of corporate banking based on multiple bank relationships are no longer present within the competitive structure that is taking shape in the banking industry.
- Internal pressures in the competition in the industry, due to the growing importance of creation of value for bank shareholders and policies of concentration. This also results in the search for greater efficiency in the production function in terms of lower operating costs of intermediation. This means creating strategies with a customer focus, in order to reduce operating costs related to the management of a number of relationships and to increase revenues from the relationships that the bank has with them, implementing the value of the packages of offered products and services.
- The reduction in the general level of interest rates and the consequent decrease in relative and absolute terms of the rate spread has made the granting of credit "traditional" activities increasingly less profitable for the bank and led to the "disengagement" of the price as a competitive variable. This is especially true for those banks that want to continue to be competitive within the corporate sector, while they are less important for banks that intend to specialize in the niche market of retail and/or private banking.

Likewise for SMEs, the changed competitive landscape has made it more and more critical for the company to maintain competitive advantage over time expressed in terms of:

- The extending of the boundaries and of the competitive geographic area of the product/customer/technology combination, imposing a review of long-term strategies. To this we must add the need to have a financial structure which is less rigid than in the past; one that it is able to maintain a greater scale of investment and a growing uncertainty on the timing of production of company cash flows.
- The need for self-financing that forces companies to reduce the financial leverage relationship, both to lighten the income statement

from the burden of borrowing costs and to have a debt capacity of "reserve" in periods of need.
- The ongoing sophistication of financial needs that guides companies with demand for customized and financial products towards the service component. This includes a new role for the credit intermediary, no longer perceived as a mere supplier of commodity, but gradually seen as strategic suppliers/partners of the company.

All this involves a shift in the relationship towards the quadrants of sophistication and extraordinary, depending on the relevance and speed of the changes taking place.

The shift to the right quadrant of the matrix of the positioning of the relationship will change gradually even the distinctive elements because the benefits associated with the practice of multi-reliance could be lost while, conversely, its disadvantages gain importance. This results in a gradual rationalization of the relationship that the company has with banks, or rather in their concentration and parallel strengthening of the contents of the relationship (Ruozi and Zara, 2001).

An important consideration must be made about this competitive change. While it is possible to say that it concerns the totality of banks – at least the ones that want to operate in the corporate segment, as noted – it is not claimed that this involves all SMEs in Italian industry, but the ones that operate in particularly dynamic environments. Indeed, given the particular financial structure that characterizes SMEs, those that will not be forced from the environment to review the financial management viewpoint will remain in traditional lending, although the scope of Basel II at a cultural level is general, and certainly it also affects the more traditional realities rooted in the most stable environment.

4.3 The specificity of the financial structure of Italian SMEs, from financing to the contribution of capital

The characteristics of an Italian SME can be summarized as follows:

- Modest company size, although there is an ongoing gradual development of the concept of corporate networks.
- Management of the company almost exclusively by the entrepreneur and other family members.
- Lack of strategic planning.
- Modest attention to operational planning of the activity (investment and financial requirements).

- Poor financial culture.
- Little attention to institutional communication (not with regards the product).[7]

The discussion on the relationship between banks and SMEs has expanded to new themes in recent years; certainly the best known and debated one concerns the diversification of funding sources through the establishment of a regulated security market aimed specifically at SMEs.

Among the reasons most frequently cited for the creation of a regulated market of securities issued by SMEs, there is the need to reduce their "under capitalization," that is, their excessive reliance on debt, especially on short-term debts to banks.[8] If we notice the structure of the activities of companies according to their size, two main differences can be seen between SMEs and the other larger companies:

- SMEs consider fixed assets of greater importance compared to other fixed components (intangible and financial assets).
- SMEs are characterized by a higher incidence of net working capital.

The motivation underlying this composition of assets may be sought also in the sector appearance of efficiency. Indeed, SMEs are more prevalent in sectors with lower capital intensity compared to large companies. The greater circulating capital share may also be due to less bargaining power of SMEs with their customers, to the spread of the sub-supply relationships and lower capacity of optimization of credits and stocks.

If we look at the structure of liabilities of companies by size, the greater dependence of SMEs on debt is confirmed, in particular on short-term debt. However, linking this structure with that of assets, some important considerations are revealed:

- The relationship between permanent financial components (equity and long-term debt) and fixed components of assets (fixed, intangible, and financial assets) is favorable to SMEs compared to larger companies.
- The degree of "capitalization" of SMEs seems even higher when you consider that the fixed assets, as characterized by a lower degree of "specificity" (and therefore by a greater aptitude for liquidity) compared to intangible and financial assets, have the ability to "endure" the highest levels of debt.

- The greater use of short-term debt is amply justified by the greater share of net circulating capital share that characterizes the assets SMEs. The short-term debt of the latter is in fact largely made up of banking, drawn in the form of the discount and the advance, as these are directly linked to changes of the circulating capital. The high short-term debt is therefore motivated by the coverage of a requirement that is variable for its nature and not always easy to predict. This provides greater flexibility to the company, allowing it to vary the amount of debt in relation to the availability of internal funds.[9]

Additional elements of policy evaluation of business financing can be inferred from the analysis of financial flows.

Regarding the sources of financing, SMEs show a greater reliance on short-term debt, less burdensome than self-financing or the contribution of capital, while there were no significant differences in the use of medium- and long-term debt compared to large businesses.[10] The greater recourse to short-term debts, as already noted, is directly related to the needs arising from net circulating capital.

The increased difficulty (or the lower preference) of SMEs for the acquisition of medium-term debt is therefore denied. This is also explained by the fact that over time the supply of medium–long-term credit has met regulatory changes – the time specialization of banks being eliminated – and this has led to a change in the competitive logic of the market of intermediaries who attacked the niche market of SMEs.

It is, however, confirmed that they have greater difficulty, compared to large companies, in finding financial resources directly on the market. Yet, such difficulty is not to be attributed to the lower remuneration of the owners' equity from SMEs, but as a functional and institutional weakness of the equity market in Italy.[11]

The choices for financing SMEs are not only induced by exogenous "constraints" (difficult access to medium-term financing and to the capital market) or endogenous (desire to maintain concentrated ownership), but they are also the result of choices inclining to optimize the financial structure. From this point of view, with any theoretical approach (cost minimization or the solving of agency problems between the shareholder and the financial backer), self-financing and debt are privileged sources compared to the raising of risk capital from outside.

On the other hand, Italian tax legislation has so far encouraged the use of debt, both with respect to self-financing and to new share issues. Moreover, the absence of minority shareholders unrelated to the management and the mix of corporate and family assets encourage and make it easier for SMEs to make use of financial leverage in order to maximize the value of the equity invested in the company.

As mentioned earlier, the relationship between SMEs and the banking system indicates how the practice of multiple credits and the widespread use of warranties (business and personal ones) constitute elements of weakness in the relationship. They, in fact, do not make for responsible lending institutions and reduce their interest in the acquisition of knowledge about the situation and prospects of the company. It is desirable, therefore, that there is a change in the method of allocation of bank credit, in the sense of a greater connection to their prospects for corporate profitability; this would ensure a greater allocative efficiency by brokers and a reduction in the risk associated with their usage.

This could be one of the effects of the regulatory legislation of Basel II, which induces banks to be more careful in their measurements of creditworthiness, and companies to pay more attention to variables that can affect a reduction of the cost of debt capital (including a better diversification of funding sources, and a reduction in the number of relationships with banks, in view of their rehabilitation from financial backers to strategic partners of the company).

As far as this hope is shared, we must not forget that the connection between creditworthiness and expected profitability of the projects is an insurmountable limit in the asymmetric information between the buyer and lender. The distribution of funds based on earnings prospects of the company (that often result from low quality accounting information) involves an analysis activity, internal rating, which is particularly onerous for intermediaries in the case of SMEs. This is inevitably reflected in interest rates charged by banks, which have received a greater adherence to the individual positions with the entry into force of Basel II.[12]

This does not necessarily mean an aggravation of the conditions applied, but rather a greater diversification among SMEs regarding the cost of debt capital.

Considering, then, the difficulties in setting the relationship of debt mainly on the assessment by the banks of the quality of the investment projects of enterprises, three elements are considered critical in order to overcome the problems associated with such a contractual relationship:

1. The provision of guarantees, whose role is precisely to reduce agency costs and monitoring related to information asymmetries.

2. The limited duration of the credit, which allows the intermediary to periodically review its decisions of custody.
3. The relationship of trust between banker and entrepreneur.[13]

In summary, the bank–company relationship, as well as configuring especially in systems of small business, is not only interpretable in terms of "backwardness" of relations and of subordination of SMEs to policies of allocation of credit by banks. The ways in which this relationship is divided, indeed, are interpreted as efficient solutions to the problems of information asymmetry inherent in the relationship and as a result of the policies of business financing.

The Italian financial system, based on bank intermediaries rather than the security market, however, is more functional to a production system based on a small- and medium-sized unit. The high use of bank credit by SMEs can, then, be read not only as an element of weakness in their financial structure but also as a result of an institutional system (financial and tax) which has in fact encouraged this method of financing; it can also be considered positively, as evidence of the ability of the financial system to transfer to SMEs adequate resources to meet the opportunities for their development, given the difficulties of the latter in the use of these channels of direct deposits.

However, with respect to the possibility of direct financing through the capital market, it should be said that even in the economic reality where markets are more established (US and UK in particular), the opportunity to receive funds through direct funding is often the last alternative of financing examined by companies.

The preference by companies for the use of undistributed profits and of debt, compared to the issue of shares on the market, is traced from the theory of corporate finance in the presence of transaction costs and information asymmetries between managers and financial backer, as well as the different structure of the rights that the various forms of funding have on dealing with the company.

From the point of view of efficient allocation of resources, the use of intermediaries rather than the market provides a number of advantages:

- Allows a more efficient monitoring of funded projects.
- Promotes investments in specific activities and with long-term returns.
- Allows the financing conditions to be renegotiated more easily, thus ensuring greater flexibility to the company.

Stock markets, from their point of view, serve two main functions:

- The presence of listed companies increases the possibility of diversification of investors' portfolios.
- The stock market is set up as one of the main tools to facilitate the reallocation of company control when they are run inefficiently.

Practically, the theoretical reflection on security markets enhances their role in the exchange of property rights and the related mechanism of price formation of such rights, rather than functioning as a channel to raise capital to finance investment. This latter function is even more penalized in the case of SMEs, whose development projects may be more effectively supported by intermediaries rather than by direct appeal to the market. This statement is supported by two main considerations:

1. The presence of asymmetric information, which would be priced in a much more severe judgment on the impersonal market, rather than by intermediaries.
2. The greater privacy issues of SMEs with regard to innovation projects and development, especially in competitive environments and those with few barriers to entry. Also in this case, therefore, the relationship with the intermediary is preferable, rather than report to an audience of investors.

If these considerations are valid, it is evident that the new market for SMEs – established in 1999 by Borsa Italiana SpA and destined for the trading of equity shares of domestic and foreign issuers with high potential for development – plays a particular role of accumulation in an already established band of medium enterprises and it does not affect in any way the financial management of the smallest and traditional realities. However, the role of intermediaries (banks, merchant bank, and venture capital) is not sacrificed, rather, in some cases it is enhanced.

The characteristic of intermediary participation is one of acquisition of a significant stake in the capital of the company in view of its sale at the end of the operation. The existence of a security market with less stringent requirements and access costs than the main one, favors the possibility of disinvestment of investments in SMEs.

The changes taking place in the systems of small business emphasize, on the one hand, the emergence of new organizational realities (networks and business groups) and, on the other, the growing importance of innovative activity. Overall, the system seems to evolve towards organizational structures that make up a flexible and decentralized model of capitalism, based on integrated systems of SMEs.

It is with reference to the ability to support and develop such a model, that actual or expected adjustments in the financial system should be assessed.

As for intermediaries, it appears essential to accelerate the changes in progress in the relationship between SMEs and banks, in the sense that the transformation of the latter also gives a good supply of credit to the enterprise partner to solve financial problems. The Italian banking system has embarked on the right path, and guided by the new regulations in terms of capital adequacy will support the development of SMEs, which are the backbone of our economic system.

4.4 The European market of SMEs

SMEs play a pivotal role in competitiveness and the creation of jobs in Europe. In fact, they constitute not only the vast majority of European companies, but are also the source of dynamism and change in the evolution of new markets, particularly those that are on the frontiers of knowledge. They were defined as "the engine of the European economy. They are an essential source of jobs, they create entrepreneurial spirit and innovation in the EU and they are therefore essential to promote competitiveness and employment" (European Commission, 2006).

The definition of SMEs developed by the European Commission includes those that have the following characteristics:

- Less than 250 employees.
- Annual turnover not exceeding €50 million or an annual balance sheet not exceeding €43 million.
- Independent, that is, not more than 25 per cent controlled by one or more organizations that are not SMEs (except public investors, financial investors operating as a bank or fund, and "venture capital" companies).

Such types of companies, although they form a diverse community, are exposed to market imperfections; in particular to increasingly fierce competition, due to the completion of the European internal market and the need to constantly innovate as well as to accommodate advances in technology. In addition, a growing number of SMEs have carried out internationalization strategies or want to do so, to find new markets and business opportunities. However, in many cases they complain about the difficulty in obtaining financial resources from capital or credit, especially in the start-up phase. This situation causes, especially for SMEs, severe limitations in terms of access to new technologies or innovation. This is reflected in a widespread climate of pessimism about the general economic situation, even if in the last period it has been softening – a pessimism that, particularly in companies, feels the negative influence created by the uncertainty about the evolution of the macroeconomic and international policy environment. In the European Union, Italy, with 5.3 million active businesses as of 31 December 2013, is the country with the largest number of micro-enterprises and SMEs at 17.2 per cent, far exceeding even the most populous countries such as Germany (10.2 per cent) and France (12 per cent), in addition to Spain (10.4 per cent) and the UK (8 per cent).

Among the active companies, analyzed from the point of view of legal form, there are 3.3 million individual businesses and over 900,000 partnerships. More than 1 million corporations, are characterized by a perfect patrimonial autonomy (in which the shareholders' meeting is separated from that of the company) and greater information requirements.

In the European context, the intensity and persistence of the economic crisis, along with the restriction of credit supply, have presented a considerable criticality for Italian production. This crisis, in addition to determining the fall in GDP, has generated a persistent stagnation in demand by limiting the growth of the system.

In this context, Italy has suffered more adverse effects than its main European partners, both in terms of the fall in gross domestic product (GDP), and for the severity of the second recession, following the one in 2008, even if this hit Spain with less force, and had no effect on Germany, France, or the UK. The weakness in demand was firstly accompanied by a slowdown, and secondly the contraction of bank credit badly affected Italian SMEs. In fact, until 2008, bank loans had grown at very high speed, then slowed down considerably until 2011 when their volume shrank. The crisis, however, has also had a negative effect on the number of Italian SMEs, despite the implementation of certain instruments of entrepreneurship incentives, created at state level. From 2008 to the first half of 2014, the number of new companies was significantly reduced, so that with the exception of 2010, the number of new registrations remained below the level of 400,00 annually. Among the new ones, those formed as limited liability companies (Srl) have a considerable influence that are potentially smaller. In particular, in 2013, only 26,000 companies were set up with paid-up capital of more than €5000 (36 per cent), a fall compared to 59,000 in 2007 (73 per cent). In the same year, 38,000 companies were created with paid-up capital of less than €5000 (53 per cent), compared to 14,000 in 2007. Also from a study carried out by Cerved on SMEs (2014), we see that the granting of bank loans over a certain threshold is crucial in the first year of establishment, in order to obtain the status of SME within three years. The statistics show that 11.2 per cent of new companies with bank debt of more than €20,000 become an SME in the three years following their enrollment. This percentage drops to 5 per cent for companies that have received loans of less than €20,000 and for those established without any bank support.

In this context, the number of those who have managed to survive by creating value for stakeholders was reduced. Those expelled from the market were in a situation of financial distress, or presenting a low level of expected profitability, and voluntarily chose to liquidate their business. Despite the difficult situation determined by the crisis, there are many Italian SMEs that are young and dynamic, especially in terms of propensity to invest, with solid fundamentals, which have the ability to grow rapidly in spite of the crisis.

Indeed, from the Cerved report of 2014 an important fact emerges: in Italy there are 3472 SMEs defined as "gazelles," which have doubled their turnover between 2007 and 2012. These businesses have implemented a process of sustained growth, while operating in sectors with a higher level of economic and financial environment, mainly in the south (this indication shows a potential growth also in southern regions), they have been active for a few years, with major investments in immaterial capital, little dependency on bank credit, and with a more daring use of leverage. Moreover, they are more profitable and more productive.

The survey also showed that the ongoing crisis has facilitated a process of selection, which has improved the financial condition of SMEs compared to the period before the crisis. In fact, the number of SMEs that had a risky budget has been greatly reduced for a whole series of factors: the selection that expelled the most vulnerable undertakings from the market; the de-leveraging linked to the credit crunch; recapitalization carried out by many companies; the decrease in interest rates, which reduced the weight of the financial charges on margins. The effects of the crisis on SMEs were amplified by their heavy reliance on bank capital for the procurement of the necessary financial resources to operate. In the financial statements of Italian SMEs, it has been found that 98 per cent of the debt is of a banking nature. This percentage represents a much higher value than that presented by German, Spanish, and French SMEs.

The high dependence on the financial system has significantly affected levels of profitability and sustainability of financial expenses as SMEs, in addition to not being able to benefit from the effects of the reduction in interest rates, have a greater fragility in facing the crisis. This situation led to a significant widening of the risk gap that existed before the outbreak of the crisis. The analysis of the levels of dependence on banking by SMEs highlights both the growth in the share of bank debt on the assets that increases the probability of company default, and in the crisis years the significant growth of the risk differential among the companies that are more or less dependent on banks.

4.5 The bank–company relationship: the importance of the risk/yield profile

The bank–company relationship is a crucial and delicate process in the development of the interrelations between the financial system and the real one. It is crucial because it is contained in it and the bank has a way of performing its contribution to the efficient allocation of resources. In other words, the distribution that it is able to guarantee, with the funding of more worthwhile initiatives in terms of expected income and taking risk into account, allows the highest rate of development of the system as a whole. It is also delicate because even just one element of imbalance is sufficient to mitigate or to nullify all the possible benefits contained in the relationship itself. From this viewpoint, the bank must always put itself in a critical position with regards investment projects and highlight all the possible points of weakness. This clearly helps to select the best initiatives in the economic and financial profiles (expected income and expected cash flows), ensuring the efficient allocation of resources. In principle, a balanced relationship can be defined as one that ensures both optimal financial structure for the company and allocative efficiency for the bank.

The bank, on the specific terms of loans, can achieve such a relationship, and thus achieve allocative efficiency, by adopting two points:

- On the one hand, the individual bank must have full knowledge of the choice of implemented financing, or rather, knowledge of the degrees of risk/return of each of the feasible operations.

- On the other hand, it would be appropriate that the bank, with its intervention, would be able to ensure a more balanced financial structure in the company.

Regarding the first point, it seems obvious, as stated by Golinelli (2012) that "the bridge over which the relationships between companies and the financial system convey, is the relationship between risk and expected return."

With this in mind, the preservation of the efficient use of resources derives from the lender's ability to choose, abstractly among the credit applicants, only guided by considerations of profitability and balance of expected cash flows; that is, respecting, in full autonomy, the risk/efficiency hierarchy in the selection of feasible operations.[14]

As it is known, in fact, lending activity is characterized by a high content of risk and, in the case of corporate finance, the risk of each loan must find expression in the expected return. In other words, there must be a direct relationship between risk and interest rate; also, to make the mediation convenient, it will be necessary that the expected return, net of the borne risk, is greater than the *risk-free* rate (the rate offered by government bonds of the same maturity).

If each bank correctly determines the risk of each loan, the rates are determined uniformly for all categories of borrowers with the same risk; if the composition of the loan portfolio is based on the evaluation of the risk/return combination for each operation, then it is possible to realize the conditions for an efficient allocation of resources (Corigliano, 1996).

As for the second point, the clear identification of the nature of the financial requirements of the financed company is particularly important because it must be able to "cut" the intervention on the real needs of the enterprise. Even if direct relationships between individual transactions of investment and financing cannot be established (companies finance themselves and not individual transactions), the impact of operations on the totality of the cash flows of the company and "draw" on the credit intervention have to be assessed, taking care to match appropriately the needs and coverage (Onado, 1996).

Moreover, as Bianchi stated (1986), "the value of the traditional guiding principles of the relationship, summarized in the concept that the excess of intermediation does not make the bank robust and healthy, but the correct finance of client companies that put in harmony the structure of assets and passive assets," leads the relationship, in the new market environment, to become even stronger, although in a comprehensive approach in which the finance of companies is directed more to markets than to intermediaries.

To achieve such results, it is necessary that banks translate the closer and ongoing relationships maintained with businesses in a better assessment of investment projects and, more generally, of the quality of the borrower, assessing the prospects of growth and income in investing companies.[15]

Deepening risk assessments, specific to a process of financing of investment projects, it is appropriate that the lender will ask if the customer that requires the funding is implementing strategies that create or destroy value. This approach leads to not focusing the analysis on the repayment capacity in the technical sense (availability of cash sufficient to support the reimbursement), but rather extending it in the direction of creating value.

The value theory argues, in fact, that the purpose to assign to management is to grow the economic value of generating benefits for all stakeholders (Maltz et al., 2011; Porter and Kramer, 2011; Rangan et al., 2012). With this, the vision of the company results is oriented to the future, because what matters is not the positive difference between revenues and costs (profits), but the potential to produce better results (Sciarelli, 2014).

Therefore, it is necessary that banks move from a system of evaluation focused on the historical balance sheet (liability method) to one based on the economic and financial prospects of the company (value method) (Brogi, 1997). The logic of the value enables key stakeholders to approach "the problems of the company with care and understanding" (Guatri and Massari, 1992). From this perspective, the banks need to better understand the changes taking place in the economic capital of enterprises and especially to strengthen their ability to follow the events of evolution of the same, as the bank–company relationship traditionally focused on the fragmentation of the relationship has certainly eroded this evaluation capacity. Monitoring business of the economic capital is therefore essential in the new configuration of the bank–company relationship, especially in operations where intervention is planned with risk capital (Golinelli et al., 2012).

It should also be pointed out that, in the current context, the relationship of bank financing is characterized in the Italian system by some aspects of allocative inefficiency that may be more burdensome for SMEs with the best prospects for growth and profitability.

These items include:

- Moral hazard and adverse selection.
- Significant difference in cost of funding that is more expensive in the south and in the center of the country than in the north-west and the north.
- High weight given to guarantees as part of the assessment of the solvency of the company.
- Splitting of credit risk achieved through the division of financing shared among multiple institutions.
- Preference for forms of control based on the short deadline of repayment of credit granted.

These are the main features of the bank–company relationship that restrict the acquisition, by the banks, of information on the projects of the company and which weaken the role of organizing investment.

The specificity of the bank in resource allocation and assessment of creditworthiness can be analyzed according to a financial theory. In support of these theories, there is the recognition of the existence of information asymmetries that dominate in almost all markets making them imperfect; information asymmetry contrasts with the theoretical diction of transparency, ensuring that trades, however, entail costs of acquisitions of information by generating uncertainty in the completion of the contract (Sciarelli, 1996).

This implies, on the one hand, that the conclusion of any exchange in itself entails acceptance of some degrees of risk; on the other hand, that beyond a certain threshold the prevalence of risk aversion can be assumed, allowing the rise to trade.

Especially in financial brokerage, the discourse gets complicated when considering the particular nature of the contract that is established between banks and businesses. The uncertainty, characteristic of the credit agreement, can determine conflicting behaviors between the two parties. Indeed, not operating under conditions of perfect information, the bank does not have certain and complete tools to grant credit on the basis of the financial structure of the applicant enterprise. Because of the uncertain conditions prevailing in the markets, the financial structure reflects the choice of allocation of business risk among those called according to diverse levels to finance the activities (managers, shareholders, and creditors). In explaining the reluctance of banks to extend credit, the so-called agency costs of debt are crucial, or rather, the costs arising from the decision of claim holders to divide the undertaken risk

(Jensen and Meckling, 1976; Scandizzo, 1999; Fontana and Caroli, 2009; Tirole, 2010; Gabbi, 2012; Dagnino and Merendino, 2013; Sarcinelli, 2014).

In financing relationships, conflicts are based on the fact that the agent, who is the party that has more information, can use the knowledge of their own characteristics or can take action in the most convenient way for themselves, but not for the other party, or rather, the principal party, which is the least informed.

According to a certain number of authors, in the light of such problems, credit brokerage appears to be the most efficient institutional solution to eliminate or reduce transaction[16] and agency[17] costs that the parties incur because of these imperfections (Williamson, 1988; Onado, 1992).

These drawbacks (informative inefficiencies) concern the possibility of making an adverse selection (adverse selection) either in the assessment of such care and taking increasing risks, or simply as a result of unforeseen opportunistic behavior on behalf of the borrower (moral hazard) over the life of custody.

By analyzing in detail these issues, let us begin with the analysis of the problems of adverse selection.

There are problems of adverse selection in a transaction when a party, the agent, is aware of relevant terms and outcome of the transaction that are not only ignored by the other side, the principal, but they pre-exist to the transaction itself and do not depend on the will of the agent.[18] The classic examples of adverse selection are found in the property market, in the case of used cars,[19] and in the case of life insurance policies where the policyholder (agent) may be aware of details about health conditions that are ignored by the insurance company. In the credit market, however, there is an adverse selection when an increase in the interest rate determines the exit from the market of risk-adverse investors, causing reductions in the average level of risk aversion of the remaining potential borrowers. The severity of a situation of adverse selection, depends on the ability of lenders to acquire all the possible elements of knowledge about debtors and their projects; if such knowledge was complete and perfect, the problem would not arise. One possible solution, in fact, can come from the conduct of the parties to the market that transmit private information in their possession through the mechanism of *signaling*[20] and *screening*,[21] according to which the transaction will be respectively the agent or the principal.

The problems of *moral hazard*, however, occur when the most informed party, the agent, takes, after the definition of the contract, discriminatory actions that have relevance to the outcome of the transaction and that the principal subject is not able to check totally or in part.

In other words, a case of hidden action takes place where one party has the full knowledge of the contract conditions, but is not able to verify its subsequent development.

In the credit market, situations of moral hazard may take place when companies that offer loans present projects to the lender where there is high uncertainty on the expected results and therefore these are more prone to failure. In this case, the creditors risk losing all or part of the loan. Businesses can easily risk failure and the greatest damage that may occur, in this case, is the possible loss of assets used as collateral. Considering these circumstances, the increasing of interest rates as a means of eliminating an excess of demand for loans may, due to the reduction of an advantage for businesses, induce the same to undertake investment projects with high profitability, but with higher risk.

In the operational reality, problems of moral hazard could be partly deleted and "could find a solution in monitoring measures undertaken by the main subject that aim to control the borrower and to prevent any prejudicial conduct of credit repayment"(Golinelli, 2000).

In practice, the fundamental role of banks lies in the function of delegated monitoring, by virtue of which the bank receives from depositors a proxy to exercise control over the final debtor, both in the evaluation of investment projects and in the verification of the results achieved.

These reflections are based on the assumption that the lender has private information on the characteristics of the risk/return of the project to be financed, on the managerial effort made to achieve that vision, as well as the final results of the project.

The function of the bank lies in the production of information aimed at overcoming this asymmetry and exercising control over the conduct of the debtor, in order not to compromise the interests of the lender.[22]

The increasing globalization of the economy inevitably involves a strong increase in competition, which is why companies are obliged to formulate new strategies and reconsider their position in the market.

This entails, among other things, the need to focus on product and process, by increasing the share of investments in order to produce at increasingly competitive costs and maintain, at the same time, high levels of quality.

For the Italian production system, this creates a new situation: many small companies will be forced to become medium-size, and many medium-sized enterprises will increase their size to adequately address the competitive challenge internationally. Companies will also increase their propensity to invest abroad and to follow policies of agreements with companies in other countries.

These policies require, of course, an appropriate financial structure with a better balance in the relationship of equity and debt financing; growth, therefore, cannot be supported as in the past, only through the banking channel or by self-financing from the family heritage, but it will rather be sought in a more active relationship with the market.

Many companies are already heading in this direction and they increasingly use financial professional management to do so.

New opportunities, in fact, can be exploited only if businesses will open up to the outside, by adopting a policy of transparency towards investors, which, however, cannot be imposed by stringent regulatory constraints, but must be primarily the result of self-determination of the companies that decide to engage with the market.

It is therefore time to reflect on what might be the ways that can help bring businesses to a more advanced financial market, with a structure of intermediaries and investors that is much stronger than the current one.

Moreover, as Ruozi stated (1998), "contrary to the opinion of those who see the relationship between banks and businesses as a situation of conflict of interests, goals and interests pursued by each of the two, travelling on absolutely parallel rails: a prosperous industrial system cannot exist, in fact, if the country lacks an effective and efficient banking system. However, the converse is true: an effective and efficient banking system is necessarily founded on an industrially profitable and growing environment."

In this regard, the potentialities arising from the removal of institutional and operational constraints of the banks certainly appear relevant. The new banking law indeed, introducing the universal bank model, outlined an institutional innovation that can help to improve the traditional bank–company relationship in a temporal and extended perspective (Baravelli, 1995b). The conversion to less fragmented and more accountable customer relations requires from banks and enterprises a considerable effort of cultural change in their *modus operandi*.

In this regard, it is believed that innovation should not be limited to the products offered, but should increase the quality of service to overcome relational barriers. What has really changed, as Giorgetti notes (1998), seems to be "the necessary nature of the companies that make up the so-called banking system: banks institutions from banks to businesses, from brokerage firms to service companies, able to place even products, that must remunerate their capital, creating value in diversified and increasingly competitive markets, with a proactive view towards a risk which is considered more an opportunity than a threat."

In this new context, then, the banks have an incentive to sell business services and therefore will have to rethink their operations, carrying out not only the usual credit activity but also consulting services, placement and underwriting of share issues, and merchant banking activities.

The reorganization of the activities is a necessary step for Italian banks that, with the euro, are facing, on the one hand, a reduction in interest margins due to the convergence of interest rates at community level and, on the other hand, the increased competition from European banks. But the competition has become fiercer, especially because customers now compare services and prices, and require new and more sophisticated products. Therefore, an important role must be played by enterprises, particularly those of small and medium size.

What seem to characterize the underlying problems of the development of a new bank–company relationship, or rather, what is called corporate banking (Corigliano, 2006; Modina and Polese, 2008), are two closely linked aspects:

- On the one hand, the emergence of a relationship that is no longer a relationship between the two entities (relationship banking) but that has been replaced by a single logical transaction of the exchange relationship (transaction banking) (Boot and Thakor, 2000; Berger and Udell, 2006; Berger and Black, 2007; Bongini et al., 2009; Scannella, 2011; Boot and Ratnovski, 2012; Bolton, et al., 2013).
- On the other hand, the fact that the large group of economic changes that are currently underway (increased competition, the euro, recapitalization needs, quality of products and processes) affect at the same time both banks and industrial companies.

However, it seems that in addition to processes of rapid change, a relationship based on traditional logic persists, for which there is a pressing need for immediate innovation – both for reasons of bank competitiveness and for the development of enterprises and the economy. What seems to hinder the change, apart from the persistence of traditional bank–company relationships, is a system of relations between supply and demand that are less sensitive to the factors that influence the relationship.

Italian companies, therefore, need to rely on a wider system of financing tools and a banking system able to assist them in supporting their innovative and internationalization strategies. The evolution of the markets in which they operate imposes demanding strategic choices that cannot be confronted with financial structures based on the prevalence of short-term debt.

In this context, intermediaries must raise the quality of their services (through diversification and specialization of content), making them competitive in a financial market, such as the European one, which in recent years has experienced a gradual unification.

This is because, in the context of modern finance, based on a developed capital market, the banking system can play a key role in defending the competitiveness of the production system, if it establishes a wider relationship with companies

In terms of tools, innovation has been extensive. Banks are now able to offer a much more comprehensive range of products and services to an audience of companies that has increased its propensity to purchase these new products and services.

In particular, there are innovations in the areas of innovative credit, corporate finance, and advisory services.

As for innovative credit, there is a larger and larger increase in medium- to long-term loans in order to raise capital to invest in a sustainable manner in companies. Investment banking, merchant banking, and risk management are new business areas that many banks, especially the large ones, have developed while others are yet to adapt.

Corporate finance is attributable to: equity loans, underwriting and market placement of shares and bonds, guarantees, underwriting and placement of securities through private placements and public offerings, commercial papers and certificates of investment, and derivative products to hedge the risks. Among the consulting services, there is the monitoring of the trend of the economic and financial enterprise, planning of financial activity in the medium and long term and planning for the short term, the preparation of complete information about the possible sources of funding and the respective costs and usage, assessment of possible decisions in order to deal with the various problems of currency (euro), the analysis and evaluation of possible mergers and acquisitions operations, and financial management of groups.

Still, credit derivatives and securitization tools are widely used in the search for more efficient solutions for the management of the default risk of borrowers, typical of credit intermediation activity.

Nevertheless, the attitude of the banks still seems too tied to products rather than innovation in its customer relations. Customers seem to acquire innovative products, more because they are pushed by the offer rather than because there is a strategic transformation in the relationship of a financial-production dimension. What must be considered is that many of the product innovations are likely to have no success unless there is a more profound and complex change that will result in a true relational innovation.

Moreover, as regards companies, the approach of risk-sharing will also rely on a renewed information transparency. From this perspective, the *rating*[23] is a variable key allowing businesses and in particular SMEs to access European financial markets. Otherwise they could be cut off not only from an increasingly global capital market but also from an increasingly competitive one.

With the introduction of the euro, in fact, there are no more barriers in terms of access to credit and savings. Having the rating is crucial; a triple-A has no nationality and, moreover, it will ensure a uniform international evaluation, putting Italian, German, and French enterprises on the same level. The rating may discriminate between being competitive or staying on the edge of the market. This happens to companies wishing to finance themselves through the issuance of debt securities, but also for those who simply want to secure a preferential channel of access to credit. To all this, we must add that the presence of a single currency, along with the progressive tax harmonization and liberalization of capital movements, allows investors to gain access to any market. Under such conditions, the rating would be the criteria most likely to be used to guide investment decisions.

It could be confirmed that, at least at first, possession of a rating assessment could be a differentiator for companies seeking financing, especially for medium-sized businesses, so that they could increase their level of visibility on the market. From what we have seen, it is possible to infer that the rating is an advantage both for issuers, who procure at lower costs, and for investors, who can diversify their portfolio with risk-certain return activities.

However, for the rules of behavioral segmentation, which involve the application of specific conditions by banks, to be transformed into opportunities for growth and consolidation for SMEs, it is appropriate that they implement a policy of financial planning and simulation for internal monitoring of their indicators.

Taking for granted that the renewed legislation favors the large companies – since they are more transparent about their finance-sheet situation and because they are more solid and solvent, guaranteeing them a more correct pricing – is a serious mistake. The winning company, big or small, will be the one that will undertake and fund a significant and profitable growth path, creating a transparent relationship with creditors and lenders (Tarocco, 2003).

The renewed Basel Accord, therefore, is definitely a challenge to be seized by both banks and companies and, if properly applied, could greatly help to evolve the relationship between bank and company arrangements to be more efficient and more consistent with a modern market economy.

Companies will be able to identify and exploit all the positivity inherent in the current process, setting a different financial culture that, however, is only part of the corporate culture. In fact, the more general objective to be pursued is the growth of the corporate culture as a whole, which means, for example, also promoting technological innovation, spreading the culture of quality, using innovative management strategies, and above all intensifying the activity of programming, not only in the production and finance area, but also in the capital area.

The business community must therefore make available all the elements that constitute a prerogative for the construction of a good dialogue with the credit system. In this context, a lighter tax aimed at the emergence of realistic income figures and that will push the convenience of debt to the assets is the most appropriate measure of economic policy.

All this should lead to a growth of the corporate culture in the medium term and a rationalizing of relations, in which the bank assumes the role of partner in the process of growth and development of the business.

4.6 The concept of capital allocation in the viable system enterprise

As already mentioned, the viable system company, during its evolutionary dynamics, is dealing with risks. These risks are divided into two classes:

1. Risks of uncertainty.
2. Risks of not knowing.

The first are risks that the governing body can predict, thanks to its cognitive variety, although it is not able to determine the intensity in terms of amount.[24] The governing body is protected from such risks, either through the transfer of the same to the outside, or resorting to insurance agencies, or providing specific internal funds to cover any losses.

The risks of not knowing are linked to the occurrence of both unknown events and events that the company does not believe it has to consider, as it is not able to assess the probability that it will manifest, nor the possible consequences on the expected results.

It is necessary to protect these risks by preparing, therefore, a garrison in charge of the property, which is called the allocated capital.

This concept, borrowed from regulatory legislation provided for financial institutions, has been adapted to non-financial companies. The basic rule is always the same, the business risk has to be borne by the property, regardless of the ways in which it occurs.

We must, at this point, summarize the ways in which the governing body determines the extent of this garrison. Firstly, it must consider that the net effective result (P_e) could present a deviation from the objective result (P_o), as provided in the budget of the investment (Golinelli, 2005).

The riskiness of the plan is determined by considering the deviation of the actual values around the target value. Assuming, then, according to a statistical approach, a normal type distribution of the net result variable (P). If σ P, or better the standard deviation of the variable P, is distributed according to a normal Gaussian, it is estimated that the maximum expected loss ($P_o - P_e$) is equal to 3 σ P, or it will be within 99.73 per cent confidence from which we associate the practical certainty of the occurrence of the deviation.[25]

$$3\delta(p) = PMA \qquad P_0 - P_e \leqslant 3\delta(p)$$

This formula represents the equation of the curve of normal distribution or Gauss, with its bell shape characteristic, which at the varying of μ (average) and σ (standard deviation) parameters implies a graphical representation which becomes more or less flattened, but always of the type shown in Figure 4.1.[26]

$$f(x) = \frac{1}{\sigma\sqrt{2\pi}} e^{-1/2(x-\mu)^2/\sigma^2}$$

The maximum expected loss being attributable to future values needs to be updated on the basis of a perpetuity. This, identifying the maximum possible loss, helps to determine the garrison that should be placed on it to protect the risk of not knowing:

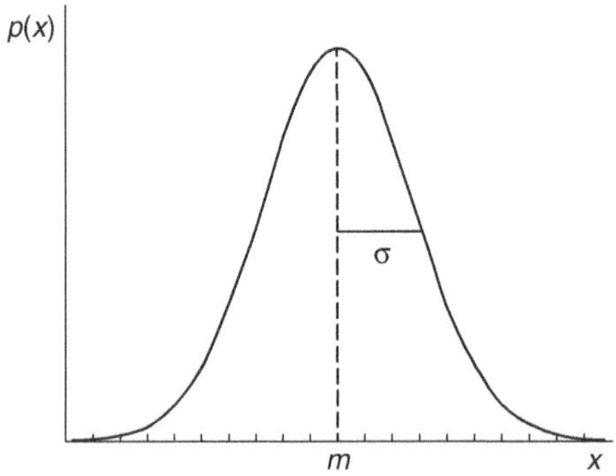

Figure 4.1 Instance of Gauss function

$$I\ \underline{3\sigma} = PMP$$

where the discount rate *I* is determined as the weighted average cost of capital debt and equity capital (WACC). These quantities are identified on the basis of the accounting records of the stated goal. So *I* is estimated according to the specific situation of the company.

However, having to calculate the maximum loss in a timely manner, it is essential to take into account the past in order to properly define the amount of allocated capital. Therefore, you must add up to the maximum possible loss (PMP), the expense recognized in the financial plans of the state of departure, or better the alleged loss in the past (PPP):

$$\text{CA} = \text{PMP} + \text{PPP}$$

To be precise, we must emphasize that the risks of uncertainty for a portion fall in the risk of not knowing if there are mistakes in the estimates or assessments made. If the separation between risk of not knowing and risk of uncertainty was actually possible, and always exact, you could define a "limit" financial structure (see Table 4.2).

Table 4.2 Types of risk coverage

Post		Coverage
Non-risky activities		Debt
Risky activities	Uncertainty	Provision
	Not knowing	Own means

Source: Author's elaboration.

In reality, allocated capital (CA) is rarely equal to the equity (MP). This situation occurs because the CA derives from estimates, particularly with regard to the discount rate. However, the estimate of allocated capital allocation finds its validity in comparison with their own means, which allows to define the level of capitalization of the company being tested.

The total invested capital in the company (K) is determined by adding the debts (D) and equity (MP):

$$K = MP + D$$

If MP = CA we are in the financial structure described above then. So:

$$K = CA + D$$

Since MP $\neq$ CA, you define a new entity EDC (excess/deficit capital) precisely equal to their difference:

$$EDC = CA - MP$$

Also in relative terms:

$$EDC/K = EDC/MP + D$$

Similarly, it is possible to define a quotient of ideal indebtedness (q*) referred to the limit financial structure, and a quotient of actual indebtedness (q) calculated on the base of the data of the balance sheet:

$$q^* = D^*/K; q = D/K$$

It is now possible to define, with regard to the parameters defined, on two financial situations in which the company could be:

Overcapitalized company, since:

$$MP > CA$$

$$EDC < O$$

$$q < q^*$$

The company, in this case, presents an excess of its own means that is able to cover both the risk of not knowing and a part of the risk of uncertainty. This surplus of resources can be used in both industrial and financial perspectives. In the first case, in order to support a policy of investments in the objective to implement the value of the structure. In the second case, the company being "solid," enjoys greater confidence on the part of the financial system; therefore, at any time it might meet the demands for the repayment of loans granted by the same.

Undercapitalized company:

$$MP < CA$$

$$EDC < O$$

$$q > q^*$$

In this case, however, generating an allocation of the garrison to the risk of non-knowledge on the part of creditors, the company presents itself as unreliable for the financial system. From an industrial viewpoint, growth projects are funded externally. This situation may preclude any possibility of development if the required risk/yield profiles by the supra-system are not met.

The new awareness of the risk, therefore, requires the viable system company to think in terms of risk/yield profiles. It is evident that in situations of underfunding, high-paying projects are required, compared to what happens in the financing of companies with a more solid financial structure. This allows us to argue on the quotient of debt in relation to higher or lower pressure that the financial system has on the system.

The quotient q^* represents a watershed between a situation $q<q^*$ where the systems resonance is ensured sovra-capitalization and a $q^*<q<q^m$ where the continuing systemic resonance conditions action is linked to the careful guidance of the government body. As q moves away from q^* to q^m the discretionary margin[27] tends to decrease with increasing essays. With the ongoing increase in the ratio of debt, the discretionary margin that the company has, tends to decrease to zero when it reaches the limit value q^m, maximum compatible value with the system's ability to convey the relationship with the company through the risk/yield profile. At the same time the degree of resonance with the SF decreases; gradually the relationship is no longer systematic, but it is related to the risk appetite of the individual intermediary.

The management tool that allows us to calculate the optimal level of debt in relation to the financial structure is leverage. This expresses the fundamental concept that it is convenient to borrow as long as the cost of debt is lower than the cost of equity.

The concept of allocated capital in the enterprise, however, is a different concept from capital allocation in banking. The latter, in fact, as we saw before, is a constraint for the banking business, with the level of lending still determined by strict rules. The corporate allocated capital placed to cover the risk of non-knowledge is an estimated measure, according to the methods that are considered most appropriate, internally and voluntarily, with the goal of evaluating the correct capitalization of the company. Therefore, significantly, it affects the ability of the governing body to perceive and read properly the complex phenomena of the environmental context. The higher the predictive power of the potential risks, the lower the garrison placed to protect the risk of non-knowledge.

In the banking sector, only with the introduction of Basel II, were the most internal interpretative skills carried out, although the estimate must still be included in quite rigid regulatory forums. Therefore, the evaluation of the risk/return profile qualifies the act of the financial intermediary; this explains the attention in government action to promoting the development of a culture of risk.

The allocated capital assumes, within government, a relevant position to the implementation of an aware management of the risk. It is, in fact, a prerequisite for the survival of the system in terms of resonance with the supra-systems and in particular with the financial one. Risk management led to the overseeing of the consequences on planned evolutionary dynamics of the business system and any adverse events – in the two classes of risk of uncertainty and non-knowledge.

The allocated capital, as a full risk capital, falls within the competence of "property." External to the system, beyond outlining the structural settings, it has qualified the governing body in relation to a planned development dynamics with the objective of increasing the chances of survival. On the other hand, the overall risk resulting from the events that the company has had the ability to identify and analyze, can be managed by the governing body through the provision of appropriate settings tending to its containment, both in the entity of the event and that of consequences. The risk can be transferred to an entity belonging to the structure of the company or to a person who, despite being part of the enterprise's transactional environment, is not included in its structure. In such a context, it is possible to have, depending on the choice, a situation of risk sharing or risk shifting.

In the first case, the risk is shared in the company by expanding the variety that characterizes its structure (for instance, outsourcing, long-term marketing contracts, a joint venture in a pool for research and development of new innovations). The risk shifting is taken into consideration, instead, assuming that the risk is transferred to a non-structural subject. Risk sharing happens, in this case, through the definition of contractual settings, used to make an assumption of risk by a third party (such as entering into a swap agreement or an insurance policy).

The possibility for the enterprise to manage risk, through the use of insurance instruments and contractual settings with third parties, located respectively in the structure or in the wider transactional environment of the company, however, depends on the ability to read complexity, in addition to defining adequate contractual settings. Ultimately, the capacity and the risk appetite of the various subjects included in the transactional environment in which the company operates.

4.7 The system of capital allocation

The system of capital allocation has the objective to allocate, in an efficient way, the capital resources of the bank, in order to assess the degree of capital utilization and measure the performance of the business units of the bank through a consistent basis for comparison. A characteristic of this system is, in fact, to highlight the current allocation of capital of the bank and determine the risk-adjusted profitability for each business area, with a homogeneous measurement of the different types of risk and associating the types of risks that are peculiar to each business unit. It can, therefore, be defined as an integrated system of policies, methodologies, and infrastructures.

With regard to the policies that directly derive from the business strategies, the systems of capital allocation must be consistent with the strategic goal aimed to maximize the economic value of the company in terms of wealth creation for the shareholder or, in any case, for the ownership. This basic strategy could become concrete, in particular, through a reorientation of the company mission to the areas of business that generate the highest return of income for the same amount of capital required. This restructuring is pursued, therefore, through the identification of well-defined business units, in competition with each other, able to think on their own with a different market segment.[28]

Regarding methodologies, these relate to the formulas for measuring the capital absorbed, methods of tipping of indirect costs and the necessary equipment.

The methodologies, both from the point of view of the calculation of the risk (VaR, historical simulations, Monte Carlo systems, confidence interval, holding period, etc.), and from the point of view of the determination of the elements of income (revenues, direct and indirect costs, system of internal transfer rates, etc.) must be consistent with the management systems already present in the enterprise, in order to provide a homogeneous key or the financial phenomena, permitting through the sharing of both databases and methodology, a reconciliation to units of the financial phenomena.

The system of reallocation of capital, as in all management systems, is identified in the various aspects of the structure and process.

Regarding the structure, the area of impact is global, as it underlies all business areas in which the bank is organized.

The latter, considering a medium-sized bank, may refer, for example, to a customer segmentation that is possible to relate to different channels (for instance families, large investors, individual companies, SMEs, corporate, government agencies), the various activities of the bank (collection, use, services, finance, investments, real estate), and the types of risk (counterparty, interest, exchange, market, operational, etc.).

The analysis that is necessary to proceed with the reallocation of capital concerns is as follows:

- Risk profiles (interest, foreign exchange, equity, credit, cooperative, etc.).
- Profiles of profitability (accrued interest income and expense, actual and figurative, direct and indirect costs reversed).
- Performance indicators: from the traditional measures to those of profitability for the risk (RORAC, RAROC, RARORAC).
- Control measures: monitoring of compliance with the limits in terms of capital allocated to each business area.

From the point of view of the process we can analyze the reallocation of capital in terms of phases, subjects, and times.

The main steps of the process are:

1. Study and the choice of the methodology.
2. Understanding of business areas.
3. Determination of the matrix areas of activity/risk.
4. Determination of the capital to be allocated.
5. Measurement of risk in terms of absorbed capital.
6. Measurement of return on assets.
7. Measurement of yields on allocated capital.
8. Definition of a reporting system.

Examining in detail the individual steps of the process, the first phase is inherent in the choice of the methodology with which to proceed, both in the measurement of the absorbed capital and the determination of income for each business area. The choices made at this stage, both in the method of measurement of absorbed capital and the technical rollover of indirect costs, carry out, by definition, the profiles of the adjusted risk/yield among their different ones. For this reason, it is necessary to deepen this time of studying in order to be able to understand the strengths and weaknesses by assessing how these harm the structure of the profit centers of the bank. The crucial nature of this phase lies, therefore, in the identification of methodologies consistent with the operational profile of the bank in relation to the size and complexity of the organization, as well as in the evaluation capacity of any distortion, in terms of results, that each choice may involve.

The second phase is inherent to the functional architecture of areas of business that must flow from the company's mission and the competitive strategy of the bank. Its purpose, therefore, is to explain in the scheme the objectives of income/capital resources and organizational structure with which the bank intends to compare itself with the market.

Once you determine the areas of business, the next step is the determination of the business areas and risks matrix. At this stage we proceed to analyze which types of risk exist in each area in order to be able to measure, in a complete and exhaustive way, the capital resources absorbed by each of them.

The fourth step is the determination of the capital to be allocated; to this aim, the quantities that can be considered relate essentially to the following:

- Market value of the assets represented by the market value of all assets, less the market value of all liabilities.
- Capital.
- Accounting assets.
- Economic capital, meaning the present value of all expected future cash flows for the various activities of the bank.

It is evident that this choice affects performance indicators because, with the increasing size of the assets taken into consideration, the risk-adjusted profitability decreases.

The next step consists in measuring the risk in terms of absorbed capital; this will therefore assess, by measuring the absorbed capital in each business unit, whether as resources the bank's capital is effectively divided among the business areas. This information, along with the analysis of income returns, provides the first quantitative indication to proceed with the reallocation of capital to the business areas with greater added value for shareholders.

The sixth phase concerns the measurement of income of each area. This results in a functional analysis of the sources of revenue and direct and indirect cost items; this activity addresses issues and aspects that are typical of traditional management control and that, therefore, it is supposed to analyze, how the process of reversal of indirect costs involves repercussions on different sizes of profitability with the changing of distribution techniques.

The next step is for the measurement of returns to profitability on allocated capital. The previous steps have been synthesized, once identified by the business units, in the determination of capital allocated to each business and the profitability achieved by each business unit. The process is therefore concluded with the calculation of the risk/yield profile (risk adjusted performance measurement indicators – RAPM) of each area. This profile, relative both to each business area and to the bank, is to be compared with the cost of capital in order to quantify the value created or destroyed for the shareholder.

The last phase implies the creation of a reporting system that is able to provide, with details for each business area and for the entire bank, information concerning:

- The size of the risk (interest, foreign exchange, equity, credit, operational) and the diversification effect for both the business area and the entire bank.
- The size of the income (revenues, direct and indirect costs reversed).
- Two-dimensional risk/income reading according to the approach of the RAPM indicators, verifying the coherence among the different business areas and between each of them and the entire bank.

From the point of view of those subjects involved, the process of reallocation of capital involves the entire organization, from the general direction to the individual responsible for the different business units through the various offices that inter-functionally collaborate on the project, such as the risk management, research, human resources, and marketing departments. As regards the timing, however, it appears evident that such a process requires an approach that is not only purely technical and methodological, but also a strong cultural sharing. This results in much shorter deadlines as there are already operating within the company other processes oriented to the two-dimensional reading of the financial issues in the key risk/yield scheme, such as the control of finance management and the control area of the system of interior controls.

The introduction of the process of reallocation of capital entails the need to maintain some fundamental coherences management.

What is relevant is to highlight the right coherence of the objectives and aims (internal coherence) with the other management systems of planning and control, reporting, human resources, and information systems (external coherences).

In the first place, the internal consistency, which must be protected, is that the process of reallocation of capital descends from the business plan of the bank and that it is consistent with the budget assumptions.

Secondly, it is necessary to maintain external coherence with other external management systems in the company.

As for the system of planning and control, defined as a coherent set of structural, process, and methodology aspects – aimed at guidance and leadership of the company, cognitive support, involvement, and cultural change – coherence is sought at all levels of the process, from strategic planning in the medium term, to the annual operational planning, to management by objectives.

The reporting system, which is a set of information made available to the various levels of responsibility in the company, must identify the different information needs of different management levels, while maintaining appropriately the requirements of consistency, transparency, completeness, and articulation, and assessing the level of destruction of compatible information with the necessary degree of timeliness of responses (timeliness/completeness trade-off).

As regards the system of human resource management, it is clearly there to ensure consistency of the reallocation of capital with the key stages of the development process of resources for the company: from intake to training, evaluation, reward, and release phases.

4.8 The bank–control body relationship

To understand the evolutionary dynamics of the relationship between the governing body of the Bank of Italy – along with the Interministerial Committee for Credit and Savings (ICRC) and the Secretary of the Treasury – and the structural component of the financial system, in particular financial bank intermediaries, it is necessary to retrace the important phases of this relationship. It has been the subject of numerous changes that culminated with the recognition of banking as a business activity and the ongoing abandonment of a structural supervision in favor of a prudential one, in addition to an attenuation of the constraints on the operation of these intermediaries.

The current relationship between the governing body and bank financial intermediaries is the result of a long and troubled evolution that has its roots in the period after World War I, in the effects of the collapse of the US stock market in 1929, and in the failure of the application, in the Italian case, of the Italian model of mixed banks imported from Germany. This model included the collection of funds in the household sector and in the medium- and long-term employment in industry, connecting in this way many times to a participation in the risk capital of the same companies.[29]

Of course, in the face of a weak financial system like the Italian one, and in the presence of a recession like the one of the 1930s, this planning, coordination, and control action of the governing body on the operational structure was characterized by a severe dirigisme, intervening in the economy and finance, in an attempt to remedy a remarkably critical situation.

The financial system is thus protected to the outside by blocking the entrance of permits imposed by the governing body to the inside by very strong segmentations that covered both the operations of banks and concentration processes.

In this climate, the bank financial intermediaries merely manage their share of the market without expansionist ambitions or concern for invasions by others, and this in the belief that this state of affairs was the most appropriate for the needs of investors, who were seen more as suppliers of raw materials than customers.

In 1937, a restructuring of the Italian financial system took place, inevitable after the great economic and financial crises of the 1920s and 1930s that resulted in the rescue of the big banks by the state, but indirectly it became their owner through the Institute for Industrial Reconstruction (IRI).[30] Such a change of ownership, which would have been initially temporary, in view of the return of investments in banks in private hands through their settlement on the market, became definitive. Indeed, the temptation to keep in public hands a business system that could be an instrument of economic policy of great importance, the possibility of establishing a credit market protected by not granting additional permissions to banking and preventing private investors from reaching the public banks, as well as the belief that there was at that time private capital able to detect the investments, not only banks, in the hands of IRI, made sure that the mission of the latter was analyzed again, making a permanent management and control structure of a system of equity to be considered permanently in public hands.

In conclusion of this restructuring process, almost all Italian banks were directly or indirectly nationalized, and the phenomenon of private entrepreneurship banking was marginalized to a supporting actor role, restricted, except in very few cases, to credit unions (banks and rural banks). The consequence of this state of affairs was the immediate censure of the model of the mixed banks and the so-called specialized banks; the latter, in fact, were distinguished as Ordinary Credit Institutions (whose loan portfolio was represented, with certain explicitly authorized exceptions by the supervisory authorities, solely by short-term loans) and Special Credit Institutions (operating in the medium and long term).

The main reason why the governing body chose this approach was to avoid the recreation of situations where excessive maturity transformation could create an uncontrollable crisis of liquidity for banks, as had happened during the chain of bank failures that occurred at the turn of the 1920s and 1930s.

The protection of the depositor and the stability of the banks were put at the top of the scale of priorities by ensuring that banks were increasingly able to cope fully and in a timely manner with their commitments with depositors. Of course, the stability came at the expense of efficiency, and the bank was seen more as a social institution, with functions of general interest, rather than as a company projected towards the achievement of profit.

In this way, however, they created entirely fictitious segmentations of the credit market, with the consequence of creating large areas of monopoly, with consequent falls of competitive tension and efficiency in the involved credit institutions.

The medium- and long-term banking sector in Italy was so characterized by mono-sectorial nature for most of the institutions, established by law. The forced operation segmentation of the banks in the medium and long term, essentially implemented for reasons of economic policy, ended up putting in serious economic difficulty the same banks operating in the sector. This is not only for the reason mentioned above, but also because of the fact that they, being unable to seek alternative forms of use of the funds raised, were often forced to grant credits under not so competitive financial and economic conditions, since the limits to the operational freedom of intermediaries gave a strong bargaining position to the only possible recipients of the credit.

In the 1990s, the path towards modernization was achieved through a process intended to promote the privatization of public institutions. In recent years, the public banks, which were the most important structural components of the financial system, have gradually abandoned the organizational model of the public budget to hire legal forms of private law. They are considered to be indispensable to make business government more careful to the results of management operations, to facilitate the collection of venture capital, to remove the obstacles that the public nature of the institution interposed to the concentration processes, and to make them less influenced by political power that systematically had occupied the management. As a result of this evolution, the governing body has recognized entrepreneurship banking, defining it as a production company that carries out systematically, institutionally on risk, a financial intermediation activity mainly using funds obtained from third parties as part of debt and to a lesser extent by way of equity capital.

The recognition of entrepreneurship banking has profoundly changed the Italian financial system, as this development concerned not only the operational capabilities of the banks through de-specialization, but also its same configuration by simplifying the varied landscape of the categories into which bank financial intermediaries were previously divided.

This has benefited the Italian financial system that, by spurning the opposition to progress that has characterized it for almost half a century through the removal of barriers that protected many segments of the industry, has been found to operate in a more competitive environment. So, it is now more market-oriented in its needs and its changes, offering customers services and products closer to real needs; or better services and products of the highest quality according to the philosophy of total quality. These goals have been achieved, as mentioned above, through two radical changes: the introduction in Italy of the bank of universal type and the institutional exemplification of the banking system.

The real breakthrough, however, occurred with the transition from a structural to prudential supervision, which allowed the gradual abandonment of a control model based primarily on the instrument of authorization. This benefit of a supervisory methodology focuses on the use of default parameters of operation related, basically, to the size of its own equity, to the compliance with capital ratios, the adequacy of the organizational structures and internal controls of the bank.

With this in mind for the governing body, the capital adequacy of the bank is the primary benchmark for both the assessment of the operational capacity of the bank and the resulting regulatory action.

The amount of equity is a quantitative element of correlation for the various supervisory rules, according to the suitability of such means to contain the different risk profiles. Unlike in the past, the governing body of the financial system exercises supervisory powers having regard to the *sound and prudent management* of bank financial intermediaries. The sound and prudent management is both an objective of supervision and a rule of conduct for supervised entities. As aims of supervision, it identifies with the other objectives (efficiency, stability, and competitiveness) the *ratio* of direction, coordination, and control of the governing body.

With regard to preventive, concurrent, or subsequent controls (permits, inspections, and monitoring of the securities) sound and prudent management is the parameter to be used to assess the validity of the business decisions of intermediaries. For this reason, it is also the rule of conduct which banks must observe. From this perspective, sound and prudent management requires observance of rules also essentially technical and, as such, subject to diversification according to the activity carried out and the space–time context of operation. Management is sound if it is based on fully functional efficiency, and probity.

Potentially, profitable management is sound, but also the financial intermediary bank that makes allocation decisions solely on the basis of merit is sound. Finally, prudent management is the one averse to risk, to an extent that can diversify obviously in relation to the activities of the intermediary.

While the purpose of sound and prudent management refers to the structural component of the financial system, in particular the bank financial intermediary, the overall stability, efficiency, and competitiveness are related to the financial system.

This differentiation helps to define the responsibilities of the governing body. It is evident, for example, that it is not its task to prevent the failure of individual institutions, but only link it to sound and prudent management, taking into account the overall system stability.

In fact, the powers of direction, coordination, and control of the governing body refer to the behavior of individual institutions; no intervention of the governing body has been adopted and reported to indistinct aggregates, but each covers and constrains the behavior of the individual, the composition of the budget (for example, it does not impose a relationship between capital and risk at the aggregate level, but it imposes on each intermediary to respect this relationship).

Therefore, the stability of the financial system must be pursued using rules, referred to individual intermediaries that incentivize them to uphold healthy and cautious behavior. Among the tools available to the governing body, the most compatible ones with the competition have to be selected, without ignoring the inefficiencies that in the financial systems characterize the same competitive game.

For what concerns more closely the supervisory functions of the governing body on the operational structure, these are divided into the following:

- Reporting requirements that are expressed on the basis of periodic reports sent by banks to the supervisory body, in the manner and within the terms established by it, and on any other data or documents requested, and on annual budgets.
- Regulatory powers, which attributes to the government, the Bank of Italy, on the basis of the resolutions of the ICRC, the power to issue general regulations concerning capital adequacy, risk containment, equity interests, administrative and accounting procedures, and internal controls that banks and other financial intermediaries are obliged to follow, as well as the power to authorize certain transactions. The Bank of Italy may also call the corporate officers of banks, as well as order the convening of the governing bodies of the same, to establish specific prudential measures for individual banks in the event that such measures are aimed to restore normal operating conditions or when individual prudential interventions are necessary.
- Inspection that allows the Bank of Italy to conduct inspections, through its officials, in banks, and to require the submission of documents and actions it considers necessary.

Regarding the control functions of the Bank of Italy, these are aimed at:

- Ensuring sound and prudent management of the banks, which must combine over time the profitability with an awareness of the risks and compatibility with the economic and financial conditions, as well as with an operating conduct based on fairness.
- Avoiding inefficiencies in operatives' practices which may affect the trust component inherent in the relationship with the public, increasing conflict and the loss of reputation that goes with it, with

consequent negative effects on the economic-financial components of the company's credit.

- Disclosing to customers, through the scrupulous implementation of the discipline of the transparency of transactions and banking services, the essential elements of the contractual relationships and their variations, as a means to promote and safeguard the regular carrying out of competition in banking and financial markets as well as protection of "weak parties," without reducing substantially the negotiating autonomy of the parts of the relationship.

Essentially the supervision of the governing body has a dual purpose. The direct purpose is aimed at protecting the efficiency of banks that with sound and prudent management pursue the objectives of an overall stability, efficiency, and competitiveness of the financial system. The indirect purpose intends to safeguard customers from abnormal behaviors of banks, in contrast with the current laws and regulations, such as those likely to cause them harm or injury.

5
Intangibles in the Assessment of Creditworthiness

5.1 Introductory remarks

The entry into force of the Basel II capital adequacy of banks, was accompanied by the adoption of more sophisticated systems for assessing the creditworthiness of companies. The Committee on Banking Supervision, in response to the globalization of the financial market, deemed that there was a need to ensure the stability of the banking system and to change business banking,[1] based on mutual trust, comprehensive and real, to be updated continuously and bound to the actual ability to generate an income, from the perspective of future growth and not just the short-term goals of the beneficiary.

Under the new agreement, the governing body of the financial system wanted to give increased coordination to the financial system, recently affected by increased competition among financial operators, with business practices that were sometimes aggressive and not always correct in behavior with savers and businesses (Golinelli, 2008).

Unlike Basel I, which established predetermined risk weights for all non-financial companies, regardless of their size and location, as well as the perception that the market had on the credit risk of the individual borrower, enshrining the role of capital in its function of covering the risks constraint to the expansion of banking (Bianconi, 2004), with Basel II each bank could determine the specific risk of the individual loans, drawing on assessments made by external rating agencies, or assessments carried out in-house (De Laurentis and Caselli, 2004), taking into account their technical-time and in view of the portfolio.

The basic element of the methodology introduced by Basel II, for the assessment of regulatory capital to be set aside, is a more accurate graduation of weighting coefficients in relation to the risk of the counterparty. This induces the banks to pay more attention to the mechanisms of evaluation, information and risk management, in addition to adopting sophisticated systems for the selection of loans and the determination of interest rates. Therefore, if a rating system based mainly on quantitative evaluations, budget, and trend analysis (how the company behaves with the bank and the financial system generally) amplifies the critical enterprise, then why not take into account the qualitative component that consists of the intangible assets, which, indeed, through more advanced systems, may be able to identify the untapped potential of the company.

In this regard, in 2009, the Governor of the Bank of Italy, Mario Draghi,[2] hoped that "banks in deciding on credit to be given should use all the available information; integrate the results of the statistical methods of scoring that lose some of their predictive ability in exceptional moments with direct knowledge of the customer, its actual potential for growth and profitability in the long run. The local roots of the banking system are valuable; these should be used, where they were lost, reconstructed. The knowledge in the field should be exploited as much as possible, avoiding an excess of automatism" and saying "we try to read a firm's positive potential, that is even if the budget figures are not really positive."

Also, on February 18, 2012,[3] the current Governor of the Bank of Italy, Ignazio Visco, strongly advised banks not to neglect the financial resources of families and businesses because it is "crucial that the economy does not become asphyxiated, with credit wasting away and taking with it the prospects of the banking system."

The problem of amplification of the fluctuations of the business cycle, which was exacerbated in the most critical phase of the crisis in business banking, between late 2008 and early 2009 (Acharya and Richardson, 2009), involves, in bad economic times like the present, the banks meeting the capital requirements of Basel II reducing commitments or raising rates for loans, due to the increasing level of risk. This results in a negative impact in terms of development, innovation, and business investment, with the consequence of further crises.

To all this, you add two critical elements in the application of the ratings in Italy:

1. In many cases, banks have adopted stringent rating systems for the evaluation of companies, and rather than bringing banks and businesses closer together, this moves them away from each other.
2. The rating is seen by PMIs only as a threat and not as an opportunity.

Therefore, in a context of high financial turbulence and worrying evolution of the business cycle, the corporatists are studying new ways to improve the impact of the rating mainly on SMEs. These SMEs are of a heterogeneous nature, each of them distinct from the other, making them difficult to assess. To give them a new rating philosophy would alleviate this issue and enhances their potential. The main criticisms are:

1. Modest use of qualitative information regarding the competitive position of the company and its prospects for development.
2. The limited scope of the quantitative accounting data, which has mainly been historical in nature and not forecast.
3. The strong weight in the overall assessment of internal performance information, making up for the limitations of punctuality and self-determination (plus the more the bank provides loans, the better are the indices of tension and use of loans).
4. The forecast horizon of the status of the debtor limited to a year.

The result is that the rating assignment is highly dependent on accurate data, based on a narrow spectrum of information that does not take into account the real value of the company – its potential for growth and evolution, complexity, skills, innovative spirit, and capabilities of government, management and marketing, entrepreneurship – failing to assess the overall economies and the benefits of a relationship with the company, conducted on a prospective basis and with a long-term view (Iannuzzi and Berardi, 2008).

In light of the above, it is essential to expand the exploitation of all available information, including it properly in the trial evaluation. This is essential to identify companies that, though suffering times of financial stress, have a competitive advantage that allows them to overcome moments of crisis. Hence the need to highlight the importance of the treatment of soft information, especially in sectors where the intangible components contribute to a greater extent to the added value and competitive advantage of the successful businesses; there is also a need to enrich quantitative data collection alongside interim information and perspectives on historical financial statements. The most important consequence, therefore, seems to be that the review and improvement of the parameters underlying the rating assessment constitute a necessary step to ensure that Basel II, and ultimately Basel III, are not perceived as dangerous developments, but as an opportunity to improve the relationship between banks and business.

In the process of assessing creditworthiness, in order to represent a spur to the capitalization of the companies, for the improvement of their technical profile and their strength, it is necessary that banks share with such counterparties any judgments assigned to them, with a view to a solid and positive evolution of the credit relationship.

5.2 The critical success factors of a business

In recent decades, economists, corporatists, accounting bodies, the financial system, trade associations,[4] the business environment, and so on, have focused their interest on the importance of intangible assets in the value chain in the current economic systems, ever more complex,[5] globalized, and characterized by highly dynamic competitive environments.

The increasing focus on intangibles is derived from many factors, including: the revolution generated by the information age, the changing international economic situation, the relevance of the statement "knowledge economy," the challenges arising from an increasingly global competition, the complexity of relations with stakeholders, the increasing importance of human capital, and the company need to survive (Golinelli, 2005) and develop in an increasingly dynamic and complex economic context (Barile, 2009b),[5] in addition to the widespread acceptance of innovative techniques of "knowledge management."

In this context, intangible resources are crucial both for corporate governance and for the process of creation and distribution of value. The resources, which are the productive assets of the company, are the basis of the process that powers the autopoietic evolution of the business.

Many authors have tried to classify these resources. For Hofer and Schendel (1978) they can be divided into five types: financial, physical, human, organizational, and technological. For Barney (1991), they can be divided into physical capital, human capital, and organizational capital. For Vicari (2008), into knowledge resources and trusted resources. Siano (2008) distinguishes between monetary resources and knowledge (which in turn can be divided into resources of knowledge and resources in the strict sense of confidence) that constitute the basic capabilities inherent in the structure of the company on the basis of unitary perspective which the systemic viable approach offers (Golinelli, 2000a; Golinelli et, al., 2002; Siano, 2001; Siano et al., 2006). Grant (2011), defines tangible and intangible human resources.

Other authors use the term "intellectual capital" as synonymous with intangible resources, dividing it into three major areas generating value: human capital, organizational, and relational, believing that through the budget, or the reporting of intellectual capital, management can have a more informed view on the company's competitiveness, technical knowledge, created innovation, and reputation. It can, therefore, pick up in advance the diverse needs of customers, responding promptly with innovative offers of products (Orlandi, 2012).

However, only since the mid-1980s, with an approach called the resource-based view (RBV) was attention focused on the analysis of the determinants of competitive advantage in internal and firm-specific resources. They are considered unique, rare, precious, non-imitable, and non-substitutable (Barney, 1991). They also allow businesses to overcome the traditional paradigm of structure, conduct, and performance and the Porteriano model, according to which the determinants of viability are attributable to environmental and exogenous factors.

According to Porter, to obtain monopoly rents, firms may decide to select and operate in the most attractive areas, or to manipulate competitive forces to their advantage, choosing between three possible strategies, to build a sustainable competitive advantage:

1. Cost advantages allow the company to provide goods and services at lower costs than competitors. A cost advantage can be obtained, for example, thanks to the efficiency of the production process, privileged access to raw materials and inputs, the location of activities, proximity to markets, achieving economies of scale and/or learning, capacity utilization, and so on.
2. Advantages of differentiation means offering a unique product or service, for which buyers are willing to pay a price that exceeds the costs of obtaining the differential characteristics. So that the variation is effective, it is necessary that its implementation is accompanied by adequate disclosure to the market: the tangible differentiation[6] shall be reported to customers through the "intangible differentiation."[7] This type of leadership depends on the possession and/or control of patents, trademarks, distribution networks, and so on.
3. Focusing on, or implementing, one of the two previous strategies in a limited segment of the competitive environment.

Porter's vision is based on the concept of the value chain that, following a sequential path, is the breakdown of activities that allow you to create value for the market in two broad categories:

1. Primary: these represent the operational activities of the company, in the early stages of purchasing, processing, and sale (inbound logistics, production, outbound logistics, marketing and sales, service).

2. Secondary or support: these consist of the additional activities related to enterprise infrastructure, human resource management, technology development, and supplies.

So, disaggregating the strategic activities of the company, we can understand where the value is generated by identifying the trend of costs and potential for differentiation. According to Porter, in carrying out activities more effectively and efficiently than the competition, the company acquires competitive advantage.

But the increase in competitive pressure, the growing contestability of markets and the shortening of the life cycle of the product, have led scholars to search for more stable parameters compared to the sector, the satisfied needs, or the target market, to identify strategic factors determining the competition, corporate positioning, and competitive advantage.

The RBV identifies the company for "what you can do" rather than "for the needs that [it] tends to satisfy" (Peteraf, 1993).

This theory, supported by the analysis of the success of many businesses on the world market, considers a wealth of resources and expertise as an essential component for the development and success of a business. According to this perspective, the environment is important as a source of resources and less important as a source of competitive advantage (Michelini, 2011).

The key points of the *Resource-Based Theory* can be identified in three fundamental propositions (Boschetti and Sobrero, 1996):

1. The heterogeneity of resources: companies are characterized by heterogeneous sets of productive resources which allow for different levels of efficiency.
2. The imperfect mobility of resources: identifies evidence rather than industrial economy, having as object the firm and not the sector.
3. The non-replicability of the resources that contributes to determining the competitive advantage.

The heterogeneity between firms, in the supply of resources that are scarce and difficult to replicate, is the reason for the achievement of differential rents compared to their competitors. Annuities can ensure a sustainable competitive advantage;[8] sustainability understood not as mere temporal duration, but as resistance to imitation, substitution, and durability.

Imitability for Cerrato (2004) allows competing companies to acquire or collect resources with attributes similar to those of the resources that are the basis of competitive advantage. Substitutability, however, allows companies access to resources that enable them to implement strategies similar to those of the company that has a position of advantage. Durability, finally, is understood as reduced likelihood of obsolescence due to changes in the environment.

Tangible resources, readily identifiable and quantifiable through the reading of financial statements, have a value that does not express a strategic value that depends on the effects of complementarity with other elements of the business system. These are resources that despite being crucial to business strategy, hardly contribute to the achievement of competitive advantages as they are easily available and transferable.

These can be divided into:

- Physical resources (technical and structural): for example, buildings, plants, machinery, equipment, and raw materials.
- Financial resources, consisting of the different funding sources that allow companies to formulate and implement business strategies, such as the capital contributed by the entrepreneurs, shareholders, or financial institutions.

Human resources, that are created and sedimented through training and learning, are made up of "the productive services that the staff makes the company" (Grant, 2011), such as skills, knowledge, individual skills, organizational skills, ability to work in teams, decision-making and analysis, planning, experience of the entrepreneur, employees and managers, interaction skills, and communication. They are a competitive advantage for the company. To all this we must add that preparation and motivation of staff are now considered two essential "ingredients" for SMEs.

The ability to attract and retain competent and motivated human resources has long been considered a key lever for business success, so that the value of human capital is a key ingredient (Rullani, 2004b; Silvestri and Pilati, 2005) for the realization of a successful strategy. If, on the one hand, human resources can be treated as tangible resources for their "physicality," on the other hand they are attributable to the intangible components for the set of skills they bring.

Intangible assets that the company is able to generate and nurture over time constitute its intangible heritage (Corno, 1996). It is characterized by a particular originality and specificity for each company, which makes it difficult to be acquired and is replicable externally only with the help of financial means, as it is strongly connected to the context in which it is developed.

Intangibles are considered the real driver (Petty and Guthrie, 2000b; Bartoli and Ossoli, 2009) of the process of value creation, able to act as levers of competitive advantage. They are essential to achieve satisfactory performance, although to date[9] there is no "space" in the budgets for several reasons, which include:

- The use of particular methods of recognition and measurement that enable proper use and disclosure. This is also because of the peculiar features of interrelation of intangible assets, which make it difficult to extrapolate them from the context in which they are used.
- The inability of management to proceed to their detection and/or understand their importance.
- The reluctance of companies to disclose outside news related to their strategic and operational profile, in the fear that this could lead to loss of competitiveness.

While well-defined property rights allow the holder to exclude others from enjoying the benefits related to physical and financial resources, it is more difficult to foreclose third party enjoyment, even partial, of intangibles, as in the case of inventions protected by patents. These generate benefits for non-owners, known as *spillover*, linked to the opportunity to imitate or actual free enjoyment of innovation after the expiry of the period of legal protection.

Numerous statistical analyses showed that most of the market value of firms is attributable to intangibles, as reported by Grant (2006), who found an incidence ranging from 70 to 99 per cent, as in the case of Disney, Johnson & Johnson, Philip Morris, and Microsoft, to name a few.

The results of a statistical survey showing that intangibles represent a key resource in determining the value of companies were already published by the American magazine *Business Week* (2002). Comparing the market value with the book value, it could be detected that, in most of the 100 cases examined, the incidence of the brand and other intangible exceeded 180 per cent of the market value of the company.

$$MARKET\ VALUE = BOOK\ VALUE + INTANGIBLE\ ASSET$$

So, since the intangibles weigh heavily on the market value of both small and large companies, it is necessary to provide adequate methods of analysis and reporting of these assets.

In Search of Excellence, by Peters and Waterman (1982), studied the most successful American companies in order to identify the critical factors that led to their excellence. They have concluded that the best performances are determined by the owned optimal immateriality conjunction rather than by using sophisticated production facilities or strategic planning. Trying to answer the following questions: *What is the secret of a successful management? How come there are companies that have extraordinary results and other inexplicably condemned to mediocrity?*, scholars have found that "excellent" companies have the elasticity and the skills necessary to recognize the needs of a changing environment through contact with the customer; to maintain flexibility with simple structures and small staff, to encourage experimentation, to give autonomy to promote entrepreneurship; to manage to achieve extraordinary levels of productivity with employee involvement; to focus on the activities that they know better and on a particular business value, such as the development of new products or services provided to customers; these are both rigid and flexible in controls.

The successful company, as identified by the authors, is therefore flexible, dynamic, viable, informal, presents characters of creative vitality, knows how to accept slight errors and a certain amount of chaos, knows how to empower and inspire confidence, is horizontal, entrusts troubleshooting to those who deal with it every day operationally, is attentive to the needs of customers and employees, acknowledges change and applies the values they believe in, in their daily lives.

Well, if tangible resources are needed to perform a task of "painting a picture," most of the intangibles and certain human resources are needed to achieve a competitive advantage, or to "paint a masterpiece" (Tardivo, 2008).

Intangibles are assets that, in addition to being free of physicality, are characterized by difficult, and sometimes impossible, monetary quantification, except in terms of value creation over time.

They are composed of elements that are often endogenous, not closely related either to a particular contract or incurring specific charges, and usually are not transferable or separable from the business system. Intangibles are company-specific and their contribution to the creation of company value is manifested in the differential performance that the company achieves compared to its competitors. Moreover, these intangibles tend to sediment over time, through various processes that take place within the enterprise system in order to support the acquired competitive position, such as through processes of experience, through the preparation and motivation of human resources supported by investment in training and internal marketing. They develop thanks to their own use that generates as a virtuous circle: the intra and inter systemic, reputation, image, and so on.

At the same time, however, they tend to deteriorate if not adequately managed by the company, as with technological resources, as they can be superseded by the innovations generated by competitors if they are not continually monitored and updated. For example, the strength of the brand must be supported by an investment in advertising, the motivation of human resources can run out if not supported by investments in training and in internal marketing.

In addition, the difficult replicability of an intangible heritage derives from the assumption that the ability of an incorporated company is based on complex organizational routines, on strong cultural beliefs, or the possibility that they are the result of long-term investments and that their replication involves very high resource requirements.

Examples of intangible assets include: the brand and trademarks, patents, licenses, copyrights, research and development, innovation, reputation or corporate image, attitude to innovation, knowledge of the market and competitors, technological knowledge, organizational capital, the stakeholder relationship, ethics management and corporate social responsibility, corporate culture, and so on – these are not easily quantifiable, transferable, or acquired on the market.

Brand and *corporate* brands, "is a name, term, sign, symbol or design or a combination of these intended to identify the goods or services of a seller or group of sellers and to differentiate them from to those of competitors" (Kotler, 1966).[10] They are intended as brands associated with products or services of a company that, being able to communicate a set of values associated with them, are a form of reputation wealth (brand equity), whose value is based on trust, the fruit of coherence, and consistency built over time.

Brand is a strategic asset for the organization (Balmer and Gray, 2003) because, if strong and well-managed, it is able to answer "yes" to the four criteria set by the RBV.

A corporate brand is an asset because:

- It is rare: it is the result of a specific historical development which is expressed by the symbolic elements of the functional characteristics of the products that are matched (quality, performance, reliability) (Balmer and Gray 2003).
- It is durable, excluding crisis situations, and it tends to lose value in a relatively slow way and over a long time (Grant, 1991).

It is imperfectly imitable because it is legally protected and is not perfectly replaceable, seeing that its construction would be a slow process, over the course of time (Siano et al., 2011).

Therefore, the brand and trademarks are able to create added value for the consumer, reinforcing the satisfaction of use, safety in the purchase and processing of information, and competitive advantage, efficiency, and so on; and for the company, with a positive impact on brand loyalty.

Therefore, thanks to brand equity, these assets give quality, validity, and value to an asset, allowing it to emerge in difficult situations, such as the extreme competitiveness of contemporary markets. Therefore, the more value they have, the more they are known (brand awareness), they generate loyalty (brand loyalty), they are distinctive and original (brand identity), they produce quality and satisfaction (perceived quality), and they have a large semantic territory of reference (brand associations).

The value of the corporate brand and relationships with stakeholders determines the value of reputation capital, given the value, credibility, and confidence that the company collects on the market, by virtue of conduct adopted over time.

Even when there is a market, reputation captures the resources on more favorable terms, as the fiduciary elements connected with it, fueling positive expectations, reducing the perception of risk in the other party. This is the case, for example, for monetary resources that are exchanged with interest rates determined on the basis of risk/return ratio, perceived by actors that express the expectations of the financial system (Golinelli, 2000b).

It is clear that this perception is conditioned, inevitably, from the elements of trustees.

So, the reputational capital of a *brand* belonging to a business unit can be shared with other *business* units of the same company or the same group of companies.

This happens when the processes of brand extension are realized (Aaker and Keller, 1990; Smith, 1992; Keller and Aaker, 1992; Sullivan, 1992; Busacca et al., 2006) where by leveraging the ability to transfer the capital of reputation, relationships, and knowledge, consolidating it – which is grounding the brand in new competitive environments and inserting it into the existing business or new business – helps to increase the value of the brand (Busacca et al., 2006).

From the sharing of the brand among business units, in fact, strategic intangible market interrelationships are derived, and they enable the achievement of competitive advantages, expressible in terms of reducing communication costs and/or reinforcing image and reputation (Porter, 1985).

Even *co-branding* programs within the company, or company group, may allow a sharing of reputational capital by generating the same results. Luxury goods are the typical case in which the brand image of the "jaws" of fashion is transferred to many other luxury goods, such as complementary clocks or jewelry, and/or to diversify its offerings. The main instruments used to achieve these effects are represented by co-branding agreements (or brand alliance, or even brand bundling) (Blackett and Boad, 1999; Busacca and Bertoli, 2003; Keller et al., 2005) and ingredient branding (Norris, 1992). These are initiatives that allow companies to sell to third parties, or obtain from others, for a certain period of time, the availability of brand equity, also called reputational capital of the brand. The reputational capital constitutes a reserve with value (Vicari, 1998) that can be used immediately or in the future, to obtain key resources and to cope with crisis situations, provided that the capital is not compromised by bad corporate conduct. Mostly, unethical or socially irresponsible behavior generates loss of value and credibility of the company from the stakeholders that results in (Gabbi, 2003; Eccles, 2006):

- Loss of customers or less loyalty from the latter (market risk).
- Loss of key human resources and talent recruitment difficulties.
- Deterioration of offered services and applied conditions (such as payment extensions) from suppliers (contractual risk).
- Difficulty in raising capital by way of loan, an increase in the cost of capital, reduction of the stock market value of the shares (credit-financing risk).
- Foreclosure of partnerships, mergers c/o strategic acquisitions, which means loss of business opportunities and improvement of operational management processes.

Today the trend is addressed, with a growing interest in business ethics, through a new ruling class made up of business owners and managers who are increasingly attentive to the ethical and social aspects of business, in addition to the environmental costs of production. They aim not only to enhance but also to convey to stakeholders modern and solid values to increase the company's intangible heritage in terms of reputation, image, environmental sustainability,[11] social responsibility, and financial credibility.

As regards to corporate image, different definitions have been offered over time in the literature. For Panati (1987), "the picture is not the mere effect of promotions and advertising campaigns developed on a market, nor is it only the distillation of its marketing mix, but it is also the epitome of some quality constituents that are a distinctive signal for the company, its remembrance of the past and its idea of the future, its own style and place on the market." For Bernstein (1988), however, it is "the perception that an individual has the personality of the company in relation identity that is transmitted in relation to the means used to bring out the personality." For Baccarani and Golinelli (2003), it can be described as "the perception that 'others' have of the company." "Others" here is understood to mean "the public," which can be classified into nine categories of stakeholders, based on their expectations of the company: "*internal public* (work force and shareholders), the *local community* (citizens, authorities, institutions), *groups of influence* (movements to protect consumers, academics, scholars), the *trading partners* (suppliers, sales force, distributors), those of *central authority* (offices in various functions, by encouraging the control and taxation), the *mass media* (newspapers, magazines, radio, television), the *financial sector* (banks or other institutional investors), *end users* (consumers or users of the product), the *general public* (the supra-local communities in which the company operates)" (Bernstein, 1988).

With regards internal relations, a strong corporate image increases the sense of belonging, cohesion, and self-esteem in people. Externally, this translates into trust, credibility, legitimacy, and simplification of the formation processes of consensus.[12]

The image comes from everyday relations that each component of the corporate structure has with its stakeholders, which should be based on common values and shared across the organization, based on specific ethical principles of behavior, in tune with social expectations (Meznar et al., 1993).

Reputation and its protection from damage to image, positively affects the company's ability to prevent risks, seeking a degree of risk exposure balanced through the use of internal control systems.

The risk related to the conduct of business can be defined as the uncertainty about the future economic results, which manifest in the difference between what is empirically observed and what is expected; this involves fundamental aspects of business life: business strategy, investments, finance, procurement, and so on.

The conditions of risk are linked both to the environment and to the strategic choices and management of enterprises, which have to operate increasingly in conditions of uncertainty and risk that is inevitable and unavoidable (Golinelli, 2008).

In the current context, characterized by a general climate of uncertainty, partly because of the economic situation that has affected the global economy, enterprise risk management (ERM), considered an innovation in management, is a framework that allows the identification, assessment, and risk management that an organization can implement in order to accumulate "reputational capital." It is able to reduce the likelihood of the occurrence of negative events for the company, promotes correct behavior towards stakeholders, and limits the likelihood of illegal actions by internal members (Miglietta, 2007).

This process is successful if it is powered by the contribution of each business area (Gaudenzi, 2006). Therefore, it is essential to consider the company as a system (Golinelli, 2000) that, while recognizing the trend towards the functions and areas of specialization, also enshrines the principle of equifinality and the importance of coordination of the various subsets.

It is therefore essential to the government of risk, in governing an enterprise, with its capacity for identification, selection, treatment, and monitoring of risks (Golinelli, 2008), that there is a mechanism of *corporate governance*.[13] This is crucial to the creation and maintenance of a durable competitive advantage. It is able to provide financial benefits to the business, management, and organization, such as:

- Better understanding of the most significant risks, their implications, and priorities for action.
- Improvement of economy management, regarding both the costs and the revenues.

Improvements in production processes allow, in fact, cost savings; while on the revenue side, increases may result, for example, in an expansion of sales as a result of the strengthening of the elements of reputation, achieved through appropriate outward communication activities. These benefits are substantiated in a dynamic evolution of the business system, which conforms to the principle of "doing well by doing good,"[14] that is, the achievement of a better value in terms of efficiency and effectiveness of the system behavior, according to Golinelli and Volpe (2012). These benefits include:

- Better assessment of the creditworthiness of financial institutions.
- Positive effects on the cost of capital and the value of the company, since the heart of the financial theory is based on the direct relationship between risk and return.

- Reduction of allocated capital meant as an entity of financial resources responsible for the risk of not understanding. This is connected to events that are unknown or that the company does not believe it needs to consider, since they fail to assess the likelihood of their occurrence and the possible effects on the expected results, and have insufficient capacity for evaluation of uncertainty risk, for which it is possible to estimate probabilistically the frequency and severity (Golinelli, 2008). Spread to all levels of the company's organizational routines and procedures that optimize the risk, increase the skills of all members, and stimulate a sense of participation (the spread of a culture of control, leading to greater commitment, accountability, and sharing of information). The control system is considered to be "the key mechanism that one side takes the role of guarantor for all stakeholders, facilitating the correct business conduct and compliance with the existing regulations, on the other hand makes possible the creation of value and the maintenance of competitiveness thus ensuring its survival and proper investment in human capital that is certainly the most valuable resource" (Miglietta, 2007).

This system is realized through the integration of the functions of internal audit, enterprise risk management, and compliance office.

Internal audit has been defined, according to the Code of Conduct of the Italian stock exchange, as "the set of rules, procedures and organizational structures aimed at permitting, through an adequate identification, measurement, management and monitoring of the main risks, in a healthy, correct and consistent way with the established goals" (Borsa Italiana SpA, 2011).

This function in the reduction of the risk profile of the company, must devote itself to the activities of:

- *Operational auditing*: verification of the compatibility of the results achieved against objectives according to the criteria of effectiveness and efficiency.
- *Financial auditing*: verification of the reliability of accounting information.
- *Compliance auditing*: verification of compliance with the regulations.
- *Management auditing*: the evaluation of business strategies and procedures in order to make a judgment on their adequacy (Zattoni, 2006).

The control system is, therefore, an integral part of the business, because by monitoring the management and operational processes of the company, it has become one of the levers available to management to manage risk, with positive effects on business performance (Miglietta, 2007).

Stakeholder relationships are the fundamental strategic resources (Lenssen et al., 2007) that allow you to generate competitive advantages. In fact, the performance of firms increasingly depends on the ability to collect accurate information on their needs and to govern relations with them.

A socially responsible company can gain competitive advantage and maximize long-term profits. However, for SMEs today, social responsibility is seen as an additional constraint, while globalization and disintermediation of communication processes have led to a very dangerous rift between those who can afford it and those who cannot.

Given the sensitivity of consumers towards responsible choices made by companies, to believe in and invest in corporate social responsibility should be considered an opportunity, a tool to implement for development and business growth, and also an investment in the medium and long term for the future competitiveness of businesses of all sizes.

However, in a highly dynamic environment, such as the current one, companies need to be flexible to carry out urgently necessary strategies to survive, actively managing the changes of the reality in which they operate, of the market, and of technology. Companies must be able to manage change, not undergo it.

Among the sources that can increase the heterogeneity between firms, creativity is a key resource to find optimism in a context of economic and financial crisis, responding with new ideas and innovation strategies for corporate change (Amabile, 1988), but especially by stimulating the differentiation of product that is a key determinant of competitive advantage (Andrews and Smith, 1996; Im and Workman, 2004).

Creativity is understood as "imagination that must rest on the shoulders of knowledge to generate innovation" (Baccarani and Golinelli, 2011).

The theoretical relevance of the topic is confirmed by the increasing importance of the most tangible result of the creative ability of an enterprise, that is, innovation; this is manifested in a growing number of sectors that make up the current economic environment (Vicari et al., 2005).

It should be noted that, for the achievement of competitive advantages, resources must be integrated with each other to create the organizational skills that have been defined as "the ability of a company to allocate resources to achieve a desired end goal" (Helfat and Lieberman, 2002). These capabilities integrate the knowledge and skills of the human factor in addition to the material, financial, and technological resources needed to achieve a competitive advantage based on resources.

They can be divided into distinctive competencies that for Selzenick (1957), are the activities that the organization carries out with more distinctive skill than its competitors, and basic skills, to Hamel and Prahalad, are those that contribute most to the creation of value and represent the basis for entering a new market.

But, also the distinctive skills or *core competencies* are able to make the company unique in the market in which it operates. These have been defined, for example, as: "the capabilities essential for the strategy and performance of an enterprise" (Hamel and Prahalad, 1990); the set of insights about the problem definition and resolution of these (Lei et al., 1996); skills that could support coordinated use of resources in effective ways to achieve the strategic goals.

Having distinctive competencies, as well as regarding the ability to dispose of tangible and intangible resources required to carry out enterprise, relate, above all to the skill of the *manager*, who should know how to combine the resources available to gain more strength or reduce weaknesses against competitors and key players of the context in which the company operates (Calvelli, 1998).

The company must possess distinctive skills, or unique ones, not owned by others; these are considered core if they meet four parameters simultaneously: rare, precious, irreplaceable, and expensive imitation.

From a resource-based view perspective, the tool that makes organizational individual skills is the organizational routine that, through coordinated actions, allows individuals to learn their duties implicitly from other individuals and replicate this within the organization to make the best skills, thus avoiding losing skills in the event of departure of key employees.

However, the easier it is to manage, replicate and transfer such skills, the less damage the loss of them could do to the company.

In order to evaluate objectively the strengths and weaknesses of the resources and expertise of a company in relation to competitors, we can use benchmarking. This tool of systematic comparison is crucial in the management of a learning organization that facilitates management in the understanding of critical success factors of the best companies and identifying the resources and expertise that the company will need to create value, to improve both the cost and the effectiveness of its internal activities.

An intangible that is focused on with growing interest by scholars of business economics is knowledge. This has been analyzed, in particular, according to the role it plays in the processes of management and business creation (Golinelli, 2000). It is regarded as the intangible resource for excellence, to be shared necessarily between all levels of the enterprise system (Rullani, 2004a; 2004b).

The company is characterized by a wealth of knowledge accumulated over time, even through experiences: the *know-how*. In this view, the human resources of a company can pursue new activities with the help of their knowledge and generate new knowledge.

Knowledge can be analyzed according to the epistemological dimension, that identifies *implicit (or tacit) and explicit, and the ontological dimension, which distinguishes it in individual and collective.*

Implicit knowledge refers to the mental models, insights, experiences, and capabilities inherent in the mind of every individual; to what is individual, subjective, and empirical (experiential) and therefore is difficult to transfer and is highly personal. This can be shared only through continuous *processes of socialization and is predominantly informal.*

In turn, tacit knowledge can be divided into *professional* knowledge, linked to the *know-how* and expertise that is not formalized, and *subjective* knowledge, which refers to individual perceptions, thought patterns, and beliefs.

This reflects both the representation of the reality of the individual, and their vision of the future, what would be, thus influencing the perception of what surrounds them.

However, both types of knowledge determine every action and/or daily behavior of individuals who are the bearers (Maggioni and Del Giudice, 2006).

Explicit knowledge, however, articulated in rules and procedures, referring to what is social, objective, and theoretical, can be easily transmitted as it is easily codified and transferable through formal study.

Individual knowledge is that part of organizational knowledge that, residing in the intellectual and psycho-motor skills in the individual, is transferable only along with the person.

The collective knowledge, however, shared and distributed among a plurality of members of an organization, is inherent in the rules, procedures, routines, and norms that guide problem-solving activities and define patterns of interaction among members.

It is important that knowledge is shared and enhanced by the relational dimension that involves individuals.

The economic heart of Italy is represented by a varied and complex universe made up of the *family business*. The family business has a fundamental role in the process of creating value through the reputation that it has in a given social context. But for the family nature of a company to exercise the role of intangible critical resource, it is necessary that it relies not only on the image of the family and/or company, understood as the perception of the public at any given instant, but on a broader perspective which sees the reputation (*family business reputation*) as the criterion of interpretation followed by the various stakeholders in the formulation of their judgments (Mainolfi, 2010).

It must therefore respond positively to three drivers of reputation:

1. The reputation of the family name (*family name*). The name can be a source of competitive advantage, especially when used in the corporate name of the company, helping to facilitate the process of acquisition of resources, both human and financial, and representing a first assessment of the reliability and respectability of the company to external stakeholders.
2. Reliability: the ability of the family to weave strong relationships in the context in which it lives (*family social capital*). This view is strongly influenced by family history. The local roots contribute significantly to give strength and value to the company (Metallo and Gallucci, 2011).
3. Differentiation, or ability to build human resources with skills recognized as unique in the social environment (*human capital*). This reflects the will of the family to uphold the interests of the family, and those of the company, to pass on to descendants such fundamental values as loyalty, honesty, mutual trust, and commitment (Metallo and Gallucci, 2011).

In an increasingly globalized economic environment, it is critical that businesses should help, even more than before, to improve their image and make sure that the information disseminated on their products and services are correct and relevant to the real *mission* and to company *performance*. An aid in this direction is provided by the digital world through new communication opportunities, which result in a number of instruments: from blogs to *social media press releases*,[15] from the *conference call* to corporate sites, the *webinar*[16] (short for web-based seminar) to newsletters. The term *beyond the line* (BTL) means the assembly of all that the company puts in place to deal with the various stakeholders.

BTL, elaborated by Caroli and Pratesi, performs the function of facilitating direct communication, personalized and relatively continuous, and will be increasingly focused on empowering the degree of "engagement" of stakeholders towards the enterprise that has direct control of the communication process.

Also, it can ensure the communication of the two characteristics considered essential today, and increasingly important in the future – speed and creativity.

The BTL can be a useful support in creating an authoritative and credible enterprise network of actors involved in the sustainable development of the environment.

The company is always regarded as a system whose dynamic evolution is conditioned, on the one hand, by the relationships that develop between the governing body and the operating structure and, on the other, with the variegated entities, with connotations more or less systemic, that populate the environment. It follows how important effective organizational communication is for the success of the company – essential for the construction and dissemination of the image, visibility, strategies, mission, and values guiding the enterprise. Notice that, within the company, it is essential to involve and motivate people, spreading knowledge and orienting subsystems towards creating value. Outside, however, it helps to maintain and strengthen the relationship with customers, suppliers, and all stakeholders (Golinelli, 2002).

A company that gives priority to listening, dialogue, and active involvement of the multiple systemic entities with which it relates, both at home and in the context of reference, and that is working to improve the conditions of this context, without being penalized for these efforts, reconciling the needs of the stakeholders with "their vital needs in the creation of shared value," is geared to sustainability.

Sustainability governance arises, for Golinelli and Volpe (2012), as a "philosophy," as an "umbrella concept" that provides guidelines, indicators, and innovative practices, in order to reconcile the tension between sustainability and profit, revealing a new stage for modern capitalism.

This philosophy of sustainability, has two consequences for those who govern the company on behalf of stakeholders. In the first case, it allows for the identification of developmental pathways that can generate profitability, context value, and therefore are more likely to lead to systemic survival. In the second case, for stakeholders, in the guidelines of the sustainability of the enterprise, a key role is played by "Sustainability Networks,"[17] that are a "more pluralistic and dialectical meter" than profits to evaluate the effects of entrepreneurial action (Barile et al., 2012; Barile et al., 2014).

In the current context, dominated by a very high level of technology that has erased distances, the company's reputation becomes a key resource to grow and protect. Business communication assumes a new and more important role, including through new media, and is essentially divisible into five areas: economic, financial, managerial, marketing, and institutional.

Financial communication is the set of communications concerning the evolution of the income and financial position of the company, which management spreads to the various categories of stakeholders.

Management communication aims to improve relations between all those involved directly or indirectly with the operational activities of the company, such as employees, contractors, professionals, distributors, and parent companies, to get involved, check, and approve the resources, skills, and cognitive abilities of the company. The objectives to be achieved are: increased staff motivation, information dissemination, the training of staff on the principles, policies, and strategies that regulate and define the behavior of the enterprise.

Marketing communication, or commercial communication, is meant to improve relations with the end customers and intermediates, raising awareness of the value of the company offer. The most important result of this is summarized in the brand.

Through institutional communication, the image of the company is projected outside the enterprise as a system, focusing on the message of its mission and its vision, to guide the behavior of audiences. Communication tools here are considered to be the social report, the sustainability report, the code of ethics, and quality certifications.

In particular, the social report,[18] which is used widely in private and public companies, although it is not required by law, nor formalized in a regulatory way, responds to the company's desire to integrate the financial statements by providing clear, transparent, and multidimensional results on the economic, social, environmental, cultural, and territorial impact generated by the company. In this document, emphasis is placed on the fundamental features of the corporate identity and its mission, strategic choices, the criteria under which it plans and implements its management, their attitude towards human resources in terms, for example, of fair remuneration and training, and its participation in the life of the community, of which it is a part in a perspective of subsidiarity of public institutions, emphasizing its link with the territory.

The territory, according to Caroli (2006a), can be regarded as a "system" consisting of a set of actors and resources, place of business, and relationships that occur in a dynamic way. It follows that, as an entity in continuous evolution, it should be interpreted as a "viable system,"[19] as characterized by Golinelli et al. (2006):

- A purpose that, for any organization, is made up of survival achieved through the creation of value for stakeholders, which can be divided according to the type of interest that feeds into the territory. The process of creating value must meet a set of heterogeneous goals, and in some cases contradictory goals in terms of competitiveness, attractiveness (that is, the ability to attract resources from external systems and "metabolize" the benefit of the actors who are part of the territory), balance, and social sustainability.
- A vocation, namely the potential for development that emerges in a given time interval, by tilting the natural, social, cultural, and economic life of the territory.
- A governance body responsible for defining strategies for the development of the area with the objective of creating value for the entire system through an ongoing interpretation and redefinition of the territorial vocation. The ability of the governing body to correctly interpret the vocation, to design a unique and unrepeatable identity, to communicate this identity by encouraging the development of an appropriate image by audiences, depends on the survival of the territorial system.

The territory must be understood not only as a physical environment that "hosts" the business entity, but also as the heritage of human settlements with identity, knowledge, and their stories, contributing to the creation of systemic value (Barile et al., 2013). "Value creation," a fundamental objective for government action – the only one always consistent with the purposes of survival and development – must brand itself as "systemic," that is, as a unit of monetary benefits and not as an enterprise system that is capable of generating enterprise for all those who, for various reasons, participate in or are interested in its story (Gennaro, 2008; Porter and Kramer, 2011). It is a function not only of its future financial results, but also the competitive and social aspects from which each category of *stakeholders*, to varying degrees, will benefit.

Indeed, the area is one of creativity and innovation; that is, resources arising from the interaction of a systemic "constellation of subjects," whose action makes any place unique and unrepeatable to discover, learn about, and appreciate. It is the place where the business is the reason of its being and of its development, drawing on the reservoir of social capital available in the forms introduced by James S. Coleman.

The territory is the field from which the competitive challenge of the company arises; is the place where innovation is formed or not formed due to the "creative atmosphere" that is breathed and to its ability to unravel entrepreneurial thinking and management's opening up to the world of the offer, and its enthusiasm for change. In fact, "the territory is a living subject of high complexity, the result of coevolutionary processes and synergy between human settlement and the environment" (Magnaghi, 2000). It can be considered as an object for which the company itself is a major player the moment it provides shape and organizational strength to resources that distinguish it, like so many areas of local development emphasize. From this conception of territory a multitude of expectations are derived, more and more pressing and trans-generational, with which the government of the enterprise is confronted, with a view to practical guidance aimed at sustainability (Golinelli and Volpe, 2012).

5.3 Intangible assets in companies and rating models

Already we have seen that studies from the literature show that the use of qualitative variables and financial data leads to a more accurate prediction of the risk of counterparty defaults,[20] because a reading of the budget alone can be detrimental, failing to fully reap the real factors of excellence or criticality of the companies, for the evaluation by other parties for several reasons:

1. The historical financial statements provide information relating to the past situation rather than the one in which the business is located at the time of applying for finance.
2. It is a type of assessment that assumes the existence of historical data, while in the case of a start-up it is based solely on prospective data, which would occur only after the disbursement of the loan.
3. It does not consider the non-accounting data that allows you to refine customer segmentation.
4. It examines data aggregates that are often unable to analyze the dynamics of flows in detail.

It is necessary that corporate balance sheets are transparent and fully representative of the business situation. They must be able to describe in a complete and exhaustive way, the economic, financial, and asset conditions.

Inadequate and incomplete information may impact on the overall economy, because it can lead to a knowledge gap between the banks and businesses that need funding, threatening to generate negative consequences in terms of lending to businesses. However, it is important to reduce the information gap by relying on a broader basis of knowledge than those inferred from the financial statements and reports (Faccincani, 2009).

Currently, banks integrate quantitative analysis with questionnaires that somehow try to draw a qualitative profile of the company, highlighting those aspects that may be relevant in the process of value creation. In the literature, the intangibles that are relevant for business competitiveness were identified. In particular, we focused on smaller companies.

SMEs, constitute 99.8 per cent of European businesses and represent 90 million workers, approximately 67.4 per cent of total employment, with an annual growth rate in employment higher than that recorded by big business (Ministero dello Sviluppo Economico, 2013). They generate about 58 per cent of total value added. Moreover, they are less risky in terms of systemic risk than large companies,[21] as established by Basel II, which provided lower absorption of capital for the loans granted to SMEs, and as confirmed by Basel III.

In this context, using credit can be convenient for both banks and SMEs, as lower capital absorption can be practiced in more advantageous conditions. However, there are several critical points due to the special "location" of the same small-to-medium enterprise that has its target in so-called niche markets, where there are risk factors other than those affecting the large enterprise. In fact, the latter work in global markets in which the risk factors, depending mainly on the economic cycle, are predictable due to automatic ratings. In niche markets, however, the risk is determined by many external factors entirely outside of the context in which a company operates and, as such, is not predictable.

All this explains the difficulty financial institutions have when disbursing credit, which also contributes to the uncertainty over the economy, which originates from the sovereign debt crisis and the credit squeeze.

In order to better understand the elements of quality that are considered strategic for the competitiveness of enterprises, in literature there is a distinction made between small, medium, and large enterprises.

In this regard, in order to prevent a "cumbersome and unreal" distinction between small and medium businesses, it has been proposed (Golinelli, 1992) to discriminate only between minor and major undertakings, "using a series of typical characters" that characterize the smaller enterprises such as "the coincidence between ownership and control, the close relationship with the family and its evolutionary stages, the development horizon limited control capacity of family members engaged in the summit."

The smaller company, is however, "the business form that is characterized not so much by the number of employees or the amount of the investment, as for the concentration in a single subject, ownership, decision-making and business risk: for the immediate participation of the property to the life of the company, a regular participation regarding all problems and aspects of management" (Golinelli, 1985). Considered as an "intermediate category between the craft business and the managerial" (Golinelli, 1974) it is then detected using the same characters that qualify equally (full integration between ownership and decision-making power, active participation in the management of the property, independence of market position and conduct active entity of sales and market share, voluntary closure to raising capital in the securities market and consequent development company closely related to the reinvestment of profits in the medium and long term), as well as with quantitative and statistical characteristics (500 employees); thus, they are smaller companies with a workforce of less than 500, and more if the number of employees is equal to or greater than 500.

Therefore, the same author, in the context of smaller companies, makes a distinction between small and medium enterprises according to whether the number of employees is below or above 100; other authors (such as Baccarani, 1987), while accepting the quantitative limits of workers first reported, further divide small businesses into two subclasses: 10–49 employees and 50–99 employees.

Empirical observation of smaller companies of territories in central and southern Italy, when compared with the data system at the national level and with the contention of the prevailing literature, allows you to draw a pyramid of success factors of a company (see Figure 5.1).

Flexibility is considered to be one of the strategic elements for the survival of enterprises. It allows you to react effectively to the economic cycle, reducing the cost structure of the company. In a very dynamic environment like the current one, flexibility can be understood as the ability of the governing body to change its strategic assets and the resulting operating procedures to respond quickly and effectively to

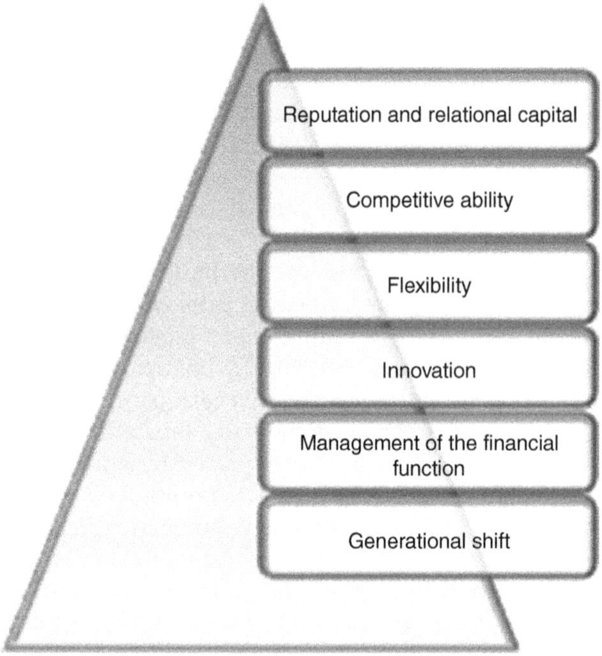

Figure 5.1 Pyramid of the success factors of an enterprise
Source: Author's elaboration.

"contingencies" that are outlined in the environment, not to lose competitive advantages, or to recover any gap with competitors. On the basis of the distinction given by Ansoff and Brandenburg (1971), it is possible to identify three types of flexibility depending on the type of change that the company intends to implement, distinguishing between the following:

- Operational flexibility, when a company is able to implement timely changes, usually temporary, covering the activities of firms in terms of production volumes, product mix, and human resources. In the latter case, the flexibility can be pursued mainly by varying the number of employees, wages and working hours, and outsourcing. This type of flexibility, which is numerical, covers three aspects: the rules governing layoffs and assumptions, the possibility of using fixed-term employment relationships and entrusting functions or phases of the production cycle to other companies, or work contracts for employees. Moreover, it is called functional flexibility when a worker within the enterprise can perform a wide range of tasks and production operations. This requires not only the absence of constraints, but also a high professional versatility and the ability of workers to accept rehabilitation processes. This type of flexibility involves production modifications in terms of quality and quantity, without incurring excessive cost increases.

- Competitive flexibility, at a time when businesses are able to react to changes that occur as a result of changing attitudes of its direct competitors. So this is realized when a company can considerably transform its position in the market, for example, by changing its product/market combination.
- Strategic flexibility, by reason of adapting to the phenomena of context, dealing with imposed conditions such as uncertain political, economic, or social environment; environmental turbulence; resource scarcity; and rising costs.

However, the systemic approach emphasizes preordained and innovative flexibility (Golinelli, 2005). Preordained flexibility is conducted through the attitude of the business system to co-evolve with the dynamics of the context in constancy of extended structure. Therefore, it qualifies as a set of alternatives to the structure adapted to contain the risk of high costs of structural intervention in correspondence with environmental changes and/or an opportunity to increase internal efficiency. Facing an increasingly inter-systemic complexity, the governing body is able to look beyond ordinary problems, will tend to modify and/or extend the variety of internal components and external relations. This is achievable to the extent that the enterprise system can leverage innovative flexibility, understood as the faculty to generate new specific structures, through interventions on the extended structure. But the aim of expanding the range of possible specific structures by strengthening internal capacity is feasible to the extent that the work on extended structure is not prevented by the inability to improve and/or change relations with banks, suppliers of raw materials, workers, and so on, as well as relationships with systems distributors, retailers, and so on. Innovative flexibility generates an active attitude on the part of companies in the face of market fluctuations (Crudeli et al., 2004).

In addition to these types, financial flexibility is significant. This represents a further critical factor that must be assessed by a careful analysis of the sources of funding. In this case, flexibility is characteristic of the financial structure, comprising all of the sources of funds used by a company. This allows it to change in relation to the evolution of requirements, as a total amount, which is a composition of financial business resources in order to improve the financial result of the management releasing or attracting capital, and with the prospects of economic return.

Flexibility is closely linked to innovation, which can only develop within structures that are able to manage processes in continuous and rapid change.

The term "innovation" is usually used in combination with a product or a new process, but to innovate the company to increase its long-term value is a much more complex process (Schumpeter, 1942; Henderson and Clark, 1990; Schilling, 2009). Innovation is, in fact, the lever to gain competitive advantages that are the source of value creation and sustainable growth, to preserve and develop as one of the key components of the intangible heritage of the company. As part of this study, it is considered appropriate to highlight that investment in research and development, innovations in the quality or range of products/services, in the production process, the company's image, operational and/or administrative procedural improvements, in light of the dynamic context in which they operate, are all often influential in the decision-making processes of the banking system on the evaluation of a business risk.

Innovation management, however, has to deal with the structures of the companies that are, in Italy, for the most part strictly controlled and of small-to-medium size.

Another key element in governance is the financial function. The difficulties associated with the management of corporate finance depend essentially on two factors: lack of equity and inappropriate use of funding sources.

In a context like the present – characterized by reduced demand, lack of liquidity, and the credit crunch – companies have to manage poor liquidity with extreme caution. It thus becomes essential to know how to plan and constantly monitor the cash flows produced by a company, as well as monitoring the financial structure to avoid excessive imbalances.

Generational shift is a focal point in the life of a company and it can generate both positive and negative effects. If managed with foresight, it can be an opportunity to rationalize and revitalize the business formula. In fact, the gradual emergence of generational synergies due to the presence of parents and children in the company can be an opportunity to rethink the ownership, management, organization, and strategy, working to create a governance quality (based on efficient communication processes), and a corporate culture that upholds rules, attitudes, values, and styles. Through the transition from one generation to another, there can also be created new productive combinations or potential enhancements, in order to seek and pursue new competitive advantages. The entrance of the new generation may represent a good opportunity to introduce new ways of managing the company; with strategies that break with tradition, they are able to overcome any technical direction based on intuition and experience. However, it is absolutely necessary to understand which elements of the "history" are still valid and therefore should be preserved, and those which, instead, are outdated and therefore need to be modified or abandoned. It follows that this process is not free from any adverse effects that may result from organizational difficulties, both legal and managerial.

From what we have seen, the problem of generational change requires the careful and deep involvement of all stakeholders. It is, in fact, a long and involved process that cannot be implemented without the full involvement of all members of the family, an enlightened attitude of the founder, adequate training of young players, and, above all, the knowledge that the interests and ambitions of individuals must give way to a primary interest – that of corporate survival.

The generational transition, with good management and proper planning, can become, therefore, the engine of growth and development for the company to the point that it is more appropriate to speak of "generational synergy" and not just generational transfer.

A good reputation is a specific resource of the most rare and inimitable type that accumulates slowly over time. It is able to represent a significant barrier to imitation (Dierickx and Cool, 1989; Barney, 1991; Amit and Schoemaker, 1993). It improves financial results, it is competitive and social, has a positive effect on costs and revenues (Shapiro, 1983; Rindova and Fombrun, 1997; McMillan and Joshi, 1997: Roberts and Dowling, 2002: Fombrun and van Riel, 2004), and is considered a strategic resource.

A successful enterprise must have the ability to maintain its competitive advantages,[22] to meet the expectations of its stakeholders by creating shared value.

The territory and the context in which the community of families, businesses and institutions operate, are both relevant to the creation of value for the implementation of business intangibles. In particular, the infrastructural facilities and the ability to generate business culture are not irrelevant to the accretion of intangible enterprise assets. It is clear that the positive performance achieved by companies that conduct their business in an area known as "disadvantaged" are more relevant than the results obtained by companies operating in more evolved territories.

However, it is believed that the performance achieved by some companies in contexts considered to be "disadvantaged" are more valuable than those which exist in others with greater structural equipment. All this should somehow be considered in the analysis of the creditworthiness of firms by banks through the use of a "territorial coefficient" which could influence the rating assignment.

It is worth repeating that the activities of the banks in the intermediation of credit also perform a development function for business territorial systems, primarily for those who are disadvantaged. It is believed, therefore, that in order to better allocate the credit to businesses, it is appropriate to include the territorial coefficient, taking into account also the context in which companies achieve their performance.

Banks can use the rating systems both for regulatory purposes and for the determination of the minimum capital, and for management purposes to measure the risks of lending. In this context, the use of models based on the rating is functional to the management of the loan portfolio, determining the pricing and allocation of capital. The rating assignment determines a risk/return profile which dictates the amount of capital that banks must allocate to the credit risks. What becomes crucial is, in this view, the concept of rating that allows banks to assign a "vote," after evaluating the quantitative information, taking into account performance and qualitative related businesses, industry trends, local context, relations with the credit system, and so on.

The rating allows, therefore, to summarize the results of analysis carried out in the traditional investigative manner, associating a risk level with each undertaking, and from this stems the decision process of the banks on the access, price-setting, and, in general, conditions of granting credit. The decision-making process takes into account other elements, such as guarantees (real and/or personal), commercial considerations, and strategic relationships, related to the development of the relationship with the customer.

From this, it follows that in certain cases any warning reported by the rating could be forced and rejected.

But the assessment of the creditworthiness of counterparties requires a strong focus not only in the selection phase of investigation and concession but also during subsequent handling of the relationship. This is to promptly identify the possible deterioration of creditworthiness and promptly take appropriate corrective action. The elements symptomatic of financial difficulty of the customer are detected, as well as periodic reviews of loans, through the monitoring of:

- Negative events (such as protests, the inclusion of the client in Interbank Alarm, prejudicial initiatives by other banks, or reports of financial suffering in Central Risk).
- Persistent situation of encroachment of the relationship and the accumulation of overdue installments of loans (unsecured and/or mortgages).
- Downgrading of creditors performing loans to the rating classes characterized by the worst credit rating.

From the graph in Figure 5.2 it can be seen that the probability of default increases with the worsening of the rating category assigned in relation to the capital entrusted.

Banks will treat severely those businesses that are less capitalized and more "opaque" in terms of information, or reject requests for funding, instead granting more favorable terms to the most creditworthy and "transparent" companies that are able to provide clear and complete information.

The conditions applied by banks are not a unique function of the rating, although this assumes an undoubted importance, because the bank will offer a better *pricing* (at-risk), not so much based on whether the debtor will be less risky, but because the same operation will result in a lower capital requirement. This requires increased sharing with banks and a more transparent dialogue based on mutual trust, where both parties bring information and assessments useful to maximize the common interest to the production of wealth (De Laurentis, 2011). In fact, adequate information allows lenders to have control over their own level of risk, reducing the cost of credit and allowing more efficient procurement procedures. It allows companies to obtain better financing terms.

In the current context, companies are having to deal with the issues that have generated obvious consequences on the real economy, with a fall in consumption, investment, and employment, due to the severe economic crisis, increasingly global competition, and access to credit being increasingly selective and expensive.

To tackle the crisis, businesses have reacted by containing operating costs, and investment and personnel costs, although this has not been sufficient to reduce the financial requirements for working capital, partly because of the stretch payment times in commercial transactions.

Despite the actions taken by the European Central Bank, there remains a high risk that the credit crunch will continue in the coming months. However, in the MEP, there has been accepted an amendment promoted by ABI, Confindustria, Italy Enterprise Network, and Alliance for the Italian Cooperative, on the introduction of a correction factor to balance the quantitative increase of the minimum capital requirement under Basel III, with the aim of alleviating the credit crunch.

This issue is of particular importance, especially in Italy and the rest of Europe, where credit banking is the channel for the economy that far outweighs other channels (75 per cent in Europe, less than 25 per cent in the US) and where this dependence is particularly strong for SMEs (about 39 per cent of total liabilities consist of bank debt; for large companies this value is about half). All this is necessary in order not to penalize SMEs, considered the fundamental "plot" of the Italian and European entrepreneurial system.

In light of the above, a correct classification of the risk/return profile affects the part of the capital that banks must allocate to cover the risk related to the supply of credit to businesses. It follows as a reflection on the regulatory capital and thus on the capital base of banks, that this is a necessary requirement to be able to carry out their banking activities.

To better understand the problem, we analyzed a panel of banks, belonging to different size classes based on the classification adopted by the Bank of Italy, which is deemed to be considered exhaustive, as the sample represents a significant share of the domestic banking system, both in relation to the total funds intermediated and the number of employees and branches operating in Italy.

In particular, with regard to banks classified as small and minor, the whole universe of representative local lenders was chosen, because this research is aimed at the analysis of the territory of the province of Frosinone.

The composition was varied in terms of size of the group of banks surveyed, differentiating interest highlights, and attitude to the improvement of relations with the SMEs, as advocated by many.

Intangibles not detected in the records can affect the sustainability of the business strategy, aimed at meeting the expectations of the stakeholders in the medium term. It follows that the judgment of the banking analyst on these elements is incorporated in the development of the rating, mainly, through a process of notching (down or up). This may impact on the credit given to companies and therefore on the level of risk associated with them. But if the rating gets worse, the banks may not be sufficiently capitalized to take on more risk and therefore would be unable to provide credit.

With the survey carried out, it was possible to detect that the methods used for the calculation of capital requirements for credit risk and counterparty for the corporate segment are identified mainly as the standard approach. Only some "big banks" resort to the advanced internal rating and foundation internal rating. This occurs for two reasons: the advanced systems generate very high costs for their realization and implementation, as heavy investment is required for staff training and the purchase of suitable software, in addition to this leading to major changes in organizational structures of banking companies. Furthermore, one must remember that when the valuation methodologies are particularly complex and take a prospective orientation, you must have analytical information, which is often difficult to find, especially if the counterparty is a small business, without formal business plans, budget forecasts, and information held on its competitive positioning. It follows that the cost of a credit line based on a thorough analysis of the characteristics of the borrower, are overly burdensome for small-size counterparts.

Therefore, in Italy, the "no cost" of prospective assessments is determined by the custom of companies to resort to multiple bank lending, covering their financial needs using a variety of banking relationships. This causes fragmentation of the customer relationship and the margin on loans necessitates the use of mostly automated techniques.

In the course of investigation, it is expected that the operator has the ability to request a change of the rating of the applicant or any guarantor. All this must be motivated and supported by adequate documentation throughout the procedure, prescribed by regulation, override, which generates impacts management on expected losses.

Exclusively for management purposes and not monitoring, it was detected that different banks use an internal rating system to support these phases when renewing customers already entrusted to the bank.

The study found, also, that the more banks are able to assess the individual customer, according to objective technical criteria validated by the Bank of Italy, the more they will be able to predict risk classes for the best customers, assign a coefficient for lower weighting for the loans, and, then, have to set aside a smaller amount of regulatory capital, with the result of taking advantage of greater leverage.

The banks, as already stated, are obliged by law to hold, for prudential reasons, a capital equal to a certain percentage for each credit exposure. This capital serves to oversee the risk from unexpected losses, the largest of which is derived from the deterioration in the creditworthiness of the counterparty, as well as the required quota on the basis of the rating associated with the risk assessment.

Expected losses and the cost of regulatory capital directly depend on the rating assigned to borrowers: the customers with the best credit ratings tend to expect losses and lower capital costs that allow them to benefit from lower pricing.

While the loss is covered in allocating the debt through pricing and allocations in the budget, the unexpected loss that is not subject to specific provisions represents the credit risk of the transaction and must be covered with an adequate supply of their own equity. Unexpected losses exceeding the VaR, which is the maximum loss achievable over the horizon, are for very rare events and those of very high severity. These are considered "catastrophic" and must be managed through the provision of effective contingency plans through the transfer of assets and contracts with insurance risk. The probabilistic distribution of the losses for insolvency are illustrated in Figure 5.2.

Hence, the logic of risk monitoring by banks as a function of the level and composition of its capital, which cannot be less than the capital absorbed by all the risks that are incurred. However, the capital is also stress-tested for further absorptions emerging from worsening market conditions, as is the case in the event of changes in interest rates, as assessed according to the situation of the current and prospective scenarios.

Regulatory capital is an aggregate capital that consists of the sum of two components of the core capital (Tier 1) and supplementary capital

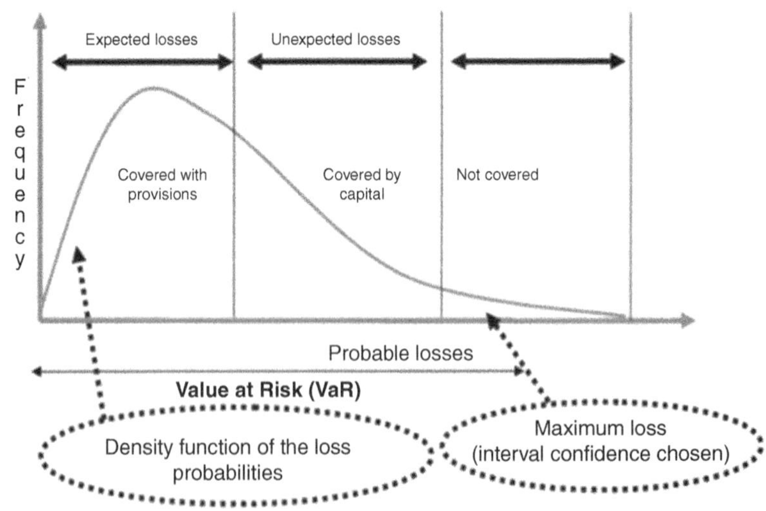

Figure 5.2 Probabilistic distribution of the losses for insolvency
Source: Author's elaboration.

(Tier 2), while the total capital ratio is the ratio between the total capital (CET1 + AD1 + T2)/RWA total. As required by the New Supervisory Instructions for Banks (Circ. 285 of December 17, 2013), the European banks are required to hold a "capital ratio" of a minimum equal to:

- Primary capital class 1 (CET1) at least 4.5 per cent of risk-weighted exposures.
- Capital primary class 1 + Additional Tier 1 (CET1 + AD1) at least 6.0 per cent of risk-weighted exposures.
- Total capital (CET1 + AD1 + T2) at least 8 per cent of risk-weighted exposures.

With the empirical analysis, we can see how the credit risk varies depending on the assignment of different ratings, because the variation of the rating changes the credit risk, the provision sheet, and the Tier. Through this magnitude, it is possible to detect whether there is an excess capital compared to the risks assumed, which is necessary for a policy of expanding credit.

From the sample analyzed, divided into four clusters according to the percentage of Tier 1 capital ratio (the ratio of core capital and RWA), it has emerged, as represented graphically in Figure 5.3, that with respect to a time horizon of five years, between 2009 and 2013, no bank has held a regulatory capital below the minimum expected by the Regulatory Authority. However, as shown in Table 5.1 and Figure 5.3, there are the smaller banks that have capital levels well above the 8 per cent minimum required by the supervisory regulations, ranking well above the average of the banking system.

Furthermore, by examining the sample, which was divided into four clusters, also a function of the average percentage of total capital ratio measured again in the period 2009–2013, as shown in Table 5.2 and Figure 5.4, earlier findings are confirmed about the fact that smaller banks hold a capitalization level higher than other types of lenders.

Table 5.1 Average percentage of Tier 1 capital ratio, 2009–2013

	2009	2010	2011	2012	2013
Bank groups	11.93%	12.99%	13.39%	14.02%	15.11%
Local banks	19.50%	19.90%	19.85%	20.10%	19.66%

Source: Author's elaboration.

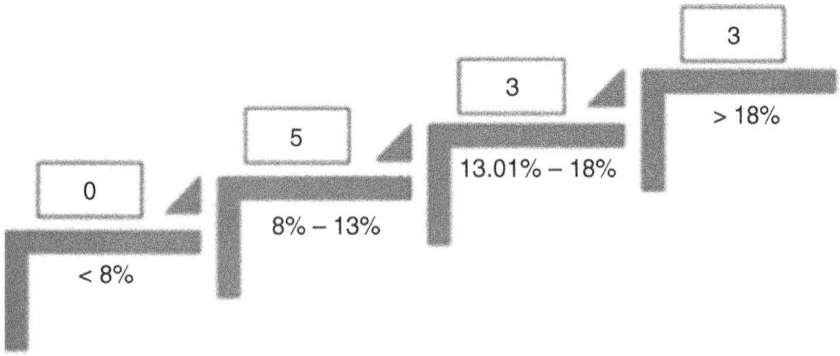

Figure 5.3 Cluster according to the average percentage of Tier 1 capital ratio, 2009–2013
Source: Author's elaboration.

Table 5.2 Average percentage of total capital ratio, 2009–2013

	2009	2010	2011	2012	2013
Bank groups	8.70%	9.17%	10.40%	11.13%	11.63%
Local banks	18.70%	19.05%	19.10%	19.40%	19.19%

Source: Author's elaboration.

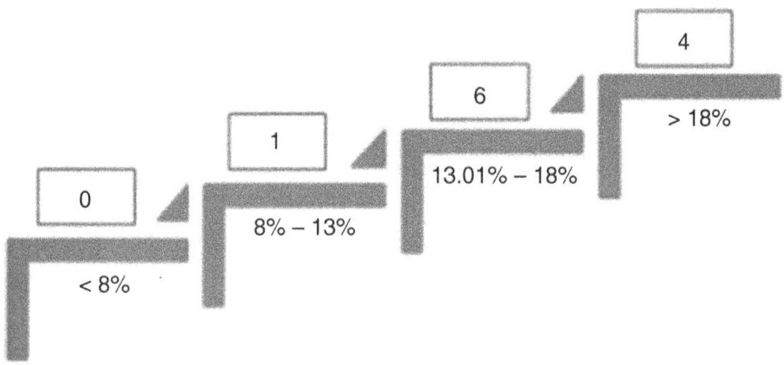

Figure 5.4 Cluster according to the average percentage of total capital ratio, 2009–2013
Source: Author's elaboration.

The banks analyzed, that determine the capital requirements for credit risk and counterparty firms using the standardized approach, very often resort to assessments issued by external evaluation. In this regard, we proceeded with examining procedures conducted within the department of CRIF Rating, aiming to broaden our vision on the company by assessing their competitive position in their industry or sector and, in the case of group membership, also checking any impact on the company's credit rating resulting from an overall analysis of the group. According to this procedure, it is no longer sufficient to use traditional instruments, it is essential to have deep and comprehensive data collated from public sources, information on territorial benchmarks, and sectorial data on payments and commercial-type credit, in addition to synthesis tools and advanced engineering statistics. In this way, you can create the best and most efficient information assets to return a complete and updated knowledge of the overall level of debt and the soundness and prospective solvency.

Therefore, the investigation showed that the intangible assets analyzed in the study affected the determination of the rating in a marginal way, given that the universe of large banks examined represents about 90 per cent of the market share.

The weight given to qualitative factors depends on the strategy of each bank and as a rule, they are able to change a maximum of one or two classes of a rating compared to the assessments arising from scoring. Recently, some large banks have revised their assessment processes to be able to "read" the best small businesses.

Local territorial banks, in particular, enjoy a privileged position, thanks to their ability to establish a long-term relationship of trust with the company. They can enjoy the availability of more information, managing to reduce information asymmetries (Corigliano, 2007, Tardivo et al., 2012) and enjoy the benefits of a so-called "relational" approach to customers: *relationship lending* (Berger and Udell, 1995, 2002; Boot, 2000; Degryse and Ongena, 2002; Gorton and Winton, 2003; Corigliano, 2007; De Mitri et al., 2010; Scannella, 2011; Modina et al., 2013; Moro and Fink, 2013). This wealth of information, gradually acquired through the confidential relationship with the customer, based on years of practice with the same, is the bank's competitive advantage over other potential lenders (theory of "relative" comparative advantage).

The availability of more information is particularly useful to banks since it facilitates the understanding of the actual *risk* profile of the company, and therefore allows a more efficient and effective access to credit by businesses.

5.4 Concluding remarks

In an increasingly competitive environment, characterized by a dynamic and turbulent economic situation, intangible assets play a crucial role in the survival of the enterprise.

The empirical analysis performed shows what are the drivers of the process of creation of value of a business and what relationships exist between the local context (environment) and enterprise.

The banks, in the assessment of creditworthiness, while taking account of such assets, give it a marginal weight in determining the rating.

The study shows also that the local banks, for their strong local roots, definitely recognize the importance of qualitative elements. However, also in this case, the process changes from bank to bank and is not fully formalized.

In light of what has emerged in the study, it is proposed that there should be an improvement of the rating system, which, moreover, cannot be ignored, with the declination of "relevant" intangible assets, by defining an algorithm able to better assess the risk level of businesses.

It is also considered desirable to combine the quantitative and qualitative elements required by Basel II in the calculation of a corrective territorial attribution of the rating, which can correlate the performance of the company and the context in which these results are achieved.

6
An Empirical Case

6.1 The credit scenario analyzed at European, national, and regional level

Within the European Union, the issue concerning the difficulties faced by small undertakings is important in terms of access to credit.[1] This criticism is especially important for small businesses in Cyprus, Slovenia, and Greece. This situation, while limiting their growth prospects, did not weaken these countries' confidence in the future, which remained at mostly optimistic levels so that, between 2009 and 2014, the percentage of SMEs with growth expectations increased from 47 per cent to 61 per cent.

According to a survey carried out by the European Commission, between April and September 2014, requests for financing from SMEs, particularly those presented by younger firms, were not always accepted. More than a third of SMEs surveyed, in fact, were not able to get the full bank financing required. However, all businesses, while noting positively the decrease in interest rates on loans, have been under increasing constraints, expressed in terms of guarantees and other requests from the European financial system.

At the sector level, it is mainly those belonging to the construction sector that, along with micro-enterprises and innovative ones, have the greatest problems obtaining funding.

However, a major issue that emerges from this study is the gap that businesses have in terms of knowledge and financial expertise; this gap narrows financing options.

At the national level, as reported by a recent survey by the Bank of Italy,[2] despite recording in the last quarter of 2014 a smaller attenuation compared to previous months, the decline in loans to companies continues to manifest itself (−1.8 per cent in November 2014 compared to −2.4 per cent in August of the same year). This performance is influenced, on the demand side, by the weakness of investments and, on the supply side, by the continuing risk of borrowers, especially with regard to certain sectors or companies. The trend of loans is affected, however, by the weakness in economic activity, due to increased tensions in international financial markets, the worsening of the economic and political situation in Greece, the economic and financial crisis in Russia, and the weakening of the economic situation in emerging economies.

In late November 2014, the decline in corporate loans was slightly lower than the same period the year before for the first five banking groups compared to other banks (−2.2 and −2.7 per cent, respectively).

As for the economic sector, the credit crunch has eased for the manufacturing sector and the service sector (at −1.7 and −2.4 per cent, respectively), which benefited most from the gradual easing of supply policies. Instead, there remains a more cautious approach towards the scope of construction (−5.4 per cent).

Moving on to analyze the conditions of supply of credit to businesses, from this study it was found that the amount disbursed improved slightly, mainly due to the benefits from increased competitive pressure that favored customers with high credit, while for riskier positions higher spreads were applied, associated to the increase in guarantees required in support of disbursements. However, these conditions are more difficult for smaller companies (those in the size class of less than 50 employees) that suffered most from the failure to grant the requested funding, compared to larger ones (14.5 per cent for the small companies, compared to 6.5 per cent for the larger ones).

SMEs, being considered by the financial system to be by nature more risky and less transparent than other companies, appear more difficult to analyze under uncertain conditions. They are affected by some factors that limit their investment choices, such as:

- Weaknesses of their financial structure, characterized by a rather high leverage.
- Heavy dependence on bank credit.
- Low ability to turn to the market.

Debt for SMEs is equal to 54 per cent of their total financial resources (debt and equity) compared to 45 per cent for other businesses. Financial payables and bank loans make up two thirds of the total, compared to slightly more than a third for larger businesses, while the weight of the bonds is virtually nil, compared with 14 per cent for other companies (AIAF, 2015).

As for the cost of credit, reduction in official interest rates, made by the ECB in September 2014, facilitated a further reduction, so that the average rate on new loans to businesses fell by four-tenths of a percentage point, to stand at 2.6 per cent. This situation has led to the decline in the differential with respect to the corresponding average rates prevailing in the euro area.

The reduction in the cost of loans to Italian companies has benefited both small companies and larger ones, so that the cost of new loans for an amount less than €1 million fell to 3.4 per cent, the top loan amount was reduced to 2.0 per cent.

The result that emerged from the analysis carried out at national and European level is essentially also found at the regional level, and particularly in the Lazio region that, for consistency with regard to the examination carried out, it was decided to investigate.[3] In fact, even in this context, regional continued reduction of bank credit to firms was equal to −5.5 per cent in June 2014, although this was to a lesser extent than at the end of 2013, when it stood at −8.8 per cent. This decrease was mainly seen in medium to large firms, rather than small ones (to June 2014, respectively, −5.9 per cent and −1.2 per cent); this performance was due to both the process of replacement of bank loans with bond issues and the outcome of certain corporate reorganizations.

However, for the main intermediaries operating in the region, demand for business loans remained weak; demand justified by the need to finance mainly the working capital and the restructuring of debts at the expense of investments, which were still falling.

As for the offer, even if the tightening of the criteria for access to credit has stopped, banks continue to maintain a prudent approach. This is reflected in less favorable conditions practiced on riskier loans and, to a lesser extent, in an increase of the required guarantees. These forms are precautionary, applied mainly to companies operating in the construction industry.

Interest rates on short-term loans applied by credit institutes on transactions with enterprises amounted to 7.0 per cent and increased slightly the differential between the average cost of short-term loans applied to small enterprises as opposed to medium to large enterprises. As for the rates charged on new loans granted to companies in the medium and long term, there was a significant reduction (from 4.3 per cent at the end of 2013 to 3.7 per cent in June 2014).

6.2 The financing of the economy analyzed in the province of Frosinone[4]

The negative trend of the Frusinate economy recorded, in 2013, a decline in value-added products that is associated with a low level of growth of finance that has an important effect on businesses.[5] This trend was caused by the collapse of the results for the construction industry that in the period 2009–2012 was reduced by 22.4 per cent compared to a 6.4 per cent reduction at the national level. The opposite trend, however, has emerged in the sectors of agriculture (+10 per cent), manufacturing (+10.4 per cent), and services (+13 per cent).

In the current economic climate – anything but favorable – at the provincial level, there has been significant stiffening of financial intermediaries in the granting of credit, which primarily affected activities of the smaller and less capitalized businesses. In 2013, there was a reduction in lending to the corporate sector by 4.9 per cent, a level associated with the cost of money amounting to 8.9 per cent, which exceeds the national average by almost one percentage point, as a consequence of the objective critical issues affecting various economic sectors. This situation has affected the ability of many companies to comply with the assumptions made by the banks, effectively increasing the level of bad debts,[6] especially among those working in the service sector (+20.3 per cent) and construction (+8 per cent).

In this context, it emerges that:

- Some businesses suffer in an economically-productive and financial sense with negative consequences for their access to credit and/or because of requests for return of credit by lending institutions, compromising the amount of available liquidity.
- To increase their propensity to access credit, businesses should increase their competitiveness, also leveraging the benefits of various forms of association, such as entrepreneurial networks, supply chains, clusters, and so on.

6.3 Sample survey carried out on a dataset of a panel of companies in the province of Frosinone

6.3.1 Premise

The sample survey was carried out with the aim of investigating the main critical factors in the approach to the financial management of local businesses and their relationship with the banking system with the entry into force of the Basel Accords.

The survey tool used to carry out this research was the questionnaire, because of its ability to standardize information acquired in different sectors. It was designed, initially, in the abstract, to the objective of the study. We proceeded then to perform a verification test at the headquarters of some companies in the dataset that were surveyed in order to grasp their impressions and suggestions. The perfected format was administered, accompanied by a letter (Appendix A) outlining the objectives of the research, to companies whose addresses were found by consulting the portal "Infoimprese.it" that contains the archives of the Chamber of Commerce and data on Italian companies. To narrow the search to companies that have their registered offices in the province of Frosinone, two filters were used: the province and the business sector.

All respondents were assured that their data, which would enrich the research, would be analyzed and used in compliance with privacy standards. Also, the results of this research would be disseminated in aggregated format (without individual reference) and would be made available to participating companies, should they request it.

The survey methodology was expressed in the following phases:

- Definition of the sample.
- Sample survey through the preparation of the questionnaire.
- Administration of the questionnaire to selected companies.
- Analysis of the responses received.
- Concluding remarks on the results obtained in relation to cognitive fixed objectives.

6.3.2 Definition of the sample

The study was focused on a dataset based on the province of Frosinone that was representative of the local economic fabric. This was performed by taking care not to obtain distorted results compared to the purposes of the research.

To achieve this goal, some filters were provided to narrow the scope of investigation and increase the significance of the sample.

The guidance criteria for the definition of the sample were the following:

- Identification of companies belonging to sectors C – Manufacturing Activities,[7] F – Construction,[8] G – Wholesale and retail trade, repair of motor vehicles and motorcycles,[9] and H – Transportation and storage[10] of the classification Ateco 2007, through the analysis of the composition by sector universe of firms listed in the Business Register.

- Located in the province of Frosinone.
- Established in the legal form of a corporation.
- With a staff of less than 300 units of employees.
- Active.

6.3.3 Sample survey through the preparation of the questionnaire

The questionnaire (Appendix B) through which information and data on the phenomenon under study was collected, was formulated through structured questions, most of which involve multiple pre-coded responses (Di Ciaccio and Borra,1996). There were 28 questions divided into five sections.

The first section dealt with the personal characteristics of the examined companies, in terms of: company name, location of the registered office, date of establishment, capital, industry Istat Ateco 2007, company size, class of turnover, number of employees, and the management.

The second section investigated what were the relations with the financial system by measuring the intensity of their exploitation of the banking channel in terms of the number of reports, seniority relations, the frequency of use of certain financial instruments in the short, medium, and long term.

The third section analyzed the companies' level of knowledge of, and any appeal to, the system of consortia. These organisms are an important channel of access to credit, especially for smaller companies and undercapitalized ones.

The fourth section focused on the Basel Accords, their impact on the company in terms of burden of bank loans, on the interventions that the governing body considers necessary and that they possibly implement to address the changes, the rating class given by credit institutions, the growing attention paid to intangible company resources in the assessment of creditworthiness, timing analysis and eventual approval of bank credit lines, the possible increase of guarantees required by the financial system, and changes regarding bank financial charges.

The last section investigated:

- The governing body's conception of the type of relationship that the company, in the last three years, had established with the banking system.

- The evolution of the number of interactions that the company intended to maintain over the next two years.
- The ability of the company to resort to alternative sources of funding, such as: self-financing, increasing the shareholding structure, funding by the shareholders, equity loan, securitization of loans, subsidized public funding and/or grants, issuing of mini-bonds, or use of private equity and/or venture capital.
- Aspects that banks must improve to be more effective.
- Communication tools that the corporate governing body will be using in the near future, to improve their relations with lenders.

6.3.4 Administration of the questionnaire to selected companies

The survey questionnaire was sent to 400 companies, selected on the basis of the criteria set out above, in the context of the entire population, updated to 28 September 2013,[11] consisting of 3308 units, divided into sectors, as outlined in Table 6.1 and Figure 6.1.

As part of this taxonomy, only businesses were selected that possessed an e-mail, as this was the chosen method of administration of the questionnaire. Likewise, the opportunity to complete and return the questionnaire was offered through the same method.

6.3.5 Descriptive analysis of the results

The valid questionnaires collected amounted to 160 and can be considered representative of the economic reality of the province of Frosinone.

Table 6.1 Subdivision of companies registered in the Business Register in Frosinone according to the economic sector

Ateco 2007 Code	Description	Number of companies enrolled with the CCIAA[12] of Frosinone, at 09/28/2013
C	Manufacturing activities	870
F	Construction	1198
G	Wholesale and retail trade; repair of motor vehicles and motorcycles	978
H	Transport and storage	262
	Total	3308

Source: Author's elaboration.

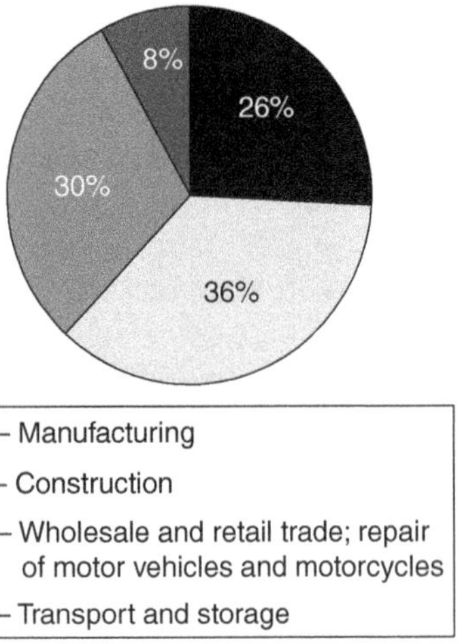

Figure 6.1 Dataset for the province of Frosinone at 09/28/2013
Source: Author's processing.

The response rate, equal to 40 per cent, is to be considered satisfactory as the factor that determines the validity of the survey is not its numerosity but the lack of distortion of the sample (Babbie, 1979). This allowed significant judgments to be made in the analysis carried out.

Examining in detail the data obtained shows that responding companies were based mainly in the city of Frosinone and the surrounding towns. They consisted almost entirely in the legal form of a limited liability company. A small percentage was made up of corporations, while no respondent belonged to the category of companies limited by shares or limited liability simplified company (see Figure 6.2).

Fifty per cent of these entities had a registered capital of less than €100,000, 30 per cent between €100,001 and €1,000,000, while the remaining 20 per cent report an amount which does not exceed €3,000,000 (see Figure 6.3).

These companies belong to the following sectors (see Figure 6.4):

- Over 31 per cent to the manufacturing sector.
- 25 per cent to the construction sector.
- 25 per cent to the sector covering wholesale and retail trade, and repair of motor vehicles and motorcycles.
- The remaining 19 per cent belong to the other sectors included in the dataset.

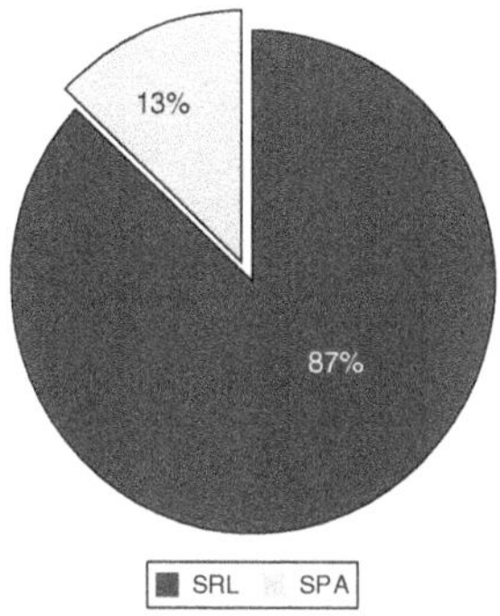

Figure 6.2 Breakdown of respondents by legal form
Source: Author's processing.

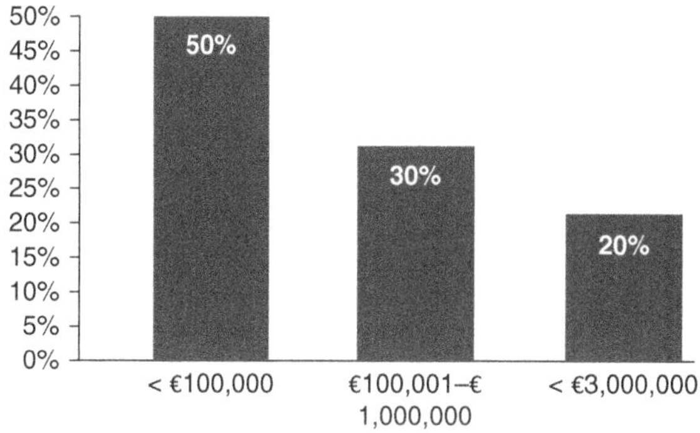

Figure 6.3 Breakdown of respondents by share capital
Source: Author's processing.

A common element in the different sectorial contexts is, no doubt, the fact that the companies analyzed are predominantly family businesses. This model encourages, in particular, the creation and consolidation, in a privileged way, of the relationships with the various stakeholders: with suppliers of resources, both financial and operational, but also with the staff.

It is family businesses that constitute today the "prime mover" of the Italian economy and, as in the past, it is believed that this will still remain so in the future. Regardless of size, they play a particularly important role in the economic landscape because they play a creative entrepreneurial role, create venture capital, and perform the activities of direction and control. These elements represent the strengths on which

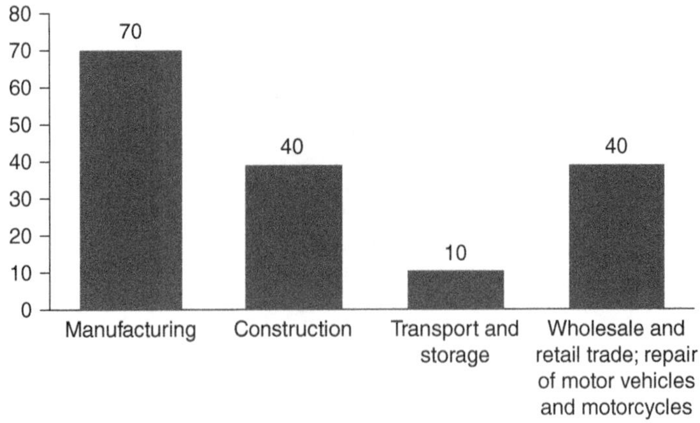

Figure 6.4 Breakdown of respondents by sector
Source: Author's processing.

rests the success of any business formula. These types of companies include all those governed directly or indirectly by family members, regardless of the legal status of the latter and their involvement in the governance. It may be the case that the property and the governing body are exclusively the prerogative of the family; this is the typical case with very small businesses, and SMEs, in which the property explicitly influences the evolutionary dynamics of the business system.

The family, in fact, plays a significant role in the governance of the company; it is entitled to define or revise the organizational scheme, plan or change the structure and steer the evolutionary dynamics with its strategic decisions. According to the "theory of social success," the purpose of business, aimed at value creation, is both oriented to ensure the survival of the company (through profit), and the assertion in the context of social class with relevant positions in the community. So the entrepreneur acts, driven by motivations of both economic and social aspects which converge within their own enterprise, orienting the dynamics. As argued by Golinelli (2005), this model shows a strong capability to "read" the supra-system, interpret systems of consumption, offer systems arrangement, technological and strategic innovation, "evolutionary management" of the structure, and ability to deal with risk.

The degree of interaction with family, company, and shareholders may undergo changes in intensity and nature, giving rise to situations

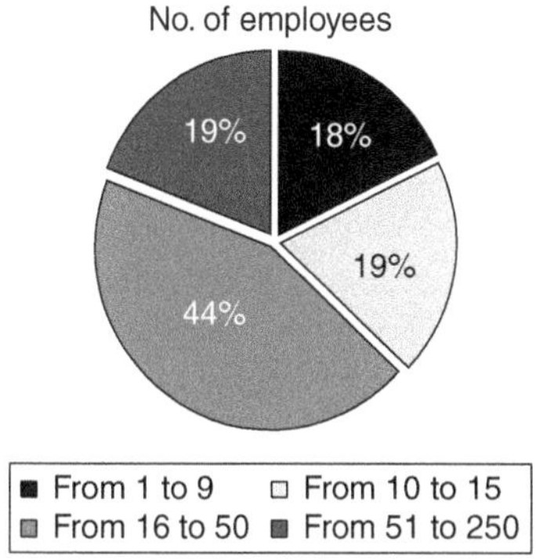

Figure 6.5 Analysis of the organizational structure
Source: Author's processing.

of mutual conditioning, which will be stronger the more effective is the presence of the family and its heritage in business management.

Also, for the business realities of large or medium to large companies there is, very often, a clear separation between ownership and control. In this case, the governing body of the company is entrusted to outside managers who have an almost absolute power and are capable of self-perpetuation. The property shall exercise the right to control *ex post* on the results achieved by the company and there is the opportunity to depose the management if the results are not in line with those expected (Marris, 1972). The companies, subject to analysis by revenue, were distributed fairly evenly among the different classes. Only in very few cases do they have a turnover in excess of €25,000,000.

With reference to the organizational structure (see Figure 6.5), 43.75 per cent employ a workforce that includes a number of employees ranging between 16 and 50 units. The remaining 56.25 per cent is distributed equally among the other classes specified in the questionnaire.

After consideration of the personal characteristics of the responding companies, we proceed with the analysis of the intensity of exploitation of the banking channel.

Businesses that have relations with a bank amounted to 6.25 per cent; of those, 12.5 per cent have relationships with two, 25 per cent with three, 6.25 per cent with four and 12.5 per cent with five banks. The remaining 37.5 per cent work with more than five lenders. This data confirms the continued use of multiple banks by companies (Ruozi, 1997), which is an anomaly of the Italian credit market, rather than the European average. The consequence of this practice is the spread of transactional models that are irreconcilable with the "labor intensive" evaluation processes that rely on a strong relationship with the company (Boot and Thakor, 2000) and induce banks to benefit from informational advantages in relationships that they establish with customers. The valuation methodologies of banks to deepen the acquisition of information on the operations of a business, especially in prospective view, are not actionable if the margins are derived from loans of a reduced amount, if you need to review a large number of loan practices, and if after a careful analysis of customer needs you want to offer integrated solutions. The multiple bank, therefore, represents a strong barrier to the establishment of solid and constant relationships in the long run between banks and businesses.

The banks with which the respondent enterprises establish relations are mainly the large banking groups (see Figure 6.6), although in recent years the local lenders play an increasingly important role as a privileged financial partner, thanks to their "proximity" to the customers, taking advantage of their in-depth knowledge of the local economy due to their local roots. Banks operating in a relatively small community can easily

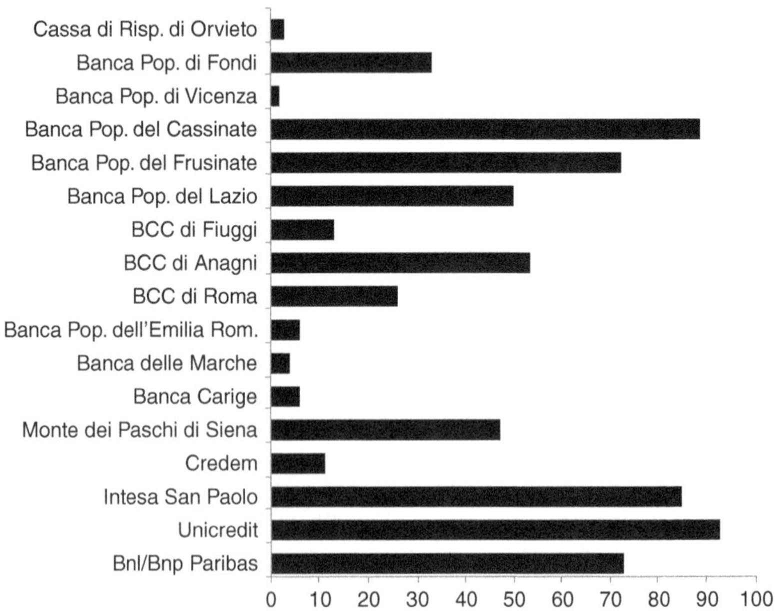

Figure 6.6 Intensity of company relations with lenders
Source: Author's elaboration.

acquire more information on the characteristics of customer risk and the quality of investment projects to be financed, thereby mitigating the problems of adverse selection (Formisano, 2002).

The analysis also indicated that the duration of the customer relationship with lenders is mainly over five years.

In order to qualify the customer behavior from the perspective of use of banking services, it was noted that companies enjoy in the usual manner only a limited number of services, mostly due to short-term financing instruments. As for forms of long-term financing, only in a few cases was a habitual recourse to unsecured loans and leases detected. The percentage increases dramatically if you also take into consideration the occasional use of both of these forms of procurement of financial resources and the mortgage loan. However, many companies stated that they had never used credit for signing, the mortgage loan and factoring.

The practice of debt consolidation, which involves the redefinition of commitments, in the medium and long term, has never been practiced by responding companies.

Moving on to analyze the level of knowledge of, and possible company relations with, the system of consortia, and evaluating the quality of services provided by these, it emerges that there is a poor dissemination of this instrument among the responding companies (see Figure 6.7). Only 37.5 per cent of companies sometimes made use of such an intermediary and considered services offered by it to be effective.

The Italian Consortium of Collective Guarantee of Trust (known as Confidi),[13] fulfilling its mandate to promote access to credit and contract terms favorable to business (in terms of volume, burden, and duration of the loan), is a valuable support – especially for the development of those

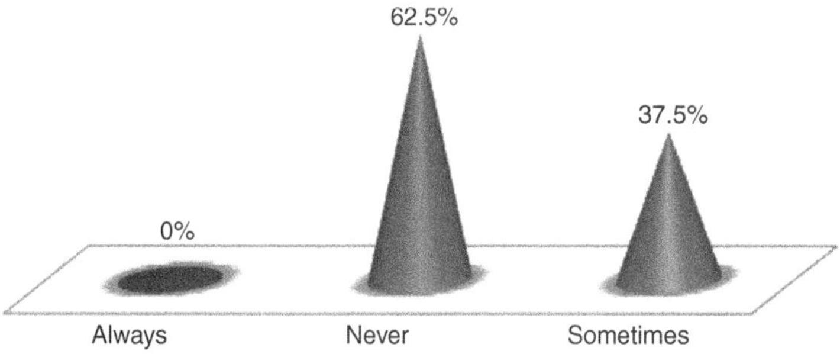

Figure 6.7 Degree of use of services offered by consortia
Source: Author's processing.

businesses of modest size. Their action is explicit through the granting of guarantees, which allow banks to:

- Have instruments that are enforceable in the event of insolvency of the borrower.
- Reduce information asymmetries, since operating a careful and thorough screening of clients is associated with simplifying how the banks engage in the acquisition of information about the potential borrower. This service is especially useful to lenders that do not have a close relationship with the territory, or that do not allow local offices to assess the risk profile of borrowers (Schena, 2004).

Confidi can, therefore, influence the process of determining the rating and reducing the capital needs of the banks, being a positive lever for the provision of credit. By outsourcing the counterparty risk that is transferred out from the perimeter bank (Costa and Costagli, 2005), "the Italian Consortium of Collective Guarantee of Trustcan play an important role in reducing the critical issues that characterize the relationship between banks and companies, especially in areas where the restriction to credit is made more severe by adverse environmental conditions" (Dell'Atti, Lopes, and Tucci, 2013). Their role is absolutely relevant for counter-cyclical situations, when the assets are reduced and consequently it is more difficult to access bank credit (Schena, 2004; Piazzo, 2006). The consortia offer to customers, among other things, support services for companies of small size in order to access venture capital.

With regards to the Basel Accords and their impact on businesses, from the responses obtained we see that the vast majority of the companies, accounting for 81.25 per cent, were aware of the popular legislation called Basel III. Some 37.5 per cent of the respondents believed that its implementation would generate negligible impact on their company. The same percentage could not answer this question, while 23.46 per cent said that the new agreement would impact significantly on their business activities; only the remaining 1.54 per cent did not expect any direct effects (see Figures 6.8 and 6.9).

The survey showed that 52 per cent of companies already believed that, following the implementation of Basel II, bank borrowing costs had affected their financial management to a greater extent than in the past, 26 per cent did not detect variations, 18.75 per cent answered that they did not know, while only 3.25 per cent had benefited from a reduction in interest rates and the cost of bank charges (see Figure 6.10).

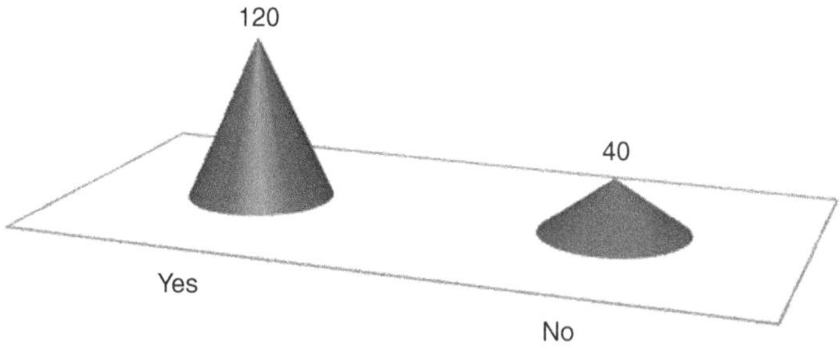

Figure 6.8 Do you know the renewed prudential regulations called Basel III?
Source: Author's processing.

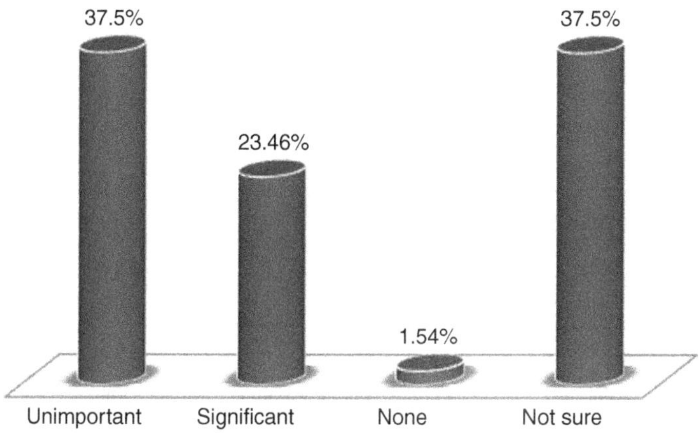

Figure 6.9 Effects of Basel III on businesses
Source: Author's processing.

According to the survey, 32 per cent believed they must take essential action to implement or strengthen their financial function, which needed greater weight, to face the changes that will result from the entry into force of Basel III. The same percentage of respondents highlighted the need to implement operations aimed at capitalization, to allow the company to provide new financial resources to be able to invest, in order to improve their competitiveness. Only a small number of respondents, 8 per cent, considered the implementation of a business information system to be important, while 4 per cent preferred forms of corporate restructuring. Sixteen per cent were not sure, while 8 per cent did not consider any intervention necessary (see Figure 6.11).

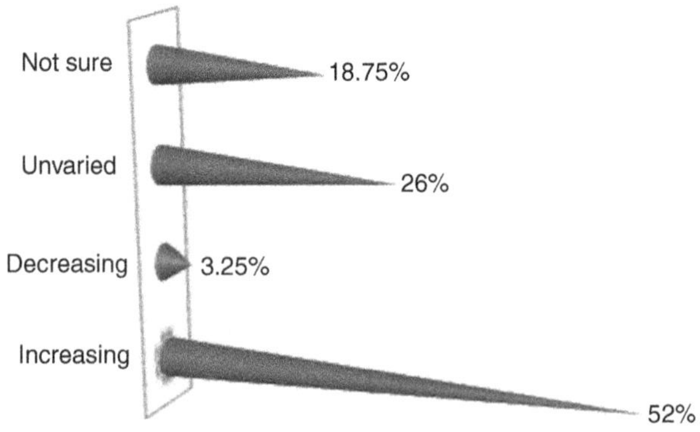

Figure 6.10 The cost of debt has changed with the introduction of Basel II
Source: Author's processing.

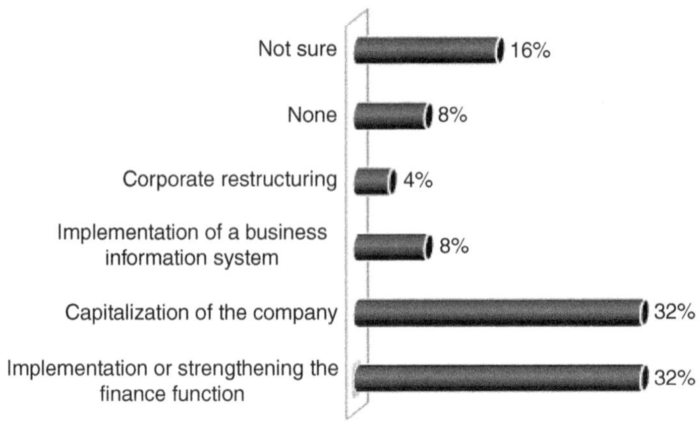

Figure 6.11 Action needed to tackle Basel III
Source: Author's Processing.

The finance function was currently active in several businesses, although, as the small and micro business realities do not always have a formalized organization, this activity is usually handled by the governing body rather than by facilities provided for the purpose. The data examined shows that this function was considered relevant by the entrepreneurs in 62.75 per cent of cases, significant in 25 per cent, and 12.25 per cent saw it as marginal. In several surveys, it was found that with this type of intervention they associate others, such as:

- The implementation of a business information system, in order to exploit the contribution from renewable information endogenous and exogenous to the company, to detect in an organic, systematic and timely manner all the heterogeneous information essential to making prudent management decisions (Lambin, 1994; Kotler, 1997).
- Recapitalization procedures to optimize its debt situation. This is necessary since the assessment of creditworthiness is based primarily on quantitative indicators derived from the analysis of the budget, in which the degree of capital strength and ability of the company to generate cash flow, which is at least sufficient to cover the financial costs, take an important place.

Recapitalization, in other cases, is an operation that is associated with forms of corporate restructuring. However, all the alternatives listed on the questionnaire were also used individually, for each of them,

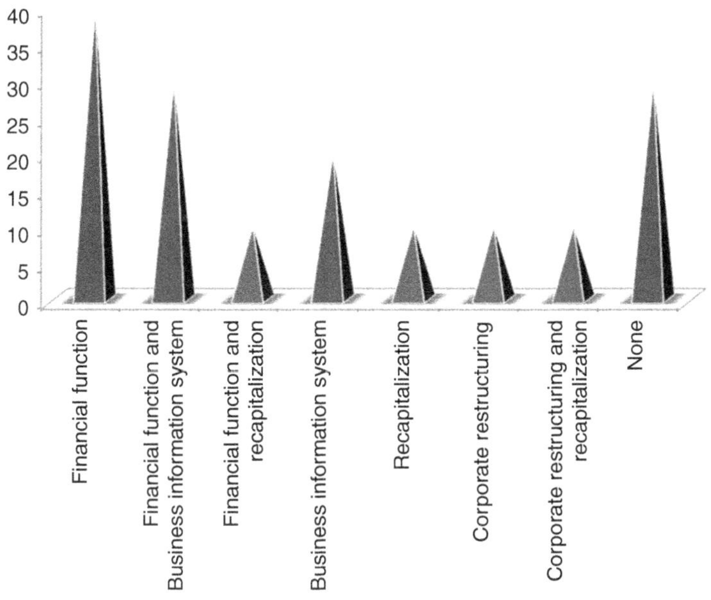

Figure 6.12 Number of interventions made by companies to cope with the changes that will come with the entry into force of Basel III
Source: Author's processing.

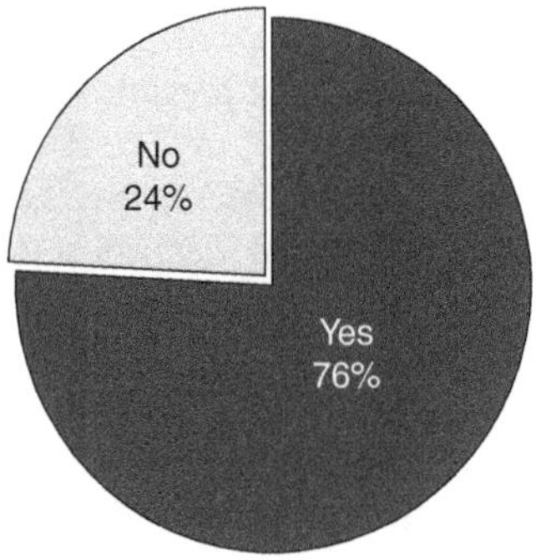

Figure 6.13 Does the company know the rating class that has been attributed by lenders?
Source: Author's processing.

only in a few companies out of the total of the respondents. Only a very small percentage of the companies did not implement any type of intervention.

Over 75 per cent of respondents were aware of the rating category that was attributed to the company (see Figure 6.13). This figure shows the increasing level of awareness of businesses of this issue, that knowledge is a critical factor in the relationship with the financial system.

Speaking of the importance of intangible assets in the assessment of creditworthiness, companies believed, in 37.5 per cent of cases, that the last three years are taken into account by lenders.

The same percentage was not aware of this possibility, while 25 per cent believed that this does not happen.

One aspect that characterizes the bank–enterprise relationship is the number of requests by the units in deficit to increase their credit lines. With reference to a period of short term (within 18 months), only 31.25 per cent of respondents, in the last three years, had requested an extension of credit, which was granted entirely in 80 per cent of cases. Such a request was made by the companies operating in the construction industry, manufacturing, wholesale and retailing, and repair of motor vehicles and motorcycles.

The same type of analysis concerned the demands of increase of credit in the medium to long term. In a very small number of instances that have been advanced, accounting for 18.75 per cent, corresponding feedback in many cases said that the funds were granted for the full amount.

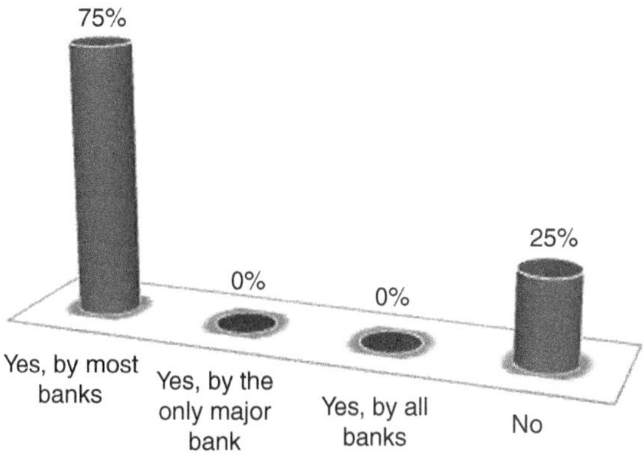

Figure 6.14 Were lengthening approval times of credit lines found in the last three years?
Source: Author's processing.

Almost 30 per cent of requests were accepted only partially and in any case for an amount greater than half of that required. Also in this case, the applicants were operating in sectors of construction, wholesale and retail, and repair of motor vehicles and motorcycles.

A further investigation was related to the evaluation of the time required for approval of the credit lines. Especially in the current economic environment, characterized by high complexity, this factor may considerably affect the survival of enterprises and their competitive strategy. In over 75 per cent of cases, over the last three years, the release of funds took a longer time with the majority of banks with which they operate (see Figure 6.14).

To complicate the situation, 81 per cent of respondents experienced a decrease in the cost of borrowing, expressed in terms of interest rate and bank commissions.

Only in a few cases, corresponding to 6.5 per cent, was the trend reversed, to the benefit of companies belonging to the manufacturing sector that have a turnover of between €10 million and €25 million, with number of employees ranging between 50 and 250. The remaining approximately 12.5 per cent did not undergo any change (see Figure 6.15).

In the past three years, 62.5 per cent of respondents did not receive any requests for increased guarantees against existing credit lines. Significantly, more guarantees were requested for 18.75 per cent, while a

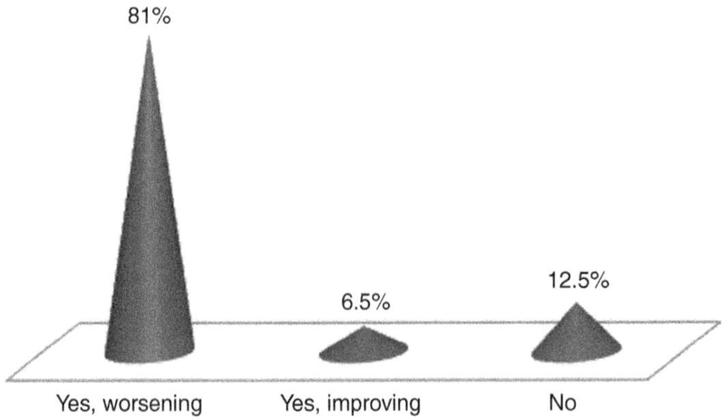

Figure 6.15 Were changes in financial and bank charges found in the last three years?
Source: Author's processing.

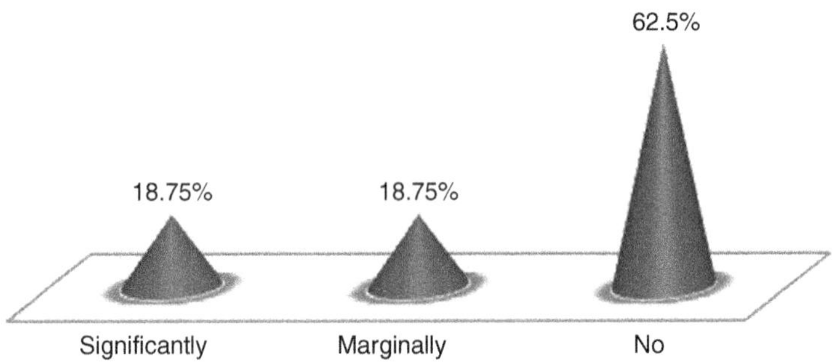

Figure 6.16 Have banks requested more guarantees?
Source: Author's processing.

further 18.75 per cent provided marginally more than in the past (see Figure 6.16).

The companies penalized in this regard have been particularly those belonging to the construction sector, wholesale and retail trade, and repair of motor vehicles and motorcycles.

Summarizing, the number of respondents who noted a deterioration in the quality of the relationship with the banks in the last three years is 31.25 per cent, the remaining 68.75 per cent believed that the relationship remained stable. No companies reported an improved relationship (see Figure 6.17).

At the sector level, the negative evaluation is due to the construction sector, and in some cases to those operating in the wholesale and

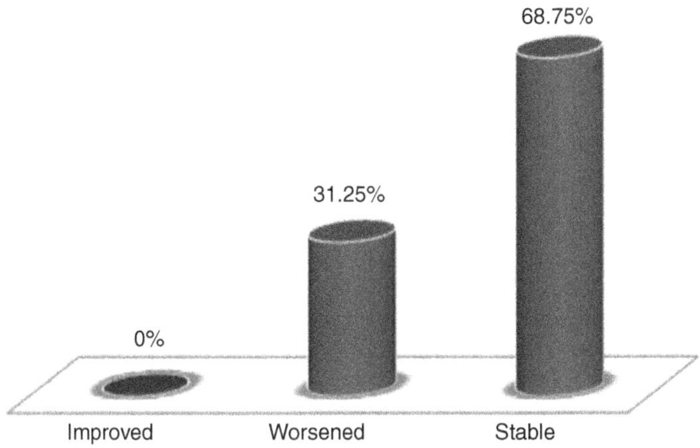

Figure 6.17 Change in relations with the banking system over the last three years
Source: Author's processing.

retail sector, as well as in the repair of motor vehicles and motorcycles. Another fact that emerges is that the critical issues are concentrated in companies that resort to multiple banking, operating with a number of financial intermediaries of about four to eight units.

Analyzing the future prospects, the research shows that:

- Almost 70 per cent of respondents believed that the number of lenders with whom they deal will remain stable in the next two years, while the others believed this number will reduce.
- 63 per cent of companies surveyed are not considering the possibility of using alternative sources of funding. Those, however, who responded positively, believe that the most appropriate for their businesses were forms of public financing (subsidized and/or grants), followed, to a lesser extent, by loans made by shareholders and only in the last resort through self-financing. All other opportunities listed in the questionnaire were not taken into consideration (see Figure 6.18).

Banks, in order to provide a more effective service to businesses, must:

- Greatly reduce response times as often as the units in deficit have an instance of financing.
- Strengthen the transparency of information.
- Improve the professionalism of the interlocutors.

- Increase the frequency of contact with the managers of the relationship.
- Increase the efficiency of telematic products.
- Reduce the technicalities.
- Pay more attention to the issues of economic and social fabric of the territory.

Finally, in order to improve the relationship with the relevant stakeholders, such as credit institutions, in the near future, companies wishing to use a range of quantitative and qualitative input, from accounting documentation (especially budgets), should ensure that it is complete and clear, so that the investor can make a fair assessment of the risk they must take.

All this must be accompanied by additional communication tools, such as a business plan that is not "wishful thinking" but that constitutes a realistic representation of the strategies, the market, the competitive environment, the strengths, weaknesses, opportunities, threats, and financial data on which the investment projects will rest.

This confirms the need for a "business strategy of open information, in order to achieve a satisfactory degree of 'transparency'. The 'transparency' makes the field of observation closer, reduces the possibility of the spread of rumors, allows the 'public' to form opinions that are not entirely subjective" (Esposito De Falco, 2003).

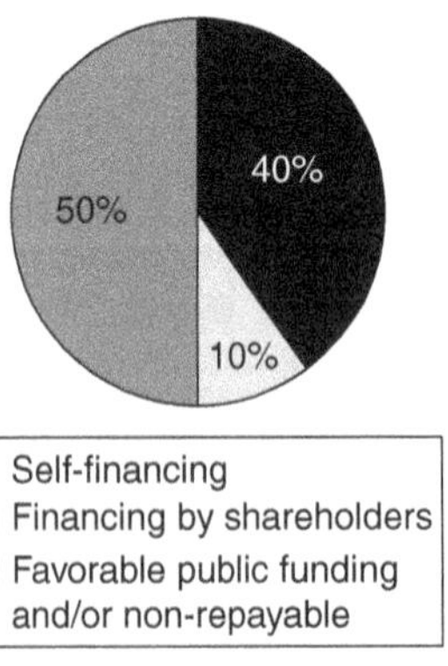

Figure 6.18 Types of funding sources that companies are considering for the future as an alternative to banks
Source: Author's processing.

Effective communication is a prerequisite for building a transparent and constructive relationship, aimed at creating a common path of growth by reducing information asymmetries.

6.3.6 Final considerations and conclusions

The renewed prudential regulation called Basel III as highlighted by Proietti (2012), is fulfilled through government action in the financial system. Such action is addressed to both the operating system and the different entities it interacts with, namely deficit units typically represented by companies.

In order to protect the solidity and stability of intermediaries, it imposes constraints and rules on the operational structure, the former concerning the capital adequacy of each entity, according to the assumed risks.

This agreement strengthens the crucial role played by the risk report in the relations between the credit institution and the businesses it interacts with, in order to adapt the expected return to the risk actually born by the lender.

Another interpretation of this regulation is due to the scientific approach of the government action concerning the "decision area" of the financial system, consequential to past experiences, contingent facts, cognitive increases, and improvements in business practices. It is realized, then, in providing the governing body with a theoretical framework aimed at supporting the interpretive and decision processes following the principles of a rationality that is aware of its own limits as well as the improvement possibilities (Golinelli, 2009).

Such a scientific approach reveals itself through:

- Adoption of an increased regulatory system.
- Undertaking of a well-structured *framework* based on the three *pillars*.
- Expansion of a range of risks to be included in the quantification of the liable equity capital.
- Development of more specific and strict methods to be applied so as to determine the creditworthiness of clients. These changes brought about a growing participation, consistent with the objectives of the system, at the level of the self-organization of the operative structure components concerning the financial system.
- Affirmation of the effectiveness principle: each lending institution is allowed to choose the method to be used in the risk-measurement (standard method or internal method) concerning all the borrowers

and/or the procedures related to a determined category, aiming at determining the minimum prerequisites.
- Predisposition to innovation according to the environmental complexity.

Such innovative regulation has led businesses to dwell on the importance of creating an effective and efficient financial function to cope with the changes taking place and from a long-term perspective.

In a nutshell, it is believed that, in order to start and maintain a relationship compliant with the financial system, companies have to:

- Increase the risk-taking culture.
- Activate concrete government measures concerning risks consistent with their own specific structure and the designed business evolutionary dynamics.
- Rebalance their own fiscal framework through a strengthening of the assets, aimed at reducing the level of *leverage*. A higher level of debt compared to the risk capital makes the firms vulnerable during negative economic-financial circumstances or in the event of any shock affecting the banking system.
- Select carefully the financing sources according to needs, in order to ease the realization of business projects.
- Value the available intangible resources.
- Invest in IT systems.
- Arrange an effective flow of information, especially from a prospective point of view, and make this available to the bank in order to facilitate "communication" in a co-development way.

In the end, following the evolution of Basel Accords, a need has emerged for companies to develop a greater "financial culture" in order to be introduced to the credit market as a reliable counterparty.

6.4 Closing remarks

In the banking system, risk management is both an activity that has as its main objective the preservation of heritage and at the same time an essential prerequisite for creating value.

As with all types of businesses, risks are covered by the assets. Given their particular activity, such an aspect for banking companies takes on greater importance. In fact, supervisors of lending institutions provide minimum capital endowment to cover different types of risks (credit risk and counterparty risk, operational risk, market risk, concentration risk, interest rate risk on the banking book, cash risk, strategic risk, residual risk, reputation risk, etc.).

The focus here has been on credit risk management (which normally absorbs most capital), and in particular the role of soft information in the rating allocation for the assessment of creditworthiness. Currently, a very limited weight, compared to the performance of banking relationships in place and quantitative indicators inferable from the analysis of the balance sheet, is attributed to the qualitative elements in the assessment procedure of creditworthiness.

Qualitative information is acquired by banks through the preparation of questionnaires that, being very synthetic and standardized, are affected by an assessment that is strongly subjective on the part of the operator, and above all they do not allow you to access the real critical success factors that the evaluating company is equipped with. This problem is particularly evident for SMEs that, despite dominating in Europe and accounting for over 99 per cent of the Italian production system, very often have difficulty accessing bank credit, on which they depend to a greater extent than the bigger companies. This highlights an inadequate diversification of the sources of financing concerning such companies.

Furthermore, SMEs are subject both to the cost of debt, that in recent years has affected their financial management to a greater extent than in the past, and to the extension of time in the approval of credit lines. These critical situations can significantly affect the survival and competitive strategy of companies themselves. In many cases, these factors limit the ability of SMEs to cover their financial requirements, with negative implications in terms of growth, development at international level, implementation of innovative strategies, and growth in employment levels.

This tendency highlights, also, a greater aversion and/or an increased risk control exercised by the lending institutions.

To fix this situation, and in accordance with the guidelines provided by the renewed prudential Basel regulation, which has also introduced more important restrictions on the capital endowment banks must hold in order to control the risk of lack of knowledge and possible inadequate ability in assessing the unplanned risk, it is necessary to expand the number and the weight given to relevant factors that, by allowing banks to get access to the real intangible assets of the company, favors the latter's adequate flow of funds. This context also supports lending institutions that by reducing the level of assumed risks will be able to set aside a smaller share of capital for each counterparty, increasing the efficiency of procurement procedures, applying a lower pricing cost and exploiting a greater financial leverage.

In this context, a special role is played by the local banks that, as stated in the study, have a capital level definitely greater than the minimum level established by the supervisory regulation, ranking well above the average for the banking system. This advantage also derives from their ability to mitigate the risk of lack of knowledge, thanks to proximity and local roots. This allows local lending institutions to acquire in-depth and complete information, establishing a long-term trust relationship with the company and enjoying the benefits of a relational approach with customers.

This results in the reduction of risks related to the phenomenon of so-called informative asymmetry that in many cases does not allow a proper assessment of the creditworthiness and the real estimate of PD (probability default) of customers.

The study shows also that the current rating systems, developed with a greater weight of intangibles, could be associated with the so-called "territory" analysis.

In substance, it would take into account, in assessing company performance, the local context in which the company itself operates.

In this sense, the evolution of the research, on the base of the present work, could lead to the identification of a calculation algorithm called the "territorial corrective."

Appendices

Appendix A – Letter of presentation of the questionnaire

Dear Manager,

the undersigned Formisano Vincenzo – associate Professor of Business Economics and Management at the Department of Economics and Law of "University of Cassino and Southern Lazio" – concerning his involvement in the scientific research is carrying out a survey titled **"Non-knowledge risk and bank-company management: the role of intangibles in rating models."**[1]

This research includes a sample survey focused on a set of data representing the economic structure related to the province of Frosinone, which is the aim of the study. It aims at analyzing the main critical factors in the approach to the financial management of the firms and their relationship to the banking system after the entry into force of Basel Accords.

Therefore, Your Excellency is called on filling in the enclosed questionnaire, which is crucial to the purposes of this research, and sending it back to the following email address (v.formisano@eco.unicas.it).

The analyzed data will be used in accordance with the privacy policies. It will enrich the survey and hopefully it will offer worthy food for thought in the field of developing relationships between bank and firm. This data will be spread only in aggregated form along with the current research results (without any individual reference) and it will be available to the participating companies asking for it.

For any information and/or further explanation please contact the undersigned through the above mentioned email address.

Thanking in advance for the valuable collaboration, I extend my best regards.

Prof. Vincenzo Formisano

Appendix B – Questionnaire

Business name

....

Legal head office

....

Date of the establishment

....

Corporation stock

....

Area (Ateco 2007):

Instructions
Express your answer(s) using an X

1. **Is the company mainly a family-run business?**
   - Yes
   - No

2. **What size is your business?**
   ...according to the class of turnover (values in €):
   - up to 2 Mln
   - from 2.1 Mln to 5 Mln
   - from 5.1 Mln to 10 Mln
   - from 10.1 Mln to 25 Mln
   - from 25.1 Mln to 50 Mln
   - beyond 50 Mln

   ...according to the number of employees:
   - up to 9
   - from 10 to 15
   - from 16 to 50
   - from 50 to 250
   - beyond 250

3. **How many banks do you have a relationship with?**
   - 1
   - 2
   - 3
   - 4
   - 5
   - beyond 5

4. **What are the main lending institutions you have relationships with?** (Point out even more than a preference enumerating them: 1,2,3,4,..., 10.)
   - Bnl/Bnp Paribas
   - Unicredit
   - Intesa San Paolo
   - Credem
   - Credit Agricole
   - Monte dei Paschi di Siena

- Other banking Groups:...
- Banca di Credito Cooperativo di Roma
- Banca di Credito Cooperativo di Anagni
- Banca di Credito Cooperativo di Fiuggi
- Banca Popolare del Lazio
- Banca Popolare di Ancona
- Banca Popolare dell'Etruria e del Lazio
- Banca Popolare del Frusinate
- Banca Popolare del Cassinate
- Banca del Fucino
- Carispaq - Cassa di Risparmio della Provincia dell'Aquila

Other:
....
....
....
....

5. **For each bank you maintain a relationship with, specify how long you have been a client.** (If greater than 10 specify only the main 10.)

Relationship in years with banks						
Bank	**1**	**2**	**3**	**4**	**5**	**beyond 5**
1						
2						
3						
4						
5						
6						
7						
8						
9						
10						

6. **For each of the following financing instruments, express its frequency of use.**

Financing instruments	**Not sure**	**Never used**	**Occasionally used**	**Regularly used**
Credit opening/overdraft				
Anticipation on promissory note				
Advance invoices				

(Continued)

Financing instruments	Not sure	Never used	Occasionally used	Regularly used
Advance subject to collection				
Commitment appropriations				
Unsecured loan				
Mortgage				
Leasing				
Factoring				
Debt consolidation at a medium/long term				
Other (to be specified)				

7. **Does the company take advantage of guarantee consortium trust (Confidi)?**
   - o Always
   - o At times
   - o Never (go to question number 9)

8. **How do you consider the quality of the services provided by Confidi?**
   - o Appropriate
   - o Not suitable for the period
   - o Not suitable for the costs
   - o Not suitable for the guarantees
   - o Not suitable for the amounts granted

9. **Are you aware of the new Basel Accords concerning the capital requirements of the banks, known as "Basel III"?**
   - o Yes
   - o No

10. **Do you consider that the fulfillment of Basel III will bring about consequences on your company?**
    - o None
    - o Unimportant
    - o Significant
    - o Not sure

11. **After the fulfillment of Basel II, bank financing cost for your company has been:**
    - o Unchanged
    - o Lower

- Higher
- Not sure

12. Among the interventions listed below, which ones do you consider necessary to cope with the changes deriving from the new Basel Accords?
- Financial function[2]
- Implementation of the business information system
- Corporate restructuring
- Capitalization of the company
- None
- Not sure
- Other

....
....

13. Among the interventions listed below, which ones is your company already implementing?
- Financial function
- Implementation of the business information system
- Corporate restructuring
- Review
- None
- Not sure
- Other

....
....

14. How important is the financial function within your company?
- Remarkable
- Significant
- Secondary
- Unimportant
- Not sure

15. Are you aware of the rating category that is attributed to your company by lending institutions?
- Yes
- No

16. Over the last three years, have the lending institutions taken into account the intangible assets available to your company, aiming at the assessment of creditworthiness?
- Yes
- No
- Not sure

17. Over the last three years, has your company asked for an extension of a short-term borrowing facilities (until 18 months)?
- Yes
- No (go to question 19)

18. **Were the further borrowing facilities granted?**
    - Yes, for the overall amount required
    - Yes, for an amount greater than half of the required amount
    - Yes, for an amount lower than half of the required amount
    - No

19. **Over the last three years, has your company asked for an extention of medium/long term borrowing facilities (beyond 18 months)?**
    - Yes
    - No (go to the question 21)

20. **Were the further borrowing facilities granted?**
    - Yes, for the overall amount required
    - Yes, for an amount greater than half of the required amount
    - Yes, for an amount lower than half of the required amount
    - No

21. **Over the last three years, have you observed any prolongation in the approval of your credit line?**
    - Yes, by the only major bank
    - Yes, by most of the banks I am in a relationship with
    - Yes, by all banks I am in a relationship with
    - No

22. **Over the last three years, have you observed any requests for guarantees increase?**
    - Yes significantly
    - Yes marginally
    - No

23. **Over the last three years, have you observed any variations of the financial and bank charges?**
    - Yes, worsening
    - Yes, improving
    - No

24. **In a nutshell, over the last three years, your relationships between your company and the banking system have:**
    - Worsened
    - Improved
    - Remained stable

25. **In reference to the next 2 years, you consider the number of banks you will maintain a relationship with**
    - Will remain stable
    - Will decrease
    - Will increase

26. **Are you considering the possibility of having recourse to funding sources different from the banking ones?**
    - Yes
    - No

27. **If so, which among these:** (point out even more than a preference enumerating them: 1,2,3,4)
    - Self-financing ....
    - Increase in social shareholders ....
    - Financing by shareholders ....
    - Shareholder loan[3] ....
    - The loan establishment ....
    - Favorable public funding and/or non-repayable ....
    - Issuing of mini-bonds ....
    - Recourse to private equity activities ....
    - Recourse to venture capital activities ....
    - Other (to specify):

    ....
    ....

28. **Which aspects do you consider banks must improve in order to offer a more effective service?**
    - Response times
    - Technical terms
    - Professionalism of the interlocutors
    - Efficiency of telematic products
    - Frequency of contact with the relationship supervisors
    - Transparency of information
    - Other (to specify):

    ....
    ....
    ....

29. **Which communication tools do you intend to use in the next future in order to improve the relationships with the other lending institutions?**
    - Accounting material (such as balance sheet)
    - Business plan
    - Rating files drawn up in accordance with the rules set by the Basel Agreements
    - Other (to specify)

    ....

Notes

1 The Context: The Financial System

1. It is important to underline that in financial services companies, there is the presence at the same time of financial intermediaries in the meaning specified and of other financial institutions that that are distinguished for a similar activity both in content and operational tools. Generally, financial intermediaries can be divided into:

   - Depository intermediaries, where banks have a dominant position.
   - Investment intermediaries, where mutual investment funds have a position or relevance.
   - Contractual intermediaries, where insurance companies have a central position.

2. With reference to such activity, the financial intermediaries have two main functions: to compensate the temporal equilibrium between an offer of money and a request for financing; and to create liquidity and payment tools for a partially active intangible.
3. See R. Costi (2001) *L'ordinamen to bancario* (Il Mulino: Bologna); M. Pipitone (2005) "La disciplina giuridica delle banche popolari e i modelli alternativi di banca," in R. De Bruyn and G. Ferri (eds) *Le banche popolari nel localismo dell'economia italiana* (Rome: Edicred).
4. Consider that in the 1980s the activities of banks under public control was close to 70 per cent of total funds, wholly intermediated by the banking system.
5. See P. Alessandrini (2001) *Il Sistema Finanziario Italiano tra Globalizzazione e Localismo* (Bologna: Il Mulino); A. Giannola (2002) *Il credito difficile* (Naples: L'Ancora del Mediterraneo); A. Giannola (2007) "Vigilanza prudenziale, consolidamento del sistema bancario e divari territoriali," *Svimez, Rivista Economica del Mezzogiorno*, XXI, no. 2; P. Bongini and G. Ferri (2005) *Il Sistema Bancario Meridionale* (Bari: Laterza editore).
6. For a complete definition of local bank, please see: Alessandrini (1994 and 1996), moreover, the works and contributions of Corigliano (2006); P. Alessandrini and A. Zazzaro (2000) "L'evoluzione dei sistemi finanziari locali nell 'era dell 'euro'," *Moneta e Credito*, vol. 53; P. Alessandrini, L. Papi and A. Zazzaro (2003) "Banks, regions and development,"*BNL Quarterly Review*, vol. 224; A. Zazzaro (1997) "Regional banking system, credit allocation and regional economic development," *Economie Appliquée*, vol. 50, no. 1; A. Zazzaro (1998) "L'articolazione territoriale del sistema bancario: aspetti teorici e alcune evidenze empiriche per la Campania," *Moneta e Credito*, vol. 51, p. 203; P. F. Russo and P. Rossi (1999) "Costo e disponibilità del credito per le imprese nei distretti industriali," *Banca d'Italia – Temi di Discussione*; P. F. Russo and P. Rossi (2001) "Credit

constraints in Italian Industrial Districts," *Applied Economics,*vol. 33, no. 11; Z. Rotondi (2005) "Banche, finanziamento dello sviluppo e dell 'innovazione e internazionalizzazione," in G. Bracchi and D. Masciandaro (eds) *Decimo Rapporto SFI. Le banche Italiane e la finanza per lo sviluppo: territori, imprese e famiglie* (Edibank-Bancaria Editrice), pp. 75–100;E. Ughetto (2007) *Industrial Districts and Financial Constraints to Innovation* (Mimeo); E. Beretta and S. Del Prete (2007) "Aggregazioni bancarie e specializzazione nel credito alle PMI: peculiarità per area geografica," Temi di discussione del Servizio Studi di Banca d'Italia, no. 644; S. Lugaresi and Z. Rotondi (2007) "Internazionalizzazione e finanziamento dei distretti industriali," *Economia Italiana*, 1.

7. Credit realities, still autonomous in management, have surely become, in a few years, a minority reality, almost a marginal one, that can control no more than 30 per cent of the overall market of Southern credit(Butzbach and Lopes, 2006).
8. See for instance, A.N. Berger, A.K. Kashyap, and J.M. Scalise (1995) "The transformation of the U.S. banking industry: What a long, strange trip it's been," Brookings Papers on Economic Activity, 2; J. Peek, andE. S. Rosengren, (1998) "Bank consolidation and small business lending: It is not just bank size that matters," *Journal of Banking and Finance*, vol. 22, issues 6–8, pp. 799–819; A.N. Berger, L. Klapper and G.F. Udell (2001) "The ability of banks to lend to informationally opaque small businesses," Federal Reserve Board working paper; A.N. Berger, N.H. Miller, M.A. Petersen, R.G. Rajan, and J.C. Stein (2002) "Does function follow organizational form? Evidence from the lending practices of large and small banks," Paper No. W8752 (NBER Working); A.N. Berger, W.S. Frame, and N.H. Miller (2002) "Credit scoring and the availability, price, and risk of small business credit," Board of Governors of the FR System FEDS 26, April.
9. The first cooperative bank system was created in Germany in the 19th century by Schultze-Delitsche.
10. In cooperative banks, there are four typologies of members: shareholders, manager members, users who are careful as to the quality of the service for saving and credit, and employee members who, as employees, provide their activities in the credit institute (Masciandaro, 1999).
11. In a cooperative bank, the pursuit of long-term profitability is an "indicator of the high protection of minority shareholders" (Pittaluga et al., 2005).
12. The traditional banking model based on relationship lending tends to traditionally counteract the one based on transaction lending. The literature suggests that a model based on the relationship with customers does not constitute a competitive advantage for the large size bank, specialized in transaction technology.
13. Corporate financial statements of cooperative credit, 2007.
14. Ferri (1997) shows, on data reported to the Italian banking system, that the mobility of bank managers is in fact higher for large banks and that the greater mobility is associated with a deterioration in credit quality.
15. Degli Antoni and Portale (2007) argue that the *multi-stakeholder* approach promoted, thanks to measures of corporate responsibility, can generate share capital for the territory and reputation for the organization that implements it.

16. CABEL was formed in 1985, on the initiative of three Tuscan rural banks, and aimed to create a "multi-purpose center for local banks."

2 The Evolution of Prudential Regulation

1. Please refer to F. Tutino (2005) *La performance delle banche* (Milan: Bancaria Editrice).
2. The bank will offer a better pricing (at-risk) for the operation, not so much when the debtor will be less risky, but because the entire operation will require a lower capital requirement.
3. For further information, please see the studies of: E. Altman (1966) "Financial ratios, discriminant analysis and the prediction of corporate bankruptcy," *Journal of Finance*, 23; W. F. Treacy and M. Carey (2000) "Credit risk rating systems at large US banks," *Journal of Banking & Finance*, special issue, vol. 24, nos. 1–2. For further information on the identification, measurement, and management of credit risk, please see among others: G. Lusignani (1996) *La gestione dei rischi finanziari nella banca* (Il Mulino); A. Sironi and M. Marsella (1998) (eds) *La misurazione e gestione del rischio di credito. Modelli, strumenti e politiche* (Bancaria Editrice); R. Masera (2001) "Il Rischio e le Banche," *Il Sole 24 Ore*; A. Resti (2001) "Misurare e gestire il rischio di credito nelle banche. Una guida metodologica," *Alpha Test*; P. Leone and C. Boido (2004) *Rischio di credito e credit derivatives. Modelli e strumenti* (CEDAM).
4. On this topic, please see among others: C. Borio, C. Furfine, and P. Lowe (2001) "Procyclicality of the financial system and financial stability: Issues and policy options," BIS Papers, No. 1; D. W. Ervin and T. Wilde (2001) "Procyclicality in the New Basel Accord," *Risk Magazine*, October; E. Catarineu-Rabell, P. Jackson, and D. P. Tsomocos (2003) "Procyclicality and the New Basel Accord, the banks' choice of loan rating system," Bank of England Working Papers, No. 181; Bank of Italy (2009) "Financial sector pro-cyclicality: lessons from the crisis," Occasional Paper 44, by F. Panetta and P. Angelini (coordinators), U. Albertazzi, F. Columba, W. Cornacchia, A. Di Cesare, A. Pilati, C. Salleo, and G. Santini, April; F. Cannata (2010) *Il metodo dei rating interni: Basilea 2 e il rischio di credito: le nuove regole, la loro attuazione in Italia, le proposte di revisione dopo la crisi finanziaria* (Rome: Bancaria Editrice).

   It is also interesting to see the study by Cannata and Quagliariello (2009) that traces, critically, the main charges referred to Basel II due to: the level of minimum capital induced by the forecasts of the Agreement, the role of rating agencies, the problem of pro-cyclicality, the use of internal models by banks, the possibility of normative regulatory arbitrage and the evaluation at fair value of financial activities.
5. This happens when the reserves accumulated during the expansion phase are not sufficient to cover the risks associated with these stages. Conversely, in periods of economic expansion, reducing the risks even the capital requirements for banks will diminish. With the introduction of Basel III, the pro-cyclicality of the financial sector will be mitigated, ensuring that banks will accumulate additional capital to the regulatory minimum (buffer)

in periods of growth and therefore they will able to deal with downturns without interrupting finance and economy and without falling below the minimum capital requirements. Compared to previous agreements, this will reduce the possibility of a vicious cycle of loss and reduction in credit disbursement.

In addition, banks will have to comply with a second buffer sheet, the counter cyclical capital buffer that has been calibrated in the range of 0–2.5 per cent, as determined by the document that establishes the guidelines for national authorities in the application of *novo regime*: "Guidance for National authorities operating the counter cyclical capital buffer," published in December 2010 by the Basel Committee.

6. This latest data is retrieved by drawing on the database of Central Risk. The Central Risks are used to collect information on the reliability of the companies in their relationship with the entire banking system. The most important in Italy is the Central Credit Bank of Italy, which contains and receives reports on loans greater than €30,000. The uses of such information shall be made in accordance with the regulations, also with reference to the service of the first information.
7. The literary landscape offers multiple classifications relevant for the identification of company intangible resources. On the topic, see, among others, the contributions of E. Comuzzi, S. Marasca and L. Olivotto (2009) *Intangibles. Profili di gestione e di misurazione*(Milan:Franco Angeli); A. Del Bello and A. Gasperini (2006) *Il valore del capitale intellettuale. Aspetti teorici e casi aziendali di reporting* (Milan: Ipsoa); M.S. Chiucchi (2004) *Sistemi di misurazione e di reporting del capitale intellettuale: criticità e prospettive* (Turin: Giappichelli); L. Edvinsson and M. Malone (1997) *Intellectual Capital* (London: Piatkus); H. Itami (1988) *Le risorse invisibili* (Turin: Isedi); B. Lev (2001) *Intangibles. Management, Measurement and Reporting* (Washington, DC: Brooking Institution Press); A. Lipparini (2002) *La gestione strategica del Capitale Intellettuale e del capitale sociale* (Bologna: Il Mulino);P. Lizza (2005) *Il Capitale Intellettuale: profili di gestione e di valutazione* (Milan: Giuffrè Editore); L. Marchi and S. Marasca (2010) *Le risorse immateriali nell'economia delle aziende. Profili di misurazione e di comunicazione* (Bologna: Il Mulino); K. Sveiby (1997) *The New Organizational Wealth* (San Francisco: Berrett-Koehler).
8. In particular, see the contributions of: M. Porter (1985) *Competitive Advantage: Creating and Sustaining Superior Performance* (New York: The Free Press); R. M. Grant (1999) *Strategic Analysis for Business Decisions* (Bologna: Il Mulino; M. Porter (2011) *The Competitive Advantage* (Collana Piccola Biblioteca Einaudi. New Series, Giulio Einaudi Editore).
9. European Commission: "How to interact with the new rating culture: Practical guide to bank financing for small and medium enterprises," http://europa.eu.int/comm/enterprise/entrepreneurship/financing/basel_2.htm.
10. For studies on this, see: T. Onesti and D. Previati (2007) *Basilea 2 e la struttura patrimoniale delle imprese*(Franco Angeli); C. Iacopozzi (2009) *L'applicazione di Basilea II in Italia. Aspetti tecnici ed elementi di riflessione* (Padova: CEDAM).
11. The Bank of Italy issued the "New Minimum Capital Requirements for Banks" (Circular 263 of December 27, 2006) for implementation of the legislation contained in the Directives 2006/48 / EC and 2006/49 / EC of June 14, 2006, where such systems are regulated.

12. See Bank of Italy Circular no. 263of 27/12/2006, TITLEII, Chap. 1, par. 2. It should be specified that retail and mortgage loans are excluded from this rule.
13. The Bank of Italy has recognized SACE as the ECA, a company wholly owned by the Ministry of Economy and Finance. The bank, when making a loan in an operation to export, if there is the presence of SACE, does not consume capital and its funding is weighted "to zero." It could be easily imagined that, in situations of serious liquidity crisis in the markets, the intervention of SACE is, at times, absolutely strategic.
14. See par. 2, Title II, Ch. 1, Section VIII of the Circular of the Bank of Italy, 263 of December 27, 2006, and subsequent amendments, with which EU directives2006/48/CE and 2006/49 / CE were transposed.
15. Ibid.
16. On December 24, 1913, Fitch Investor Services was founded by John Knowles Fitch, based in New York. In late 1997, after a series of acquisition sit became Fitch IBCA. In 2000, it became Fitch IBCA Duff & Phelps (following the acquisition of Duff & Phelps Credit Rating Co.), and soon after, Fitch Ratings. In subsequent years, the company through further acquisitions increased in size, creating the Fitch Group, although it still remains the smallest of the three major rating agencies internationally.
17. Moody's Investors Service, founded in 1909 by John Moody, a business journalist interested in the financial transparency of companies, began his work by evaluating the titles of the US federal government. He opened the office in Milan in April 1999, following the creation of the Economic and Monetary Union and the approval of the Italian law n.130 / 1999 on securitization, but it has operated in Italy since 1986, when the first rating was assigned to Republic and the Italian Working National Bank. Currently, Moody's ratings in Italy are awarded to corporate groups, banks and financial institutions, local authorities, insurance groups, investment funds, property funds, and management companies of real estate funds.
18. Founded in 1976, it has its headquarters in Toronto.
19. Standard & Poor's began its activities in 1860, when its founder Henry V. Poor proposed to US investors an analysis on the reliability and quality of credit of US companies engaged in projects related to the construction of canals and railways.
20. By resolution No. 40 of 19/01/2010 held by Cerved Group SpA, the Bank of Italy issued the ECAI recognition. Moreover, the Cerved Group is recognized as a rating tool within the schema ECAF, that is, the recognition in Europe that allows use of the ratings issued by the Group to determine the high credit standards for loans submitted by banks as collateral, to access financing from the Bank of Italy or of other central banks of the European Union.
21. The simultaneous recognition and solicited ratings may be required, limited to assessments of public finance(central governments and central banks, public sector entities, territorial sector entities, multilateral development banks) for unsolicited ratings.
22. If the application for an endorsement has been submitted by 12/31/2009, the time span of two years has been considered for the AIRB approach and one year for the FIRB approach and for retail exposures.

23. For the description of this method of assessment as provided in the "Enforcement of the new international prudential regulation. IRB approach to calculate the capital requirement for credit risk," by the Bank of Italy, in July 2006.
24. It performs functions of strategic supervision, management, and control.
25. Banks define the organizational characteristics of the rating system they intend to adopt by providing appropriate forms of assessment and feedback at all levels that make up the control activities. In the rating systems focused on automatic components, the verification concerns the completeness of the valuation elements taken into account and extends to the treatment methods of the qualitative information objectified. As part of the rating systems that provide for the integration of automatic judgments with a discretionary component, checks on the consistency of the reasons for the proposed override, with the criteria defined by internal regulations, are necessary. See Bank of Italy (2006) "Implementation of the new international prudential regulation: IRB approach to calculate the capital requirement for credit risk."
26. This consists of a formalized set of activities, tools, and procedures to assess the accuracy of the estimates of all relevant risk and make a judgment about the proper operation, the predictive ability, and overall performance of the IRB system adopted. Through the validation task, then, the bank monitors continuously and iteratively the reliability of the results of the rating system and the maintenance of its consistency with the regulatory requirements, with operational requirements, with business and market developments of reference. The validation consists of both quantitative and qualitative analyses, then, in addition to the comparison of the actual risk measures with the *exante* estimates, the conducting of analysis is extended to all members of the IRB system, including processes, operational control tools, documentation, infrastructure, and the assessment of their overall consistency. See Bank of Italy (2006)"Implementation of the new international prudential regulations: Method of internal ratings to calculate the capital requirement for risk credit."
27. See Circular no. 263 of December 27, 2006, "New Minimum Capital Requirements for Banks," Title IV, Chap. 1.
28. For banking portfolio, it is intended "all types of diverse positions from other than those included in the trading portfolio for supervisory purposes" (see Chap. 4, Part I, Section I, par. 3.1).
29. The Bank of Italy defines it as "an automated system adopted by banks and financial intermediaries to assess applications for financing customers (generally for the granting of consumer credit). It is based on automated systems that provide the application of methods and statistical models to assess the credit risk, and the results are expressed in the form of synthetic judgments, numerical indicators or scores, associated to the person, directed to provide a representation, in predictive or probabilistic terms, of its risk profile, reliability, or timeliness of payments." (https://www.bancaditalia.it/footer/glossario/index.html?letter=c).

    Therefore they are evaluation systems that draw their judgment exclusively from a quantitative analysis, based on objective data for which the weight of the analyst evaluator is irrelevant as it has no weight of the qualitative factors. To obtain a "score," it is sufficient to introduce the required parameters in a properly set spreadsheet.

Many banks, when measuring the company's score, use the CeBi-Score, a module of System CeBi aimed at diagnosing the financial risk profile of the company. In 2011, there was a fourth release of this scoring model, whose contents are highly innovative:

- It examines jointly the last three balance sheets based on 30 specialized functions for economic activity.
- It assigns the company to a risk category according to a scale divided into ten classes, grouped in three main areas: solvency, vulnerability, and risk.
- It estimates a probability of default (PD) at one, three, and five years.
- The risk profile of the company is placed in the reference sector (Istat Ateco the 3rd digit).
- It is a forward-looking measure: the risk of the enterpriseis adjusted on the basis of its current and prospective economic area of reference (sector and geographical location).

30. In the case of exposures to retail, as well as the PD (double entry), LGD and EAD must also be estimated.
31. In this sense, this is also expressed by G.M. Golinelli (2011) *L'approccio sistemico vitale (ASV) al governo dell'impresa, vol. II, Verso la scientificazione dell'azione di governo* (Padova: CEDAM).
32. In G. De Laurentis and R. Maino (2010) "I rating interni durante e dopo la crisi: rapporti banca-impresa, vincoli regolamentari e modelli di business," *Bancaria,* no. 1.
33. In addition to the Bank of Italy Central Risks, the Central Risk Amount Content and private forms of this service, such as CRIF, Experian, CTC, and so on, exist.
34. Some useful information can be obtained from reports submitted by cyclical and structural relationship: associations of category. To Confindustria, Confartigianato, Confcommercio, CNA, Confai, Confcooperative adjoin; associations related to the specific sector: Confetra, Altech-Assinform, and so on.
35. Reports from the field allow us to assess its evolution in periods characterized by economic cycles of the economy.
36. Giovanni Carosio, Deputy Director General of the Bank of Italy and President of the CEBS (Committee of European Banking Supervisors), wrote along these lines in the preface of F. Cannata (2010) *The IRB Approach: Basel 2 and the Credit Risk: The Rules, their Implementation in Italy, Review Proposals after the Financial Crisis* (Milan: Bancaria). On this, par. 411 of Basel II provides that "all the information directly available from the banks because of the magnitude and continuity of their customer relationships should be used to estimate the risk underlying a transaction."
37. In this way, the General Manager of ABI, during the presentation of the guide, "Understanding the Rating," spoke of an initiative conducted within the Permanent Observatory on bank-business relationships, involving the ABI (Italian Banking Association) and all the major representatives of business.

38. G. Gabbi, M. Matthias, and M. De Lerma (2006) "CART analysis of qualitative variables to improve credit rating processes," *Computing in Economics and Finance*, vol. 179, Society for Computational Economics.
39. "Although the crisis was the consequence of many concomitant facts, certainly there gulatory apparatus and supervision of the financial industry has not been able to prevent the excessive expansion of the risks or to harness the transmission of financial turbulence." In this sense, G. Carosiospoke, in'The reform of prudential rules. Participation of the Deputy General Manager of the Bank of Italy' at the ABI conference "Basel 3: Banks and businesses around 2012," Rome, 4 May 2010, pp. 1–2.
40. Concerning this, see F. Cannata and M. Quagliariello (2009) "The role of Basel II in the sub prime financial crisis: guilty or not guilty?" CAREFIN Working Paper, No. 3, p. 8.

3 The Banking Business: The Governing Body and the Operational Structure

1. The Bank of Italy refers to*credit scoring*as "an automated system to be adopted by banks and financial intermediaries to evaluate the request of financing of customers (in general the concession of credit to consumption). It is based on automated systems that foresee the application of statistic models or methods to evaluate the credit risk, and the results are expressed in short considerations, numbers of scores that are associated to the interested, which directly give a representation of its risk profile, form a prevision or probable point of view, reliability or precision in payments."
2. These are evaluative systems that elaborate their judgment based on a quantitative analysis, based on objective data. Therefore, the role played by the appraiser analyst is irrelevant, and the weight of qualitative factors is invalid. To obtain a "score" it is enough to introduce required parameters on a properly set-up calculation paper.
3. Istruzioni di Vigilanza (G.U. Serie Generale no.245 del 20-10-1998 – Suppl. Ordinario n. 175)

4 The Bank–Company Relationship

1. See R. Ruozi and C. Zara (2001) "Il rapporto tra banca e Pmi: caratteristiche strutturali e tendenze evolutive," *Contributi in Bancaria*, no. 10.
2. The simple/complex variable gives a more articulated reading key of the reality of the company than the traditional discrimination based on the dimension of SMEs vs. big business. The main assumption is that there could be some small complex companies also in the financial function (let us think of the start-up in a new economy, of some world niche leader, etc.). The complexity is a concept which is understood in the observation of diverse elements that characterize the management formula of a company, in terms of typology of customers, markets, and technology.
3. With the ordinary/extraordinary variable, the area of operativity of the financial function is defined. The term "ordinary" refers to the satisfaction of the financial requirements and of the linked services related to the

investments in circulating and fixed capital of a company, necessary for the realization of a precise strategy for the conservation of the competitive equilibrium. Alternatively, the term "extraordinary" refers to the operations that, involving the company structure or entailing a growth in the size of the company, cause changes in the company strategy.

4. For further details on the financial culture of SMEs, see Confindustria (2001) "Survey on Small Italian Business," par. 4.
5. A banking product cannot be patented while the use of brand policies is still problematic, especially in relation to the level of development of competitive policies that the industry presents.
6. In Italy, there are about 850 banks, and although the process of concentration is very present, the relative simplicity of the production function also allows very small operators to compete on a regional scale, reduced to tools substantially at the same level of larger banks.
7. See F. Tarocco (2003) *Basilea 2: nuovi scenari del rapporto banca – impresa* (Giappichelli).
8. The subject was dealt with during the seminar, "Credit and Savings: Intermediaries, Markets, Institutions," organized by ABI on March 17, 2000 in Perugia, in the speech by C. Fissola, "Banks – Small and Medium Business in an Evolution Relationship."
9. Overall, this would be a balanced financial structure. The considerations made take into account the balance sheet of a typical Italian SME, and have therefore no claim to be valid for the whole of the national realities. The study – the result of processing of the data provided by the Central Financial throughout the 1990s – in fact, does not take into consideration the gap between north and south, and other components, such as cultural, which can greatly affect the quality of financial balance.
10. If you look at the composition of the debt in the medium and long term, it is interesting to note that SME debts due to banks are not lower than those of large enterprises, while the bonds increase with the firm size.
11. "Appropriate standards to those of other countries, a system of efficient public services, a less expensive banking system and one pension able to survive, a capital market oriented to small and medium-sized enterprises, a modern labor market and a less oppressive tax system." Billè therefore wanted to reply to those who believe that there would be an over-representation of SMEs in the Italian business, with the consequence of insufficient competitiveness of our country. "We passed – he said – from the praise of small size and productive districts to open criticism to that size of the company. But we forget almost the failure of major initiatives of public industry, the crisis of large enterprises, the capacity, conversely, of small and medium enterprises to continually adapt to changing market conditions." SMEs, the President of Confcommercio said, are not only the result of Italian entrepreneurship, but also "the answer to the constraints that the state has built for decades in spite of the competitiveness and the chronic dysfunction of our system." It is so that "an expression of exasperation, italic individualism to put the index as non-value" cannot be considered.
12. The associated costs with these activities are largely fixed with respect to the size of the loan: their incidence is therefore increasing with the decreasing amount of the loan. The higher cost of managing the relationship with SMEs

is considered by banks especially in the application of interest rates on short-term loans, while it seems completely irrelevant to the definition of the rates on loans with longer maturities, where the weight of the guarantees is more decisive.

13. The importance of this issue highlights how the new scoring systems absolutely cannot prescind the consideration of the quality elements that characterize the relationship of trust. The personal "trust," result of the experience of direct reports and repeated between entrepreneur and intermediary, but also the more general knowledge on the part of the latter of the economic and social environment in which the entity operates, constitutes an implicit guarantee of financial assets and helps to reduce the costs of collecting and processing information. The personalization of the relationship between bankers and local entrepreneurs can therefore be interpreted as a strength of lending because it can lead to greater availability and lower cost of credit. This can also be amplified by reducing the number of banking relationships between entrepreneurs.
14. In reality, if the bank has actually interest to give life to lending balanced operations, there will be an abstract hierarchy of bank projects, within which you must make a choice. This choice must be made based on the risk/yield profile of each transaction. Necessarily, then, elements of divergence and conflicts of interest arise, between lender and financier that, under the conditions described, are essential for the validity of the employment decisions of banks and, therefore, the allocative efficiency of the entire system.
15. For a discussion of the problems of evaluation and organizational solutions prepared by banks to improve access to information on companies see Baravelli (1997).
16. The cost of the transaction should not be confused with the cost (price) of the exchanged object (or information): it is the cost incurred to implement the exchange (intake and exchanged information on the nature of the object of the counter party, the stipulation of the contract) plus incurred costs to control and possibly to impose the *ex post* realization (monitoring the execution of the transaction, damages resulting from the failure to perform the transaction costs incurred to enforce the execution of the transaction in the event that a party fails to comply with the commitment). Transaction costs include, therefore, all costs required to design, negotiate, and protect an exchange agreement (Grant, 1991).

    Transaction costs are the costs related to the exchange of financial resources between employers and borrowers (research costs of the other party, the production costs of the contract, the costs of screening and monitoring). In fact, the poor transparency of information in the financial market hinders the direct transfer of resources and increases the burden of the exchange. In this sense, financial intermediaries are an efficient response to the asymmetric information related to transaction costs as they are able to exploit economies of scale in the production of existing financial assets (Onado, 1996).
17. The first contribution of research into the effects of agency costs is due to Jensen and Meckling (1976). They start from the conception of the company as a set of contracts between parties that define relationships between their agency where a *principal* person delegates another *agent* person to make

on his behalf and in his interest, a given task. Since as a rule the agent tends to work to satisfy their own interests and not those of the principal, inevitable conflicts are produced. To eliminate conflicts of interest arising from the opportunistic behavior of the agent likely to damage the principal, it imposes the costs incurred by the agency. In this context, agency costs are the costs imposed on the company by lenders to make sure the right and not opportunistic execution of a financing contract, either in the form of capital risk or in the form of borrowed capital. So, agency costs may occur in two directions: in the relationship between shareholders and creditors of the company or between managers and shareholders. In this second case, the use of debt allows shareholders to make a more careful check on the work of managers as the need to cope with the debt service reduces the discretion of management and then the intent of the latter to pursue personal rather than business goals. It is evident, however, that this type of asymmetry is of little value in a PM1 where usually the owner is also the one who has the control, therefore it can be considered to be less than a further theoretical justification for the use of a too high leverage for SMEs (Scandizzo, 2000). The effects of asymmetries that are present in the relationship between the company and its lenders are more significant for SMEs. The use of a high debt determines the occurrence of implicit or explicit charges, for which the owners have incentives to engage in excessively risky strategies that can result in redistributions of wealth with damage to the creditors, who, not being insiders, have no decision-making power. In the presence of information asymmetries that favor the emergence of opportunistic behavior by the firm, the optimal financial structure is one that minimizes agency costs associated with debt and equity (Jensen and Meckling, 1976). It is evident that the more the company uses internal sources to cover its investments or reduce the asymmetry through a closer relationship with its lenders, including through participation in the venture capital business by the latter, the lower the agency costs it may incur.

18. See P. Milgrom and J. Roberts (1994) *Economics, Organization and Management* (Bologna: Il Mulino).
19. The problem of asymmetric information and adverse selection was presented by Akerlof (1970), based on the used car market that represents a market characterized by a high degree of asymmetry of information. The actors in this market are buyers that, unless they are mechanics or testers, are the least informed, and the sellers, who know the true value and the wear of the machines. Akerlof suggested the presence of a third actor who evaluates used cars, giving a quote based on the average value of some features such as seniority, wear, defects and accidents. In this way, only those sellers who feel that their cars are worth less than the average market price, will be presented on the market. This then establishes a chain, so as the lower the quality standard of the car, the lower the price of the market and, vice versa, until you get to a market comprised solely of *lemons*, a term used to describe a purchase that turns out to be defective and therefore of no value. This example, because of its simplicity, explained by the phenomenon of adverse effective selection that can be applied in other markets, including that of credit and insurance.

20. In the case of signaling, the parties, privately informed, adopt a behavior that reveals the information possessed by them; the aim is to enter into a contract with the principal who awards the best quality of agent and separates them from those with the worst characteristics, obtaining a separating equilibrium.
21. The screening refers to the activity of investigation that is carried out by investors to collect the necessary information for a correct evaluation of investment projects in terms of risk and reward.
22. In this perspective, it seems useful to use an incentive mechanism. The principal, that is unable to control unequivocally, neither the type nor the degree of commitment by the agent in respect of the obligations arising from the transaction, will be interested to structure the contract so that the agent has an incentive to take actions that maximize its convenience and at the same time that of the principal. The contracts with incentives must be defined in such a way that we can maximize the expected utility of the principal under two constraints: firstly, the one of participation, for which agents find convenient to accept the contract; secondly the one of incentive compatibility, for which agents should be encouraged to engage, in their own interests, in choices and actions that correspond well to those preferred by the principal.
23. The rating of a debt is a form of independent certification, which awards a capacity of solvency of a debtor (whether a state is a business etc.) in relation to certain benchmarks, measuring the deviation of credit compared to optimal reliability standards (Golinelli, 2000).
24. Important ideas for the realization of the following paragraph are taken from the work of G. M. Golinelli (2011) *L'approccio sistemico vitale (ASV) al governo dell'impresa, Volume II, Verso la scientificazione dell'azione di governo* (Padova: CEDAM).
25. In practice we consider the almost total area under the density function p sigma representing the degree of variability that characterizes the distribution of the net results.
26. What makes this "formula" spectacular and remarkable, or to be more precise, the distribution characterized by this feature, is that it is a real bridge between mathematics and the real world. The only missing link is the only passage to infinity, which belongs to the mathematics and the science of the real. Here are some special features of the curve: 1) As the number of data used for the construction of the Gauss curve the more the distribution that is obtained is similar to a continuous curve (theoretically needed, in fact, infinite data); 2) In any bell distribution the media, fashion, and the median coincide. We remind ourselves here that in a series of numbers the arithmetic mean is the intermediate value between the upper and lower bounds which summarize the overall trend, fashion is the value in which it appears several times as it gives the highest frequency of an event or behavior or condition and it is therefore indicative of the general trend of the event itself, the median is, finally, the result which occupies the central place of the numerical series; 3) In the theory of errors and always in the accidental field, it is said that small errors are the biggest ones; 4) In addition to a certain limit, there are no more errors; 5) The algebraic sum of the wastes, given from the difference between the middle value, which is the most probable in a measurement, and the individual observations carried out, is zero, that

is to say that the sum of positive deviations is equal to the sum of negative differences ; 6) The sum of the squares of the deviations is minimal, that is, if you add up the squares of the differences between any value that is not the arithmetic average and all measurements, you always get a larger value.

27. The discretionary margin is revealed as reserve capacity, ensuring the company the necessary room for activities in the context of increasing complexity.
28. It mentions only that the choices of capital allocation of the different areas of business must maintain a medium term consistent, considering the markets/channels/emerging and mature client segments.
29. In this way the bank was often in the position of group leader of an industrial group and, therefore, deeply involved in the fate of the companies belonging to the group.
30. In fact, what would have weighed heavily on the history of Italian banks, was represented by the drastic transformation of their ownership base: the big investment banks, Comit, Credit, and Banco di Roma, came together in the public system through the Institute for Industrial Reconstruction; issuing banks of the Bourbon Kingdom, the Bank of Naples and Sicily were joined by the Institute of Agricultural Credit, which evolved in the new configuration of the Tour of Sardinia; the two "state and municipality banks" (as defined by Raffaele Mattioli) Monte dei Paschi di Siena and San Paolo di Torino, began its expansion without sacrificing the public dimension of its statutes. Many savings banks and numerous banks completed the picture, mainly concentrated in the local communities of the center-north, and a very small number of private banks, joint stock companies that over the years will be partially reabsorbed from the much more dynamic and popular banks.

5 Intangibles in the Assessment of Creditworthiness

1. The survey carried out by the Research SWG, on behalf of the National Confederation of Artisans (CNA), conducted from October 12 to 25, 2011, through interviews with a sample of 400 companies with fewer than 50 employees, showed that the entrepreneurs consider the current situation more serious than the credit crunch of the years 2008–2009.
2. Speech by the Governor of the Bank of Italy, ABI Ordinary Meeting, July 8, 2009, p. 4.
3. Speech by the Governor of the Bank of Italy at the conference dell'Assiom-Forex.
4. Reaffirming that the banks return to being truly "Banks of the Territory," with assessments of creditworthiness that depart from "data blocks" of a company, not the quantity of the last two budgets, but qualitative, intangible and design, to ensure a future micro and small medium enterprise that is the widespread Italian wealth (Marseglia, 2011).
5. Even Vicari (1992) argues that the viability of the company in the long run depends on the type of intangible resources owned, which are identified by the same sources as successful.
6. The visible characteristics of a product or service that are relevant in the preferences and processes of consumer choice (size, shape, color, weight, design,

material, and technology). It also includes the performance of a product or service in terms of reliability, consistency, taste, speed, durability, and safety.

7. Social, emotional, psychological, and aesthetic considerations are present in the choices of all products and services, along with extremely strong motivational forces, such as the desire for status, exclusivity, individuality, and security.
8. The concept of income is central in setting a conceptual resource-based view. In particular, it must be understood in the "Ricardian" sense, that is, as income that flows by the uniqueness of the inputs available to the company, rather than by the market power and the pattern of demand. Next to the classical notion of rent, which is round on the comparison between static productivity of different resources or of the same resource used in different uses, it should be emphasized the concept of "annuity business," understood as income that comes from the discovery of new combinations of resources (Rumelt, 1987).
9. While this effort has been in force for many years, in the US and other countries such as Denmark, where since 2001 the listed companies operating in "knowledge-intensive" sectors draw the "Intellectual Capital Statement," only in Italy since 2000 has the IAFA (Italian Association of Financial Analysts) addressed the problem of the evaluation of intangible capital of enterprises and its proper communication with stakeholders through the project, "IAFA Intangibles."
10. Translation is by Kotler.
11. In 2011, for the third consecutive year, Fiat was recognized as a sustainability leader and was confirmed in the Dow Jones Sustainability World and Dow Jones Sustainability Europe, the most prestigious equity indexes that only admit companies with the best economic, environmental, and social performance. Source: 2011 Sustainability of FIAT SPA.
12. Coda (1990) notes that "a strong image and attractiveness is an intangible asset of great importance, which is the focus of critical links driving business development, provided that the direction conceives this image as a powerful but delicate instrument generator always new consensus, to be used with caution; as a constant objective of the investment policy: as the focal point of an integrated system of communications converging on it."
13. The weight of this magnitude increases with the size and complexity of the company structure, as the rules of good corporate governance is a factor of competitiveness. Of particular importance, for example, are ownership structure, the statutory rules and options chosen with reference to the organs of administration and control, the organizational assessment of internal control systems, planning, and management control, as well as the estimation of the probability of risk resulting from a conflict between the shareholders and the effectiveness of possible subsequent actions. See the studies of O. Brunninge, M. Nordqvist, and J. Wiklund (2007) "Corporate Governance and Strategic Change in SMEs: The Effects of Ownership, Board Composition and Top Management Teams," *Small Business Economics*, vol. 29, no. 3, pp. 295–308.; S. Barile and M. Gatti (2007) "Corporate governance and creation of value in the systemic-vital viewpoint," *Sinergie*, nos. 73–4, pp. 151–68.

14. This expression is taken from the poster of the 2007 Annual Meeting of the Academy of Management, which states: "More importantly, there is no reason to believe that a firm which spends its energies trying to improve the world around it, will necessarily suffer for those efforts. In fact, there is evidence that firms which 'do good' are often the same firms that 'do well.' Furthermore, many of the 'best practices' our colleagues from all parts of the Academy have suggested can lead to both financial success and social success. Thus there would seem to be micro, macro and international research topics that are consistent with these ideas."
15. The social media press release is a press release written on a web page using the typical language and content of social media (blog, microblog, social network) to reach a broad range of audiences using the power of word of mouth and exchange of information.
16. The webinar is used to conduct business meetings, training courses, and so on, in which each participant accesses it by their own PC and is connected with the other participants via the Internet. It is an interactive web conference where participants can interact with each other and with the coordinator of the seminar (hearing officer) through tools such as: chat, audio and video chat, electronic whiteboards, available from the web conference system.
17. According to Golinelli and Volpe (2012), the integration scenarios of knowledge coming from different sources, networks providing collaborative workspaces and based on shared values and goals. Often sponsored by industry associations, these networks take on character both formal (hard) and informal (soft), showing strong ability to lobbying about issues of geographically territorial, often with effects of increased competition among enterprises.
18. About it, see the studies of F. Manni (1994) *Responsabilità sociale ed informazione esterna d'impresa. Problemi, esperienze e prospettive del bilancio sociale* (Turin: Giappichelli); G. Catturi, (2000), "Bilancio sociale e cultura aziendale. Premesse e sviluppi, in Quaderni Senesi di Economia Aziendale e di Ragioneria," Serie Interventi, n. 61, Siena; A. Chiesi, A. Martinelli, M. Pellegatta, (2000) "Il bilancio sociale, stakeholder e responsabilità sociale di impresa," *Il Sole 24 Ore*, Milano; L. Hinna (2002) "Il bilancio sociale," *Il Sole 24 Ore*; L. Hinna (2005) "Come gestire la responsabilità sociale dell'impresa. Manuale pratico operativo. Processi, strumenti e modelli. La redazione del bilancio sociale," *Il Sole 24 Ore*.
19. Golinelli (2005) illustrates how the postulates of the viable systems approach good for business and human organizations in general are also applicable to the territory interpreted as a system. The postulates are: 1) a system is viable if it can survive in a particular type of environment with which it exchanges resources; 2) the viable system possesses the property of isotropy (relative invariance of its basic characteristics with respect to the subject observer); 3) the viable system pursues certain goals and objectives and results to be connected to supra and sub-systems from which and to which, respectively, draws and provides guidelines and rules; 4) a viable system has the possibility, on the basis of conditions before and consonance of resonance processes then, to dissolve itself, understood as an autonomous entity, supra in which, in a specific time period, refers.

20. See M. De Lerma, G. Gabbi, and M. Matthias (2007) *CART Analysis of Qualitative Variables to Improve Credit Rating Processes* (Mimeo).
21. Risk generated by factors that affect the overall progress of the market and that cannot be eliminated or reduced through a diversified portfolio.
22. The competitive advantage is the ability to develop and sustain long-term core competencies can generate a differential that can be received positively by the market in which the company operates (Porter, 1987).

6 An Empirical Case

1. The data was drawn from a European Commission survey on the access to finance by enterprises (SAFE). Analytical Report 2014, November.
2. The data was taken from the Banca d'Italia, *Bollettino Economico*, no. 1, 2015.
3. For the region indicated, reports updating cyclical economic trends in the Italian regions were examined: "The economy of Lazio," *Banca d'Italia*, no. 34, November 2014.
4. The data reported in this section was taken from data on the economics of the province of Frosinone, prepared by the Institute Tagliacarne in 2014, on behalf of the Chamber of Commerce of Frosinone.
5. Financing of the economy here means the tendency of growth of finance, in the long run, rather than production. On this issue, see the studies of R. G. Rajan and L. Zingales (2003) *Saving Capitalism from the Capitalist*s (New York: Crown Business); A.Roncaglia (2010) "The cultural origins of the crisis," *PSL*, vol. 63, no. 250, pp. 10–118.
6. The Bank of Italy defines the distressed bank, as part of its "Changes to the Circular 139/9" Central Credit. Instructions for credit intermediaries areȘthe entire sheet exposure to borrowers in default, even if not legally ascertained, or in similar situations, regardless of any loss forecasts made by the company.
7. This section, as indicated by Istat (2009), includes "the physical or chemical transformation of materials, substances or components into new products. The materials, substances, or components transformed are raw materials that come from agriculture, forestry, fishing, mining or quarrying are the products of other manufacturing activities. The alteration, renovation or reconstruction of essential products are generally considered to be manufacturing. These activities are often described as plants, factories or mills and characteristically use power-driven machines and materials handling equipment. Included in this section also units that transform manually materials and substances into new products, those that carry out manufacturing in the home of the worker and the units that sell to the public products manufactured in the same premises where the sale takes place, such as bakeries and dressmakers tailored suits. The manufacturing units are: working directly the materials, subcontract part of the processing of materials, subcontract the whole materials processing own and not keeping the legal property and patents of the product, to complete the work subcontracted mentioned above. The new product process may be finished, that is ready for use or consumption, or it may be a semi-finished product intended for further manufacturing. The boundaries of the manufacturing sector and other sectors of the classification system can be somewhat

blurry. As a general rule, the activities of the manufacturing section involve the transformation of materials into new products. Their output is a new product. Included in this section: the food, the drink industries, the tobacco industry, the textile industries, the packaging of clothing, the packaging of leather and fur, manufacture of leather goods and the like, the Manufacture of wood and of products of wood and cork (except furniture), manufacture of articles of straw and plaiting materials, manufacture of paper and paper products, printing and reproduction of recorded media, manufacture of coke and products derived from petroleum refining, the manufacture of chemical products, the manufacture of basic pharmaceutical products and pharmaceutical preparations, the manufacture of rubber and plastic products, the manufacture of other non-metallic mineral processing, metallurgy, manufacture of metal products (except machinery and equipment), manufacturing of computer and electronics products and optical; medical equipment, measuring instruments, watches and clocks, manufacture of electrical and non-electrical equipment for domestic use, manufacture of machinery and equipment NCA, the manufacture of motor vehicles, trailers and semi-trailers, manufacture of other transport equipment, manufacture Furniture, other manufacturing, repair, maintenance and installation of machinery and equipment."

8. This category includes "the general and specialized activities for the construction of buildings and civil engineering works. It includes new work, repair, additions, alterations, the erection of prefabricated buildings or structures and the construction of a temporary nature. The construction of general concern the construction of housing complexes, office buildings, shops, and other public buildings and services, farm buildings, etc., as well as the construction of civil engineering works such as highways, roads, bridges, tunnels, railways, fields aviation, harbors and other water projects, the construction of irrigation systems and sewage, industrial facilities, pipelines and electric lines, sports facilities and so on. These jobs can be carried out on own account or for third parties. Part of the work or the whole can be subcontracted out. Are classified in the division, including the units responsible for a construction project in its entirety. Also included is the repair of buildings and engineering works. Equipment rental with operator Construction is ranked among the specific construction activity carried out with this equipment. This section also includes the development of plans for the construction of buildings or civil engineering projects through the collection of financial, technical and physical in order to achieve real estate units. Included are also the activities of cooperatives aimed at finding financial resources, technical and physical to realize real estate units. Included are also the activities of cooperatives aimed at finding financial resources, technical and physical to realize real estate projects, residential and non-residential use for their own." (Istat, 2009)
9. This section includes "activities of wholesale and retail trade (ie sale without transformation) of any type of goods and the provision of services related to the sale of goods. The sale of Wholesale and retailing are the final steps in the chain of distribution of goods. It also includes the repair of motor vehicles and motorcycles. The sale without transformation includes the steps

of moving goods usually associated with trade, for example sorting, grading and assembling of goods, mixing of goods (eg wine or sand), bottling (preceded or less bottle cleaning), packing, splitting breaking of bulk and repacking for distribution in smaller lots, storage (whether or not frozen or chilled), cleaning and drying of agricultural products, cutting of fiber or metal sheets as related activities. Wholesale (without transformation) of new and used goods sold to retailers, to industrial users, commercial, institutional or professional, to other wholesalers, or to dealers who sellgoods to such persons or companies. It is made from wholesalers holders of traded goods, from industrial distributors, exporters, importers, and cooperative buying associations, sales and sales offices (but not retail stores) held by manufacturing or mining units separate from the production plants, targeted to the sale of products, and do not merely take orders to be filled by direct shipments from the plants or mines. Included in this section also commercial intermediaries, agents, associations between buyers and cooperative associations engaged in the marketing of farm products. Wholesale suppliers often collect, select and physically divide the goods in large lots, repack the goods and redistribute in smaller lots, for example pharmaceuticals; store, refrigerate, deliver and install goods. Retail (without transformation) of new and used goods sold to the final consumer for personal or household use and consumption. It is carried out in shops, department stores, banks, mail order companies, from street vendors, consumer cooperatives, auction houses and so on. Most retailers take title to the goods they sell, but some of them sell on consignment or commission." (Istat 2009)

10. This category complements "the activities of carriage of passengers or goods carried out on a regular basis or not by rail, by pipeline, road, by water or air and auxiliary activities such as services to the terminals, parking lots, handling and storage goods etc., the rental business of transportation with driver or operator. Also included are activities postal and courier services. This also includes the transport of passengers for recreation, food services and bars made by such companies perform transport. Are excluded, however, repairs or modifications made to transportation (excluding motor vehicles); the construction, maintenance and repair of roads, railways, ports, airfields; maintenance and repair of motor vehicles; the hiring of means of transport without driver or operator." (Istat 2009)
11. Companies registered as active in the Companies Register of Frosinone, having the legal form of companies and a number of employees less than 300 units, at 09/28/2013, amounted to 4299 units.
12. The Chamber of Commerce (and industry, agriculture, and small business)
13. The Confidi, according to the Bank of Italy (https://www.bancaditalia.it/compiti/vigilanza/intermediari/confidi/index.html#1), are qualified to take part in a totally exclusive activity of "mutual benefit and entrepreneurial guarantees to encourage the involvement of small and medium-sized enterprises associated with borrowing from banks and other stakeholders in the financial sector (art. 13, paragraph 1, of Decree Law no. 269/2003 converted by Law no. 326/2003). These operators are therefore barred from exercising provision of guarantees other than those stated and, in particular, the issue of guarantees to the public as well as the exercise of other activities

reserved to financial intermediaries ex art.106." These consortia are configured as entities able to perform a kind of "intermediary" between bank and enterprise to reduce the impact of asymmetric information and operational conditions that currently impact on this relationship. Since, in fact, given the difficulty and cost for banks in dealing with small businesses, and the lack of documentary sources that are qualitatively significant and reliable, it very often becomes essential to make the qualitative judgment on the entrepreneur rather than on the company itself. This determines the importance of the role of consortia, as connoisseurs closely associated with enterprises and entrepreneurs, that have already been evaluated for their reputation, morality and "credibility," first on their admission to the group and later through performance monitoring. Therefore, the strengthening of partnerships between banks and consortia allows the first to take advantage of the most comprehensive information while also reducing the burden of operating costs related to the lending process. Substantial benefits are also felt by the member companies in terms of reduced response times, greater chance of being evaluated "for what they are worth" and mitigation of the administrative costs related to the granting of the credit line. See the studies of R. Ruozi, (2002) "Ancora sul rapporto fra banche e PMI: prospettive dei consorzi fidi," *Banche e Banchieri*, no. 5, pp. 432–39; C. D'Auria, (2005), "Il ruolo dei Confidi nel finanziamento delle piccole e medie imprese alla luce delle modifiche del regolamento internazionale di Vigilanza," in *Newsletter Aifirm*, no. 1, pp. 3–5; L. Gai, (2005) "Prospettive delle garanzie dei confidi verso le PMI dopo la riforma del settore e Basilea 2," *Rivista Bancaria – Minerva Bancaria*, no. 1, January-February, pp. 29–60; C. D'Auria (2008) "Le sfide per i confidi alla luce della nuova normativa prudenziale," *Bancaria*, no.10, pp. 54–8.

Appendices

1. "Risk of non-knowledge and management of the bank company: the role of intangibles in rating models."
2. The item Financial function implies the complex of decisions and operations aimed at finding financing sources and planning investments. in particular it includes the following activities:

    - planning and checking short, medium and long term financial resources;
    - finding financial resources;
    - management of cash and general financial requirements;
    - managing relations with banks and other investors;
    - investments assessment and management.

3. It is a form of bank financing that requires the borrower to refund, at maturity, the assets and to pay a percentage of the net income for the year in addition to interests. It is feasible for restructuring measures and expansion of the company.

References

Aaker, D. A. and L. K. Keller (1990) "Consumer evaluations of brand extensions," *Journal of Marketing*, vol. 54.

ABI (Associazione Bancaria Italiana) (2009) Intervento del Governatore della Banca d'Italia – Assemblea Ordinaria, https://www.bancaditalia.it/pubblicazioni/interventigovernatore/integov2008/draghi_090708.pdf, 08 luglio 2009.

ABI (Associazione Bancaria Italiana) (2015) *Indagine conoscitiva sul sistema bancario italiano nella prospettiva della vigilanza europea, Audizione del Direttore generale dell'ABI Giovanni Sabatini al Senato della Repubblica,* http://www.abi.it/DOC_Info/Audizioniparlamentari/Aud_Sabatini_Indagine_Sistema_Bancario_10_3_2015.pdf.

Acharya, V. and M. Richardson (2009) *Restoring Financial Stability: How to Repair a Failed System* (Chichester: Wiley).

Aguiari, R. and P. Di Nauta (2012) "Governing business dynamics in complex contexts," *Mercati e Competitività,* 1, pp. 39–59.

AIAF (Associazione Italiana degli Analisti e Consulenti Finanziari) (2015) "Crescita economica e finanziamento delle imprese," Intervento del Vice Direttore Generale della Banca d'Italia Fabio Panetta, Rome, 27 January 2015, https://www.bancaditalia.it/pubblicazioni/interventi-direttorio/int-dir-2015/AIAF_gennaio_2015_testo_finale_REVISIONATO.pdf.

Akerlof, G. A. (1970) "The market for lemons: qualitative uncertainty and the market mechanism", *Quarterly Journal of Economics*, no. 89.

Alessandrini, P. (1994) *La banca in un sistema locale di piccolo e medie imprese* (Bologna: il Mulino, Collana Studi Finanziari e Bancari).

Alessandrini, P. (1996) "I sistemi locali del credito in regioni a diverso stadio di sviluppo," *Moneta e Credito*, vol. 49.

Alessandrini, P. (2001) *Il Sistema Finanziario Italiano tra Globalizzazione e Localismo* (Il Mulino, Bologna).

Alessandrini, P. and A. Zazzaro (2000) "L'evoluzione dei sistemi finanziari locali nell'era dell'euro," Moneta e Credito, vol. 53.

Alessandrini, P., L. Papi and A. Zazzaro (2003) "Banks, regions and development," *BNL Quarterly Review*, vol. 224.

Allee, V. (2000) "Reconfiguring the value network," *Journal of Business Strategy*, no. 4.

Allen, F. and D. Gale (2000) *Comparing Financial Systems* (Cambridge, Mass: MIT Press).

Altman, E. I. (1966) "Financial ratios, discriminant analysis and the prediction of corporate bankruptcy," *Journal of Finance*, no. 23.

Altman, E. I. (2002) *Revisiting Credit Scoring Models in a Basel 2 Environment: "Credit Rating: Methodologies, Rationale and Default Risk"* (London: Risk Books).

Amabile, T. M. (1988) "A model of creativity and innovation in organizations," in B. M. Staw and L. L. Cummings (eds) *Research in Organizational Behavior* (Greenwich, CT: JAI Press).

Amatori, F. and F. Barca (1997) *Storia del capitalism italiano dal dopoguerra ad oggi* (Rome: Donizelli).
Amel, D., C. Barnes, F. Panetta and C. Salleo (2004) "Consolidation and efficiency in the financial sector: a review of the international evidence," *Journal of Banking and Finance*, no. 28.
Amit, R., L. Glosten and E. Muller (1990) "Does venture capitalist foster the most promising entrepreneurial firms?," *California Management Review*, Spring.
Amit, R. and P. J. H. Schoemaker (1993) "Strategic assets and organizational rent," *Strategic Management Journal*, vol. 14.
Anderson, R. (2007) *The Credit Scoring Toolkit: Theory and Practice for Retail Credit Risk Management and Decision Automation* (New York: Oxford University Press).
Andrews, J. and D. C. Smith (1996) "In search of the marketing imagination: factors affecting the creativity of marketing programs for mature products," *Journal of Marketing Research*, 33.
Ansoff, H. I. and R. G. Brandenburg (1971) "A language for organization design," *Management Science*, 17, pp. 705–31.
Antonucci, A. (2007) "La responsabilità sociale dell'impresa bancaria" in F. Capriglione (ed.) *Finanza Impresa e Nuovo Umanesimo* (Bari: Cacucci Ed.).
Arcelli, M. (1994) *Economia e politica monetaria* (Padova: CEDAM).
Avery, R. B., K. P. Brevoort, and G. B. Canner (2009) "Credit scoring and its effects on the availability and affordability of credit," *The Journal of Consumer Affairs*, vol. 43, no. 3.
Babbie, E. R. (1979) *The Practice of Social Research* (California: Ed. Wadsworth).
Baccarani C. (1987) "Alcune osservazioni sul valore segnaletico del concetto di impresa minore in una prospettiva organizzativa," *Il Risparmio*, no.1.
Baccarani, C. and G. M. Golinelli (2003) "L'impresa inesistente: relazioni tra immagine e strategia," *Sinergie*, nos. 61–2.
Baccarani, C. and G. M. Golinelli (2011) "Il vento del cambiamento," *Sinergie*, no. 86.
Badinelli, R., S. Barile, C. L. Ng Irene, F. Polese, M. Saviano, and P. Di Nauta (2012) "Viable service systems and decision making in service management," *Journal of Service Management*, vol. 23, no. 4, 498–526.
Bailey, M. (2001) *Credit Scoring: The Principles and Practicalities* (Kingswood, Bristol: White Box Publishing).
Balmer, J. and E. Gray (2003) "Corporate brands: what are they? what of them?," *European Journal of Marketing*, vol. 37, Nos. 7/8, pp. 972–98.
Banca d'Italia (2014) "L'economia del Lazio. Aggiornamento congiunturale," no. 34, November.
Banca d'Italia (2015) "Bollettino economico," no. 1.
Banerjee, A. V., T. Besley and T. W. Guinnane (1994), "Thy neighbor's keeper: The design of a credit cooperative with theory and a test," *Quarterly Journal of Economics*, vol. 109, pp. 491–515.
Bank of Italy, http://www.bancaditalia.it/compiti/vigilanza/intermediari/#altri_soggetti
Barabási, A. L. (2002) *Linked: The New Science of Networks* (Cambridge: Perseus).
Baravelli, M. (1995a) "Modelli organizzativi della gestione finanziaria delle banche," *Il Risparmio*, no. 5.
Baravelli, M. (1995b) "Rapporto banca-impresa. Le relazioni privilegiate," *Finanza & Mercato*, no.1.

Baravelli, M. (1997) *Le strategie competitive nel corporate banking* (Milan: Egea).
Barile, S. (2008) *L'impresa come sistema – Contributi sull'Approccio Sistemico Vitale, Volume II* (Turin: Giappichelli).
Barile, S. (2009a) *Management sistemico vitale* (Turin: Giappichelli).
Barile, S. (2009b) "Verso la qualificazione del concetto di complessità sistemica, il governo dei sistemi complessi tra creazione e distruzione di valore. L'impresa e oltre l'impresa," *Sinergie*, no. 79, part one, May-August.
Barile, S. (2009c) "The dynamic of information varieties in the processes of decision making, proceeding of the 13th world multi-conference on systemics" (Cybernetics and Informatics: WMSCI).
Barile, S. (2011) *Management sistemico vitale: Decisioni e scelte in ambito complesso* (Avellino: International Printing Srl Editore).
Barile, S. and M. Gatti (2007) "Corporate governance and creation of value in the systemic-vital viewpoint," *Sinergie*, nos. 73–4, pp. 151–68.
Barile, S. and M. Saviano (2010) "A new perspective of systems complexity in service science," *Impresa, Ambiente, Management*, vol. 4, no. 3, pp. 375–414.
Barile, S. and M. Saviano (2011) "Qualifying the concept of systems complexity," in *Contributions to Theoretical and Practical Advances in Management. A Viable Systems Approach* (VSA) (Avellino: ASVSA, Associazione per la ricerca sui Sistemi Vitali International Printing), pp. 27–64.
Barile, S., M. Calabrese and F. Iandolo (2012) "Sostenibilità e paradigmi service-based: possibilità e criticità per l'economia d'impresa," *Sviluppo e Organizzazione*, no. 252, pp. 45–59.
Barile, S., M. Saviano, F. Iandolo, and M. Calabrese (2014) "The viable systems approach and its contribution to the analysis of sustainable business behaviors," *Systems Research and Behavioral Science*, vol. 31, pp. 683–95.
Barile, S., M. Saviano, F. Polese and P. Di Nauta (2013) "Il rapporto impresa-territorio tra efficienza locale, efficacia di contesto e sostenibilità ambientale," *Sinergie Rivista di Studi e Ricerche*, vol. 91.
Barney, J. B. (1991) "Firm resources and sustained competitive advantage," *Journal of Management*, vol. 17.
Bartoli, F. and G. Ossoli (2009) *Valore d'impresa e valore intangibile. Una metodologia per la valutazione delle aziende: guida alla misurazione e alla pianificazione del valore* (Milan: Franco Angeli).
Beaver, W. and G. Parker (1995) *Risk management. Problems and solutions* (Stanford University Press, McGraw-Hill).
Becchetti, L. (2005) *La felicità sostenibile* (Rome: Donzelli).
Beck, T. and R. Levine (2004) "Stock markets, banks and growth: panel evidence," *Journal of Banking and Finance*, vol. 28, no. 3, pp. 423–42.
Benedetto XVI (2009) *Caritas in Veritate.*
Beretta, E. and S. Del Prete (2007) "Aggregazioni bancarie e specializzazione nel credito alle PMI: peculiarità per area geografica," Temi di discussione del Servizio Studi di Banca d'Italia, no. 644.
Berger, A. N. and G. F. Udell (1995) "Relationship lending and lines of credit in small firm finance," *Journal of Business*, vol. 68, pp. 351–81.
Berger, A. N., A. K. Kashyap and J. M. Scalise (1995) "The transformation of the U.S. banking industry: What a long, strange trip it's been," Brookings Papers on Economic Activity, 2.

Berger, A. N., A. Saunders, J. M. Scalise, and G. F. Udell (1998) "The effects of bank mergers and acquisitions on small business lending," *Journal of Financial Economics*, vol. 50, no. 2.

Berger, A. N., L. Klapper and G. F. Udell (2001) "The ability of banks to lend to informationally opaque small businesses," Federal Reserve Board working paper.

Berger, A. N., N. H. Miller, M. A. Petersen, R. G. Rajan and J. C. Stein (2002) "Does function follow organizational form? Evidence from the lending practices of large and small banks," Paper No. W8752 (NBER Working).

Berger, A. N., W. S. Frame and N. H. Miller (2002) "Credit scoring and the availability, price, and risk of small business credit" (Board of Governors of the FR System FEDS 26, April).

Berger, A. N. and G.F. Udell (2002) "Small business credit availability and relationship lending: the importance of bank organisational structure," *Economic Journal*, vol. 112, no. 477, pp. 32–53.

Berger, A. N. and G. F. Udell (2006) "A more complete conceptual framework for SME finance," *Journal of Banking and Finance*, vol. 30, pp. 2945–66.

Berger, A. N. and L. K. Black (2007) "Bank size and small business finance" (FMA Annual Meeting Working Paper).

Berndt, A. and A. Gupta (2009) "Moral hazard and adverse selection in the originate-to-distribute model of bank credit." Available at SSRN: http://ssrn.com/abstract=1290312 or http://dx.doi.org/10.2139/ssrn.1290312.

Bernstein, D. (1988) *Company image* (Milan: Guerini e Associati).

Bessis, J. (2011) *Risk management in banking* (John Wiley & Sons).

Bhattacharya, S. and A. V. Thakor (1993) "Contemporary banking theory," *Journal of Financial Intermediation*, no. 3, pp. 2–50.

Bianchi, M., M. L. Di Battista and G. Lusignani (1998) "Assetto proprietario e performance delle banche italiane," *Banca Impresa Società*, vol. 17, no. 1, pp. 85–146.

Bianchi, T. (1986) *Nuovo e antico nell'economia delle aziende di credito* (Banche e banchieri).

Bianconi, M. (2004) "Basilea 2 – La nuova sfida di banche e imprese," at the convention, "Basilea 2 e l'economia locale - Quale Banca per il territorio? Quale credito per l'impresa?," Auditorium di Palazzo Montani Antaldi, Pesaro, 23 April.

Bizer, D. S. and P. M. Demarzo (1992) "Sequential banking," *Journal of Political Economy*, no. 100, 41–61.

Blackett, T. and R. W. Boad (1999) *Co-branding: The Science of Alliance* (London/Basingstoke: Palgrave Macmillan,).

Bolton, P., X. Freixas, L. Gambacorta, and P. E. Mistrulli (2013) "Relationship and transaction lending in a crisis", No. W19467 (National Bureau of Economic Research).

Bonaccorsi di Patti, E. and G. Gobbi (2001) "The changing structure of local credit markets: are small businesses special?," *Journal of Banking and Finance*, vol. 25.

Bonaccorsi di Patti, E. and G. Gobbi (2003) "The effects of bank mergers on credit availability: evidence from corporate data" (Temi di discussione, Banca d'Italia).

Bonaccorsi di Patti, E., G. Eramo and G. Gobbi (2005) *Piccole e grandi banche nel mercato del credito in Italia*, vol. 1 (Banca Impresa Società).

Bongini, P. and G. Ferri (2005) *Il Sistema Bancario Meridionale* (Bari: Laterza editore).
Bongini, P. and G. Ferri (2007) *Governance, Diversification and Performance: The Case of Italy's Banche Popolari* (Mimeo).
Bongini, P., M. L. Di Battista and L. Nieri (2009) "Relationship banking: una soluzione antica contro la crisi recente?," *Bancaria*, no. 5, pp. 2–20.
Boot, A. W. A. (2000) "Relationship banking: What do we know?," *Journal of Financial Intermediation*, vol. 9, pp. 7–25.
Boot, A. W. A. and A. V. Thakor (1994) "Moral Hazard and Secured Lending in an Infinitely Repeated Credit Market Game," *International Economic Review*, vol. 35, no. 4, pp. 899–920.
Boot, A. W. A and A. V. Thakor (2000) "Can relationship banking survive completion?," *Journal of Finance*, vol. 62, pp. 679–713.
Boot, A. W. and L. Ratnovski (2012) "Banking and trading," Paper No. 85 (Amsterdam Law School Research).
Borghesi, A. (1985) *La gestione dei rischi di azienda* (Padova: CEDAM).
Borghesi, A. (1994) "Chindinica e risk management," *Sinergie*, no. 35.
Borio, C., C. Furfine and P. Lowe (2001) "Procyclicality of the financial system and financial stability: issues and policy options," BIS Papers, no. 1.
Borsa Italiana (2011) "Codice di autodisciplina," http://www.borsaitaliana.it/comitato-corporate-governance/codice/2011.pdf.
Boschetti, C. and M. Sobrero (1996), "Risorse e vantaggio competitivo: ricorsi storici o nuove prospettive di analisi," *Economia e Politica Industriale*, vol. 91, pp. 63–93.
Brighi, P. (2008) *Credito e finanza d'impresa. Aspetti teorici ed evidenze empiriche* (Bonomia University Press).
Brogi, M. (1997) *L'evoluzione del rapporto banca impresa in Italia: dal pluriaffidamento alla banca moderna* (EGEA).
Brown, J. R., S. M. Fazzari, and B. C. Petersen (2009) "Financing innovation and growth: Cash flow, external equity, and the 1990s R&D boom," *The Journal of Finance*, vol. 64, pp. 151–85.
Brunninge, O., M. Nordqvist, and J. Wiklund (2007) "Corporate governance and strategic change in SMEs: the effects of ownership, board composition and top management teams," *Small Business Economics*, vol. 29, no. 3, pp. 295–308.
Bugera, V., H. Konno and S. Uryasev (2002) "Credit cards scoring with quadratic utility function," *Journal of Multi-Criteria Decision Analysis, Special Issue on MCDA Methodologies in Finance*, 11, pp. 197–211.
Busacca, B. and G. Bertoli (2003) "Co-branding e valore della marca," *Atti del III Convegno Internazionale "Le tendenze del Marketing"*, Università Ca' Foscari, Venice, 28–29 November.
Busacca, B. and G. Bertoli (2006) "Brand extension & Brand loyalty," *Atti del V Convegno Internazionale "Le tendenze del Marketing"*, Università Ca' Foscari, Venice, 21–22 January.
Business Week (2002) "The 100 top brands. Special Report," August 5, http://www.businessweek.com/pdfs/2002/0231-brands.pdf.
Butzbach, O. and A. Lopes (2006) "Mutamento degli assetti proprietari e performance del sistema bancario nel Mezzogiorno," in A. Giannola (ed.) *Riforme istituzionali e mutamento strutturale. Mercati, imprese e istituzioni in un sistema dualistico* (Rome: Carocci).

Cafferata, R. (2009a) "Il cantiere aperto della responsabilità sociale dell'impresa," *Electronic Journal of Management*, no. 1.

Cafferata, R. (2009b) *Management in adattamento. Tra razionalità economica ed imperfezione dei sistemi* (Bologna: Il Mulino).

Calcagnini, D. (2009) *Banche e PMI: "Le regole dell'attrazione". Spunti di riflessione su vincoli e opportunità di Basilea 2 per lo sviluppo delle piccole e medie imprese* (FrancoAngeli).

Calvelli, A. (1998) *Scelte d' impresa e mercati internazionali* (Turin: Giappichelli).

Camera di Commercio di Frosinone (2014) "Osservatorio economico della provincia di Frosinone," http://www.fr.camcom.it/files/Studi/Osservatorio/Commercio%20Fr_2014_DEF.pdf.

Campanella, F. (2014) "Assess the rating of SMEs by using classification and regression trees (CART) with qualitative variable," *Review of Economics and Finance*, vol. 4, no. 3, pp. 16–32.

Cannata, F. (2010) *Il metodo dei rating interni: Basilea 2 e il rischio di credito: le nuove regole, la loro attuazione in Italia, le proposte di revisione dopo la crisi finanziaria* (Rome: Bancaria Editrice).

Cannata, F. and M. Quagliariello (2009) "The role of Basel II in the subprime financial crisis: guilty or not guilty?," CAREFIN Working Paper, no. 3.

Capra, F. (2002) *The Hidden Connections* (London: HarperCollins).

Caroli, M. (2006a) *Il marketing territoriale. Strategie per la competitività sostenibile del territorio* (Milan: Franco Angeli).

Caroli, M. (2006b) "Pubblico e privato nella logica di marketing territoriale," *Sinergie*, no. 70.

Carosio, G. (2010) 'La riforma delle regole prudenziali. Intervento del Vice Direttore Generale della Banca d'Italia al convegno dell'ABI *"Basilea 3: Banche e imprese verso il 2012,"* ' Rome, pp. 1–2.

Carter, R. L. and G. N. Crockford (1999) *Handbook of risk management* (London: Croner).

Caselli, C. (2003) "Etica e responsabilità d'impresa nelle relazioni internazionali," *Symphonya: Emerging Issues in Management,* no.1.

Caselli, L. (1997) *Per una società del lavoro libero, dell'impresa e della partecipazione*, in S. Zamagni (ed) *Economia, democrazia, istituzioni in una società in trasformazione. Per una rilettura della Dottrina Sociale della Chiesa* (Bologna: Il Mulino).

Castells, M. (1996) *The Rise of the Network Society* (Oxford: Blackwell).

Catarineu-Rabell, E., P. Jackson, D. P. Tsomocos (2003) "Procyclicality and the new basel accord, the banks' choice of loan rating system," Bank of England Working Papers, No. 181.

Catturi, G. (2000) "Bilancio sociale e cultura aziendale. Premesse e sviluppi," *Quaderni Senesi di Economia Aziendale e di Ragioneria. Serie Interventi*, no. 61, Siena.

Cerrato, D. (2004) 'Natura e determinanti del vantaggio competitivo sostenibile nella prospettiva resource-based: alcune riflessioni critiche', *Sinergie*, no. 63.

Cerved Report on SMEs (2014) https://area.cervedgroup.com/news/approfondimento/Rapporto_Cerved_PMI_2014_ExecutiveSummary.pdf.

Cesarini, F. (2003) "Banca Etica e impresa sociale," speech at the conference held in Varese on 28 February, as part of a series of meetings organized by the University of Insubria on "Quale solidarietà?"

Chiesi, A., A. Martinelli, and M. Pellegatta (2000) Il bilancio sociale, stakeholder e responsabilità sociale di impresa (Milan: Il Sole 24 Ore).

Chiucchi, M. S. (2004) *Sistemi di misurazione e di reporting del capitale intellettuale: criticità e prospettive* (Turin: Giappichelli).

Church, K. B. (1992) "Properties of fundamental equilibrium exchange rate models of the UK Economy," *National Institute Economic Review*, August, pp. 62–70.

Coda, V. (1985) "Valori imprenditoriali e successo dell'impresa," *Finanza, marketing e produzione*, no. 2.

Coda, V. (1990) "Le analisi di bilancio a fini di valutazione strategica dell'impresa," in *AA.VV. Studi in onore di Ugo De Dominicis* (Trieste: Edizioni LINT).

Coleman, J. S. (1998) "Social capital in the creation of human capital," *The American Journal of Sociology*, vol. 94.

Comuzzi, E., S. Marasca and L. Olivotto (2009) *Intangibles. Profili di gestione e di misurazione* (Milan: Franco Angeli).

Conti, V. and A. Fabbri (1996) "Proprietà e controllo degli intermediari finanziari," *Bancaria*, no. 9, pp. 2–11.

Corigliano, R. (1996) "Letture di economia degli intermediari finanziari," CLUEB.

Corigliano, R. (2006) *Corporate banking, credito e finanza delle imprese* (Rome: Bancaria Editrice).

Corigliano, R. (2007) "Banca e impresa in Italia: caratteri evolutivi del relationship lending e sostegno dello sviluppo," Banca Impresa Società, vol. XXVI, no. 1.

Corno, F. (1996) *Patrimonio intangibile e governo dell'impresa* (Milan: Egea).

Costa, S. and S. Costagli (2005) "Finanza per le piccole e medie imprese: il ruolo dei Confidi" in G. Bracchi and D. Masciandaro (eds) *Le banche italiane e la finanza per lo sviluppo. Decimo Rapporto sul sistema finanziario italiano* (Rome: Edibank).

Costi, R. (2001) *L'ordinamento bancario* (Bologna: Il Mulino).

Cravera, A. (2009) *Competere nella complessità* (Etas Libri).

Crockford, N. (1986) *An Introduction to Risk Management*, 2nd edition (Cambridge: Woodhead-Faulkner).

Crouhy, M., D. Galai, and R. Mark (2001) *Risk Management* (New York: McGraw-Hill).

Crudeli, L., G. Guidetti and M. Mazzanti (2004) *Dinamiche occupazionali e formazione nelle imprese* (Milan: Franco Angeli).

Culp, C. (2001) *The risk management process* (New York: Wiley).

Culp, C. (2002) *The Art of Risk Management – Alternative Risk Transfer, Capital Structure, and the Convergence of Insurance and Capital Markets* (New York: Wiley).

Cuneo, S. and R. Maino (2010) "Internal rating and economic cycle: a structural approach towards Basel 3 regulatio," *Bancaria*, vol. 66, no. 12, pp. 43–58.

D'Auria, C. (2005) "Il ruolo dei Confidi nel finanziamento delle piccole e medie imprese alla luce delle modifiche del regolamento internazionale di Vigilanza," *Newsletter Aifirm*, no. 1, pp. 3–5.

D'Auria, C. (2008) "Le sfide per i confidi alla luce della nuova normativa prudenziale," *Bancaria*, no. 10, pp. 54–8.

De Bruyn, R. and G. Ferri (2005) *Le banche popolari nel localismo dell'economia italiana* (Rome: Edicred).

De Laurentis, G. (2011) Il credito alle imprese dopo la crisi. Politiche e strumenti di dialogo banca-impresa: rating, analisi e previsione finanziaria (Rome: Bancaria Editrice).

De Laurentis, G. and S. Caselli (2004) *Miti e verità di Basilea 2. Guida alle decisioni* (Milan: Egea).

De Laurentis, G. and R. Maino (2010) "I rating interni durante e dopo la crisi: rapporti banca-impresa, vincoli regolamentari e modelli di business," *Bancaria,* no. 1.

De Lerma, M., G. Gobbi, and M. Matthias (2007) *CART Analysis Of Qualitative Variables to Improve Credit Rating Processes* (Mimeo).

De Mitri, S., G. Gobbi, and E. Sette (2010) "Relationship lending in a financial turmoil," Bank of Italy Temi di Discussione, working paper, no. 772.

Degli Antoni, G. and E. Portale (2007) "Organizzazioni del terzo settore e creazione di capitale sociale: il caso delle cooperative sociali e il ruolo della responsabilità sociale d'impresa," Aiccon Working Papers, no. 47.

Del Bello, A. and A. Gasperini (2006) *Il valore del capitale intellettuale. Aspetti teorici e casi aziendali di reporting* (Milan: Ipsoa).

Dagnino, G. B. and P. Merendino (2013) *L'interazione fra capacità d'impresa, opportunità strategiche, risorse finanziarie e performance: un'analisi multivariata su un campione di piccole e medie imprese operanti nel mezzogiorno* (Piccola Impresa/Small Business).

Degryse, H. and S. Ongena (2002) "Bank-firm relationships and international banking markets," *International Journal of the Economics of Business*, vol. 9, no. 3, pp. 401–17.

Dell'Atti, S., A. Lopes and G. Tucci (2013) (eds) "Rapporto SVIMEZ su relazioni banca-impresa e ruolo dei Confidi nel Mezzogiorno," *Mercato, regole e prospettive di sviluppo, Quaderni SVIMEZ*, no. 36.

Demirgüç-Kunt, A. and R. Levine (1999) "Bank-based and market-based financial systems: cross-country comparisons," World Bank Policy Working Paper no. 2143, pp. 1–41.

DeYoung, R., D. Glennon and P. Nigro (2008) "Borrower-lender distance, credit scoring, and loan performance: Evidence from informational-opaque small business borrowers," *Journal of Financial Intermediation,* vol. 17, no. 1, pp. 113–43.

Di Ciaccio, A. and S. Borra (1996) *Introduzione alla Statistica Descrittiva* (Milan: McGraw-Hill).

Diamond, D. W. (1984) "Financial intermediation and delegated monitoring," *Review of Economic Studies*, vol. 51.

Dierickx, I. and K. Cool (1989) "Asset stock accumulation and sustainability of competitive advantage," *Management Science*, vol. 35.

Doherty, N. (2003) *Integrated Risk Management: Techniques and Strategies for Reducing Risk* (London: Mc Graw-Hill).

Dominique, C. (2011) *Complexity: Against Systems* (New York: Springer).

Draghi, M. (2009) Considerazioni Finali del Governatore sul 2008, https://www.bancaditalia.it/pubblicazioni/interventigovernatore/integov2009/cf08_considerazioni_finali.pdf.

Duffie, D. and K. J. Singleton (2012) *Credit Risk: Pricing, Measurement, and Management* (Princeton: Princeton University Press).

Eccles, R. G. (2006), "Reputation and its risks: the necessity ofmanaging reputational risk," Symposium on Managing Reputation and Risk, Corporate Communication Institute (New York).

Edvinsson, L. and M. Malone (1997) *Intellectual Capital* (London: Piatkus).

Ervin, D. W. and T. Wilde (2001) "Procyclicality in the new basel accord," *Risk Magazine,* October.

Esposito De Falco, S. (2003) "Competizione Globale e forme di potenziamento della governance," *Sinergie,* no. 60.

European Commission (2006) La nuova definizione di PMI, http://ec.europa.eu/enterprise/policies/sme/files/sme_definition/sme_user_guide_it.pdf.

European Commission (2007) "Come interagire con la nuova cultura del rating: Guida pratica al finanziamento bancario per le piccole e medie imprese," Directorate-General for Enterprise and Industry.

European Commission (2014) "Survey on the access to finance of enterprises (SAFE)" *Analytical Report,* November.

Faccincani, L. (2009) *La valorizzazione della proprietà intellettuale d'impresa nel corporate lending. Metodologie di analisi del merito di credito e operazioni di IP Finance* (Milan: Giuffrè).

Fama, E. (1980) "Agency problems and the theory of the firm," *Journal of Political Economy,* vol. 88.

Fazzi, R. (1982) *Il governo d'impresa, Volume I* (Milan: Giuffrè).

Felisari, G. (2008) *Valutazione strategica e previsione finanziaria nel rating interno delle imprese* (Milan: Franco Angeli).

Ferreira, F. A., R. W. Spahr, I. F Gavancha, and A. Çipi (2013) "Readjusting trade-offs among criteria in internal ratings of credit-scoring: an empirical essay of risk analysis in mortgage loans," *Journal of Business Economics and Management,* vol. 14, no. 4, pp. 715–40.

Ferri, G. (1997) "Mobilità dei dirigenti ed efficienza allocativa: banche locali e nazionali," *Quaderno di Moneta e Credito,* March.

Ferri, G., D. Masciandaro and M. Messori (2001) "Corporate governance, board turnover and performance: the case of local banks in Italy," SSRN Working Paper.

Ferri, G. and U. Inzerillo (2002) "Ristrutturazione bancaria, crescita e internazionalizzazione delle PMI meridionali. Indagine su un campione di imprese manifatturiere," Centro Studi Confindustria, Working paper, no. 10.

Fombrun, C. J. and C. B. M. van Riel (2004) *Fame & Fortune. How Successful Companies Build Winning Reputations* (Upper Saddle River: Prentice Hall Financial Times).

Fontana, F. and M. Caroli (2009) *Economia e Gestione delle Imprese* (McGraw Hill).

Forestieri, G. (2011) *Corporate & investment banking,* 2nd edition (Milan: Egea).

Forestieri, G. and M. Onado (1998) "Governo societario e imprese bancarie," *Banca Impresa Società,* no. 1.

Formisano, V. (2002) "La dinamica evolutiva dell'impresa bancaria: una lettura in chiave sistemico-vitale. Dimensione, teoria delle risorse, network," *Quaderno,* no. 19, Dipartimento Impresa e Lavoro, Università degli Studi di Cassino.

Formisano, V. and G. Russo (2012) "Il ruolo degli intangibles nei modelli di rating," in M. Modina and V. Formisano, "Il rating tra impresa, banca e territorio, Rapporti di Ricerca," *Sinergie,* no. 36.

Formisano, V., M. Modina, and A. Quintiliani (2014) "The role of intangibles in improving the predictive ability of Internal Rating System," XIII Congresso internazionale SGBED, Università Politecnica delle Marche, 16–18 July.

Frame, W. S., A. Srinivasan and L. Woosley (2001) "The effect of credit scoring on small-business lending," *Journal of Money, Credit and Banking*, vol. 33, no. 3, pp. 813–25.

Frank, M. Z. and V. K Goyal (2003) "Testing the pecking order theory of capital structure," *Journal of Financial Economics*, vol. 67, no. 2, pp. 217–48.

Frels, J. K., T. Shervani and R. K. Srivastava (2003) "The Integrated networks model: explaining resource allocations in network markets," *Journal of Marketing*, vols. 6/7.

Gabbi, G. (2003) "Definizione, misurazione e gestione del rischio reputazionale degli intermediari bancari," *Newfin-Università Bocconi*, Milan, no. 2.

Gabbi, G. (2012) "Il risk management e i suoi stakeholder," *Bancaria*, no. 3, pp. 18–24.

Gabbi, G., M. Matthias and M. De Lerma (2006) "CART analysis of qualitative variables to improve credit rating processes," *Computing in Economics and Finance*, vol. 179, Society for Computational Economics.

Gabbi, G. and A. Patarnello (2010) 'Il valore della reputazione bancaria tra "risk management" e scelte strategiche', *Banca Impresa Società*, vol. XXIX, no. 2.

Gai, L. (2005) "Prospettive delle garanzie dei confidi verso le PMI dopo la riforma del settore e Basilea 2," *Rivista Bancaria – Minerva Bancaria*, no. 1, January-February, pp. 29–60.

Gambel, E. L. (2006) *Basilea 2: da problema a opportunità aziendale. Come affrontare con successo i cambiamenti nel rapporto banca-impresa con il Gambel Rating* (Milan: Franco Angeli)

Gaudenzi, B. (2006) "Nuovi approcci di gestione dei rischi d'impresa: verso l'integrazione tra imprenditore e management," *Sinergie*, no. 71.

Gennaro, A. (2008) *Finanza condizionata e teoria del valore, vol. XIII, Governance e valore* (Rome: Aracne).

Ghosh, P., D. Mookherjee and D.Ray (1999) "Credit rationing in developing countries: an overview of the theory," in D. Mookherjee and D. Ray (eds) *Readings in the Theory of Economic Development* (London: Blackwell).

Giannola, A. (2002) *Il credito difficile* (Naples: L'Ancora del Mediterraneo).

Giannola, A. (2007) "Vigilanza prudenziale, consolidamento del sistema bancario e divari territoriali," *Svimez, Rivista Economica del Mezzogiorno*, vol. XXI, no. 2.

Giordano, L. and A. Lopes (2008) "Dimensione, localizzazione ed assetto giuridico nell'analisi dell'efficienza del sistema bancario italiano," *Quaderno n° 07/2008*, Dipartimento di Scienze Economiche, Matematiche e Statistiche, Università degli Studi di Foggia.

Giorgetti, G. (1998) "Relazionalità innovativa nei finanziamenti bancari alle imprese," *Il Risparmio*, vol. 46, no. 2, pp. 237–58.

Giovanni Paolo II (1991) *Lett. enc. Centesimus Annus*.

Godbillon-Camus, B. and C. J. Godlewski (2005) "Credit risk management in banks: Hard information, soft information and manipulation," working paper, LaRGE 02.

Golinelli, G. M. (1974) *L'impresa minore tra forme artigiane e istituzioni manageriale. Verso la formulazione di un modello di comportamento* (Milan: Giuffrè).

Golinelli, G. M. (1985) "Lo sviluppo dell'imprenditoria artigiana: condizionamenti di carattere finanziario e linee di intervento per il loro superamento," in *Studi in onore di Francesco Parrillo* (Milan: Giuffrè).

Golinelli, G. M. (1989) "Per una progettualità di ricerca sul ruolo dell'artigianato per lo sviluppo del Mezzogiorno," *Credito ed Artigianato*, no. 4.

Golinelli, G. M. (1992) "I problemi strategici nelle imprese minori," *Sinergie*, no. 27.

Golinelli, G. M. (2000a) *L'approccio sistemico al governo dell'impresa, La dinamica evolutiva del sistema impresa tra economia e finanza, Volume I* (Padova: CEDAM).

Golinelli, G. M. (2000b) *L'approccio sistemico al governo dell'impresa. La dinamica evolutiva del sistema impresa tra economia e finanza, Volume II* (Padova: CEDAM).

Golinelli, G. M. (2002) *L'approccio sistemico al governo dell'impresa. Valorizzazione delle capacità incorporate, rapporti intersistemici e rischio nel governo delle imprese* (Padova: CEDAM).

Golinelli, G. M. (2005) *L'approccio sistemico al governo dell'impresa. L'impresa Sistema Vitale, Volume I edizione* (Padova: CEDAM).

Golinelli, G. M. (2008) *L'approccio sistemico al governo dell'impresa. Verso la scientificazione dell'azione di governo, Volume II* (Padova: CEDAM).

Golinelli, G. M. (2009) 'L'approccio sistemico vitale: nuovi orizzonti di ricerca per il governo dell'impresa', *Sinergie rivista di studi e ricerche*, no. 79, pp. 11–24.

Golinelli, G. M. (2011) *L'approccio sistemico vitale (ASV) al governo dell'impresa*, vols. II, *Verso la scientificazione dell'azione di governo* (Padova: CEDAM).

Golinelli, G. M., M. Gatti and A. Siano (2002) *Approccio sistemico e teoria delle risorse: verso un momento di sintesi per l'interpretazione della dinamica dell'impresa*, in G.M. Golinelli (ed.) *L'approccio sistemico al governo dell'impresa. Valorizzazione delle capacità, rapporti intersistemici e rischio nell'azione di governo*, Volume III (Padova: CEDAM).

Golinelli, G. M., M. Trunfio and M. Liguori (2006) "Governo e marketing del territorio," *Sinergie, Rapporti di ricerca*, no. 23, pp. 17–44.

Golinelli, G. M., C. Gatti, L. Proietti and G. Vagnani (2012) *I rapporti tra sistema impresa e finanziario*, in Golinelli G. M., *L'approccio sistemico (ASV) al governo dell'impresa*, Vol. I, L'impresa sistema vitale (Padova: CEDAM).

Golinelli, G. M. and L. Volpe (2012) *Consonanza, valore, sostenibilità. Verso l'impresa sostenibile* (Padova: CEDAM).

Gorton, G. and A. Winton (2003) "Financial intermediation," in G. Harris, M. Stultz, and G. M. Constantinides (eds) *Handbooks in the Economics of Finance, Volume 1* (Amsterdam: Elsevier Science).

Grant, R. M. (1991) 'Porter's "Competitive advantage of nations": An Assessment', *Strategic Management Journal*, vol. 12, no. 7, pp. 535–48.

Grant, R. M. (1999) *L'analisi strategica per le decisioni aziendali* (Bologna: Il Mulino).

Grant, R. M. (2006) *L'analisi strategica per le decisioni aziendali* (Bologna: Il Mulino).

Grant, R. M. (2011) *L'analisi strategica per le decisioni aziendali* (Bologna: Il Mulino).

Grunert, J., L. Norden and M. Weber (2005) "The role of non-financial factors in internal credit Ratings," *Journal of Banking and Finance*, vol. 29, pp. 509–31.

Guatri, L. and M. Massari (1992) *La diffusione del valore* (Milan: Egea).

Gulati, R. (1998) "Alliances and networks," *Strategic Management Journal*, vol. 19, pp. 293–317.
Hakansson, H. and G. Ostberg (1975) "Industrial marketing: an organizational problem?," *Industrial Marketing Management*, vol. 4, no. 2/3.
Hanifan, L. J. (1916) "The rural school community center," *Annals of the American Academy of Political and Social Science*, vol. 67.
Hardie, I. and D. Howarth (2013) *Market-Based Banking and the International Financial Crisis* (Oxford: Oxford University Press).
Harrington, S. and G. Niehaus (1999) *Risk Management and Insurance* (McGraw-Hill).
Hart, O. D. and J. Moore (1998) "Cooperative vs. outside ownership," NBER papers, no. 6421.
Helfat, C. E. and M. B. Lieberman (2002) "The birth of capabilities: market entry and the importance of pre-history," *Industrial and Corporate Change*, vol. 11, no. 4.
Henderson, R. M. and K. B. Clark (1990) "Architectural innovation: the reconfiguration of existing product technologies and the failure of established firms," *Administrative Science Quarterly*, no. 35, pp. 9–30.
Hesse, H. and M. Čihák (2007) "Cooperative banks and financial stability," IMF Working Paper, 2 January.
Hinna, L. (2002) "Il bilancio sociale," *Il Sole 24 Ore*.
Hinna, L. (2005) "Come gestire la responsabilità sociale dell'impresa. Manuale pratico operativo. Processi, strumenti e modelli. La redazione del bilancio sociale," *Il Sole 24 Ore*.
Hofer, C.W. and D. Schendel (1978) *Strategy formulation: analytical concept, La formulazione della strategia aziendale* (Milan: Franco Angeli).
Hoff, K. and J. E. Stiglitz (1990) *Introduction: Imperfect information and rural credit markets - Puzzles and policy perspectives, IV* (World Bank Economic Review).
Hull, J. C. (2012) *Risk Management and Financial Institutions, Volume 733* (Wiley).
Iacopozzi, C. (2009) *L'applicazione di Basilea II in Italia. Aspetti tecnici ed elementi di riflessione* (Padova: CEDAM).
Iannuzzi, E. and M. Berardi (2008) "Le PMI distrettuali meridionali nel nuovo contesto relazionale con il sovrasistema finanziario," *Sinergie*, no. 77.
Im, S. and J. P. Workman Jr (2004) "Market orientation, creativity, and new product performance in high-technology firms," *Journal of Marketing*, vol. 68.
Istat (2009) "Classificazione delle attività economiche Ateco 2007," Metodi e Norme no. 40, volume integrale, http://www.istat.it/it/strumenti/definizioni-e-classificazioni/ateco-2007
Itami, H. (1988) *Le risorse invisibili* (Turin: Isedi).
Jens, G., N. Lars and M. Weber (2002) "The role of non-financial factors in internal credit ratings," *Journal of Banking and Finance*, vol. 29, pp. 509–31.
Jensen, M. C. and W. Meckling (1976) "Theory of the firm: managerial behavior, agency costs and ownership structure," *Journal of Financial Economics*, no. 3.
Jorion, P. (2007) *Value at risk: the new benchmark for managing financial risk, Volume 3* (New York: McGraw-Hill).
Keller, K. L., B. Busacca, and M. C. Ostillio (2005) *La gestione del brand. Strategie e sviluppo* (Milan: Egea).
Keller, K. L. and D. A. Aaker (1992) "The effects of sequential introduction of brand extensions," *Journal of Marketing Research*, February, vol. 29.

Kotler, P. (1966) *A design for the firm's marketing nerve center* (Business Horizons).

Kotler, P. (1997) *Marketing Management: Analysis, Planning, Implementation, and Control* (London: Prentice Hall International).

Laffont, J. and D. Martimort (2002) *The Theory of Incentives* (Princeton: Princeton University Press).

Lamanda, C. (1994) *La società per azioni bancaria* (Rome).

Lambin, J. (1994) *Le marketing stratégique* (Ediscience Internationale).

Lehmann, B. (2003) "Is it worth the while? The relevance of qualitative information in credit rating," working paper, University of Konstanz.

Lei, D., M. A. Hitt and R. Bettis (1996) "Dynamic core competences through meta-learning and strategic context," *Journal of Management*, vol. 22.

Lenssen, G., F. Perrini, A. Tencati and P. Lacy (2007) "Corporate governance," *The International Journal of Business in Society*, vol. 7, no. 4 (Guest editorial).

Leone, P. and C. Boido (2004) *Rischio di credito e credit derivatives. Modelli e strumenti* (CEDAM).

Lev, B. (2001) *Intangibles: Management, Measurement and Reporting* (Washington: Brooks Institution Press).

Levine, R. (2002) "Bank-based or market-based financial systems: which is better?," *Journal of Financial Intermediation*, no. 11, pp. 398–428.

Lewin, A. Y. and H. Volberda (1999) "Prolegomena on coevolution: A framework for research on strategy and new organizational forms', *Organization Science*, no.10.

Lewin, A. Y., C. P. Long and T. no. Carrol (1999) "The coevolution of new organizational forms," *Organization Science*, vol. 10, no. 5, September-October.

Lipparini, A. (2002) *La gestione strategica del Capitale Intellettuale e del capitale sociale* (Bologna: Il Mulino).

Lizza, P. (2005) *Il Capitale Intellettuale: profili di gestione e di valutazione* (Milan: Giuffrè Editore)

Lugaresi, S. and Z. Rotondi (2007) "Internazionalizzazione e finanziamento dei distretti industriali," *Economia Italiana*, 1.

Lusignani, G. (1996) *La gestione dei rischi finanziari nella banca* (Il Mulino).

Maggioni, V. and M. Del Giudice (2006) "Relazioni sistemiche tra imprenditorialità interna e gemmazione d'impresa: una ricerca empirica sulla natura cognitiva delle nuove imprese," *Sinergie*, no. 71.

Magnaghi, A. (2000) *Il progetto locale* (Turin: Bollati Boringhieri Editore).

Mainolfi, G. (2010) *Il modello della country reputation. Evidenze empiriche e implicazioni strategiche per le imprese del made in Italy nel mercato cinese* (Turin: Giappichelli).

Maltz, E., F. Thompson and D. J. Ringold (2011) "Assessing and maximizing corporate social initiatives: a strategic view of corporate social responsibility," *Journal of Public Affairs*, vol. 11, no. 4, pp. 344–52.

Manni, F. (1994) *Responsabilità sociale ed informazione esterna d'impresa. Problemi, esperienze e prospettive del bilancio sociale* (Turin: Giappichelli).

Manzelli, G. (2009) "Il nuovo accordo sul capitale (Basilea 2). Un inquadramento generale e talune proposte di modifica', *Rivista Bancaria – Minerva Bancaria*, no. 3.

March, J. C. (1991) "Exploration and exploitation in organizational learning," *Organization Science*, no. 2.

Marchello, M. P. and M. Michetti (2010) "La responsabilità sociale e la cooperazione bancaria," *Credito Popolare*, no. 1.
Marchi, L. and S. Marasca (2010) *Le risorse immateriali nell'economia delle aziende. Profili di misurazione e di comunicazione* (Bologna: Il Mulino).
Marris, R. (1964) *The economic theory of managerial capitalism* (New York: Free Press).
Marris, R. (1972) *La teoria economica del capitalismo manageriale* (Einaudi).
Marseglia, L. (2011) "Il mercato del credito: analisi e andamento dei finanziamenti alle Imprese. Rilevazioni Osservatorio Credito Confcommercio – Imprese per l'Italia in collaborazione con Format RdM," www.consorziocamerale.eu/writable/.../DOC_20111013162207.ppt.
Masciandaro, D. (1999) "La corporate governance nelle banche popolari' in F. Riolo, D. Masciandaro (eds) *Il governo delle banche in Italia, IV Rapporto della Fondazione Rosselli sul sistema finanziario italiano* (Rome: Bancaria Editrice).
Masera, R. (2001) "Il rischio e le banche," *Il Sole 24 Ore*.
Matacena, A. (1984) *Impresa e ambiente. Il bilancio sociale* (Bologna: Clueb).
Mcmillan, G. S. and M. P. Joshi (1997) "Sustainable competitive advantage and firm performance: the role of intangible resources," *Corporate Reputation Review*, vol. 1, nos. 1/2.
Metallo, G. and C. Gallucci (2011) "Un'analisi del "family effect" attraverso la reputazione della famiglia imprenditoriale: asset o liability per le imprese familiari?," paper presented at the XXIII Sinergie Annual Congress, November 10–11, IULM University, Milan.
Meznar, M. B., J.J. Chrisman, and A.B. Carroll (1993) "Responsabilità sociale e management strategico: verso una classificazione delle strategie d'impresa," *Problemi di gestione*, vol. XIX.
Michelini, L. (2011) *La competitività delle imprese nei settori in evoluzione. Un modello integrato per individuare le determinanti del vantaggio competitivo* (Milan: Franco Angeli).
Miglietta, A. (2007) "I meccanismi della corporate governante," *Sinergie*, nos. 73–74.
Milgrom, P. and J. Roberts (1994) *Economics, Organization and Management* (Bologna: Il Mulino).
Ministero dello Sviluppo Economico (2013) Small Business Act. Le iniziative a sostegno delle micro, piccole e medie imprese adottate in Italia nel 2012, Rapporto 2013, http://www.sviluppoeconomico.gov.it/images/stories/pubblicazioni/RapportoSBA2013-1.pdf
Mirrlees, J. (1971) "An exploration in the theory of optimal income taxation," *Review of Economic Studies*, no. 41.
Modina, M. (2012a), "Rating e struttura finanziaria delle imprese," in M. Modina, V. Formisano (eds) *Il rating tra impresa, banca e territorio, Volume 36* (Rapporti di Ricerca Sinergie).
Modina, M. (2012b) "Rating e gestione finanziaria delle imprese: implicazioni e opportunità," in M. Modina, G. Birindelli, C. Cattaneo, V. Formisano and B. Quattrociocchi (eds) *Il rating 2.0 per una nuova relazione tra impresa e banca* (Padova: CEDAM).
Modina, M. and F. Polese (2008) "The strategic role of local banks networks for quality standards of corporate banking services for SMEs," 11th Toulon-Verona Conference on Quality and Service Sciences, Florence, pp. 643–58.

Modina, M., A. Quintiliani, and M. Arnone (2013) "Il ruolo delle banche locali e del Relationship Lending in scenari economici in profondo cambiamento," *Arethuse Rivista di Studi Economico-Gestionali, Società Editrice Esculapio*, Bologna, vol. 2, no. 2, pp. 91–106.

Molteni, M. and M. Lucchini (2004) *I modelli di responsabilità sociale nelle imprese italiane* (Milan: Franco Angeli, Collana Unioncamere-Ufficio studi).

Moro, A. and M. Fink (2013) "Loan managers' trust and credit access for SMEs," *Journal of Banking and Finance*, vol. 37, pp. 927–36.

Murè, G. (1989) "Dimensioni e processi di crescita," "Fusioni e acquisizioni delle aziende di credito," Atti del Convegno di Modena, 13–14 April.

Myers, S. C. and N. Majluf (1984) "Corporate financing and investment decisions when firms have information that investors do not have," *Journal of Financial Economics*, vol. 13, pp. 187–221.

Norris, D. G. (1992) "Ingredient branding: a strategy option with multiple beneficiaries," *Journal of Consumer Marketing*, vol. 9.

OECD (1999) Principles of Corporate Governance.

Onado, M. (1992) *Economia dei sistemi finanziari* (Bologna: Il Mulino).

Onado, M. (1996) *La Banca come Impresa* (Bologna: Il Mulino).

Onesti, T. and D. Previati (2007) *Basilea 2 e la struttura patrimoniale delle imprese* (Franco Angeli).

Ongena, S. and D. Smith (1998) "Quality and duration of bank relationship' in D. F. Birsk (ed.) *Global Cash Management* (London: Europee).

Orlandi, M. (2012) *Il bilancio del capitale intellettuale: gestione, valutazione e misurazione* (Milan: Franco Angeli).

Panati, G. (1987) *Dal mercato al marketing*, Marketing e impresa (Padova: CEDAM).

Panetta, F. (2003) "Evoluzione del sistema bancario e finanziamento dell'economia nel Mezzogiorno," *Servizio Studi Banca d'Italia, Temi di discussion*, no. 467.

Panetta, F. and P. Angelini (2009) "Financial sector pro-cyclicality: lessons from the crisis," Occasional Paper 44, Bank of Italy, U. Albertazzi, F. Columba, W. Cornacchia, A. Di Cesare, A. Pilati, C. Salleo, G. Santini (eds), April.

Paniccia, P. (1999) *Il tempo nel governo dell'impresa. Tempo e conoscenza nell'economia delle imprese* (Turin: Giappichelli), pp. 17–277.

Paniccia, P. (2002) *Dinamiche temporali e cognitive nell'approccio sistemico al governo dell'impresa* (Padova: CEDAM).

Paniccia, P. (2004) "Co-evoluzione nel rapporto impresa-ambiente: il caso Olivetti," in R. Cafferata (ed.) *Casi di economia e gestione delle imprese* (Padova: CEDAM).

Peek, J. and E. S. Rosengren (1998) "Bank consolidation and small business lending: It is not just bank size that matters," *Journal of Banking and Finance*, vol. 22, issues 6–8, pp. 799–819.

Pepe, C. (2007) Prodotti del sud del mondo (Milan: Franco Angeli).

Peteraf, M. A. (1993) "The cornerstones of competitive advantage: a resource-based view," *Strategic Management Journal*, vol. 14.

Peters, T. J. and R. H. Waterman Jr (1982) *In Search of Excellence. Lessons from America's Best-Run Companies* (New York, NY: HarperCollins).

Petty, R. and J. Guthrie (2000a) "Intellectual capital literature review: measurement, reporting and management," *Journal of Intellectual Capital*, vol. 1, no. 2.

Petty, R. and J. Guthrie (2000b) "Knowledge management and the measurement of intangibles," *Management Today*.

Piazzo, D. (2006) *Il sistema dei confidi nell'accordo di Basilea* (Cacucci).

Pipitone, M. (2005) "La disciplina giuridica delle banche popolari e i modelli alternativi di banca' in R. De Bruyn and G. Ferri (eds) *Le banche popolari nel localismo dell'economia italiana* (Rome: Edicred).

Pipitone, M. (2008) *Gli statuti delle banche popolari* (Rome: Edicred).

Pittaluga, G. B., P. Morelli and E. Seghezza (2005) "Fondamenti teorici della corporate governance e comportamento delle Banche Popolari' in R. De Bruyn and G. Ferri (eds) *Le banche popolari nel localismo dell'economia italiana* (Rome: Edicred).

Polese, F., G. Russo and L. Carrubbo (2009) "The contribute of viable system approach in directing and managing inter-firm relationships," 2nd Euromed Conference of the Euromed Academy of Business.

Porta, A. (1997) "Assetti proprietari dell'impresa bancaria: un confronto tra i diversi modelli," *Cooperazione di credito*, no. 156–7, April-September.

Porter, M. (1985) *Competitive advantage: creating and sustaining superior performance* (New York: The Free Press).

Porter, M. (1987) "From competitive advantage to corporate strategy," *Harvard Business Review*, May/June 1987, pp. 43–59.

Porter, M. E. (2011) *Il vantaggio competitivo* (Collana Piccola Biblioteca Einaudi. Nuova Serie, Giulio Einaudi Editore).

Porter, M. E. and M. R. Kramer (2007) *Strategia e società. Il punto d'incontro tra il vantaggio competitivo e la corporate social responsibility, Harvard Business Review*, no. 1/2 (Italy).

Porter, M. E. and M. R. Kramer (2011) "The big idea: creating shared value," *Harvard Business Review*, vol. 89, pp. 1–17.

Prahalad, C. K. and G. Hamel (1990) "The core competence of the corporation," *Harvard Business Review*, no. 68.

Proietti, L. (2012) *Il rischio nel governo dell'impresa, tra senso, superamento ed elusione del limite*, in G. M. Golinelli (ed.) *L'approccio sistemico (ASV) al governo dell'impresa, Vol. I, L'impresa sistema vitale* (Padova: CEDAM).

Putman, R. D. (1993) *Making Democracy Work: Civic Traditions in Modern Italy* (Mondadori, Milan: Princeton University Press).

Rajan, R. G. and L. Zingales (2003) *Saving capitalism from the capitalists* (New York: Crown Business).

Ruozi, R. (1997) *Economia e gestione della banca* (Milan: Egea).

Ruozi, R. (1998) *Quale banca per il Sud. Un'analisi a livello regionale della domanda e dell'offerta di credito* (Giuffrè).

Ruozi, R. (2002) "Ancora sul rapporto fra banche e PMI: prospettive dei consorzi fidi," *Banche e Banchieri*, no. 5, pp. 432–9.

Ruozi, R. and C. Zara (2001) "Il rapporto tra banca e Pmi: caratteristiche strutturali e tendenze evolutive," *Contributi in Bancaria*, no. 10.

Rangan, K., L. A. Chase and S. Karim (2012) "Why every company needs a CSR strategy and how to build it," working paper, Harvard Business School, pp. 12–88.

Resti, A. (2001) "Misurare e gestire il rischio di credito nelle banche. Una guida metodologica," *Alpha Test*.

Resti, A. and A. Sironi (2008) Rischio e valore nelle banche. misura, regolamentazione, gestione (Milan: Egea).

Richardson, G. B. (1972) "The organization of industry," *The Economic Journal*, vol. 82.

Rindova, V. and C. J. Fombrun (1997) "Constructing competitive advantage: the role of firm-constituent interactions," *Strategic Management Journal*, vol. 20, no. 8.

Roberts, W. and G. R. Dowling (2002) "Corporate reputation and sustained superior financial performance," *Strategic Management Journal*, vol. 23.

Roncaglia, A. (2010) "The cultural origins of the crisis, PSL," vol. 63, no. 250, pp. 107–18.

Rotondi, Z. (2005) Banche, *finanziamento dello sviluppo e dell'innovazione e internazionalizzazione*, in *Decimo Rapporto SFI. Le banche Italiane e la finanza per lo sviluppo: territori, imprese e famiglie* (eds) G. Bracchi and D. Masciandaro (Edibank-Bancaria Editrice) pp. 75–100.

Rullani, E. (2003) "La conoscenza e le reti: gli orizzonti competitivi del caso italiano e una riflessione metodologica sull'economia di impresa," *Sinergie*, no. 61–2, pp. 147–87.

Rullani, E. (2004a) *Economia della conoscenza. Creatività e valore nel capitalismo delle reti* (Rome: Carocci).

Rullani, E. (2004b) *La fabbrica dell'immateriale. Produrre valore con la conoscenza* (Rome: Carocci).

Rumelt, R. (1987) "The competitive challenge' (Cambridge: Ballinger).

Russo, P. F. and P. Rossi (1999) "Costo e disponibilità del credito per le imprese nei distretti industriali' Banca d'Italia – Temi di Discussione.

Russo, P. F. and P. Rossi (2001) "Credit constraints in italian industrial districts," *Applied Economics*, vol. 33, no. 11.

Sabatini, G. (2010) during the presentation of the guide "Understanding the rating," an initiative conducted within the Permanent Observatory on bank-business relationships, *https://www.abi.it/DOC_Info/Comunicati-stampa/127297866253486_g__servizi_1.pdf*

Sapienza, P. (2002) "The effects of banking mergers on loan contracts," *Journal of Finance*, vol. 57, no. 1, pp. 329–67.

Sarcinelli, M. (2014) "Governare la banca tra modelli e realtà," *Moneta e Credito*, pp. 50–197.

Saunders, A., E. Strock and no. G. Travols (1990) "Ownership structure, deregulation, and bank risk taking," *Journal of Finance*, vol. 45, no. 2, pp. 643–54.

Sawyer, M. (2014) "Bank-based versus market-based financial systems: a critique of the dichotomy," Working papers, Financialisation, Economy, Society & Sustainable Development (FESSUD) Project, http://EconPapers.repec.org/RePEc:fes:wpaper:wpaper19.

Scanagatta, G. (1995) "Sviluppo e occupazione: il ruolo delle piccole e medie imprese," *Mondo bancario*, vol. 6, pp. 15–20.

Scandizzo, P. L. (1999) "Growth, trade and factor endowment: a survey," *Labour*, vol. XIII, no. 2, pp. 509–47.

Scandizzo, P. L. (2000) *Le Banche Locali. Progettazione, strategie e tecniche di analisi* (Milan: Giuffrè Editore).

Scannella, E. (2011) *La catena del valore dell'intermediazione creditizia nell'economia delle imprese bancarie. Profili di innovazione finanziaria, organizzativa e tecnologica* (Milan: Franco Angeli).
Schena, C. (2004) *Il ruolo prospettico dei Confidi nel rapporto banca-impresa: mitigazione del rischio e supporto informativo,* Università dell'Insubria, Facoltà di Economia (Varese: Quaderni).
Scheuer, F. (2013) "Adverse selection in credit markets and regressive profit taxation," *Journal of Economic Theory*, vol. 148, no. 4, 1333–60.
Schilling, M. A. (2009) *Gestione dell'innovazione* (Milan: McGraw-Hill).
Schumpeter, J. A. (1942) *Capitalism, socialism, and democracy* (New York: Harper & Row).
Sciarelli, S. (1996) "Etica aziendale e finalità imprenditoriali," *Economia & Management,* no. 6.
Sciarelli, S. (2007) *Etica e responsabilità sociale nell'impresa* (Milan: Giuffrè Editore).
Sciarelli, S. (2014) *La gestione dell'impresa. Tra teoria e pratica aziendale* (CEDAM).
Scott, J. A. (2000) *Relationships, access to credit and loan pricing: An analysis of small business experience* (Temple University, Mimeo).
Selzenick, P. (1957) *Leadership in Administration: a sociological interpretation* (New York: Harper & Row).
Shapiro, C. (1983) "Premiums for high quality products as returns to reputation," *Quarterly Journal of Economics*, vol. 98, pp. 659–79.
Shleifer, A. and R. Vishny (1997) "A survey of corporate governance," *Journal of Finance,* vol. 52, no. 2, pp. 737–83.
Siano, A. (2001) *Competenze e comunicazione del sistema d'impresa. Il vantaggio competitivo tra ambiguità e trasparenza* (Milan: Giuffrè).
Siano, A. (2008) "Conoscenza e risorse monetarie: analogie e principi di management convergenti," *Sinergie*, no. 76.
Siano, A., M. G. Confetto and G. Basile (2006) Il ciclo risorse-capacità-competenze nell'approccio sistemico vitale: dall'individuo all'organizzazione, in S. Barile (ed.) *L'impresa come sistema. Contributi sull'Approccio Sistemico Vitale (ASV)* (Turin: Giappichelli).
Siano, A., A. Vollero and M. G. Confetto (2011) 'Il processo di management della comunicazione d'impresa: tra comunicazione strategica e strategia di comunicazione' in *XXIII Sinergie annual Congress IULM University, Milan 10–11 November*, pp. 1–24.
Silvestri, G. and M. Pilati (2005) "La gestione strategica delle risorse umane: un nuovo patto tra direzione del personale e management," *Economia e Management*, no. 1, pp. 97–113.
Sironi, A. and M. Marsella (1998) (eds) *La misurazione e gestione del rischio di credito. Modelli, strumenti e politiche* (Bancaria Editrice).
Smith, D. C. (1992) "Brand extensions and advertising efficiency: what can and cannot be expected," *Journal of Advertising Research*, November/December.
Smullen, J. (2000) *Risk management for company executives* (Financial Times Management Pearson Education), 13ff.
Stiglitz, J. E. (1990) "Peer monitoring in credit markets," World Bank Economic Review, IV.
Stiglitz, J. and A. Weiss (1981) "Credit rationing in markets with imperfect information," *American Economic Review*, vol. 71, no. 3, pp. 393–410.

Stiglitz, J. and A. Weiss (1983) "Incentive effects of terminations: applications to the credit and labor markets," *American Economic Review*, vol. 73, no. 5, pp. 912–27.

Sullivan, M. W. (1992) "Brand extensions: when to use them," *Management Science*, Vol. 38, no. 6.

Sveiby, K. (1997) *The New Organizational Wealth* (San Francisco: Berrett-Koehler).

Tarocco, F. (2003) *Basilea 2: nuovi scenari del rapporto banca – impresa* (Giappichelli).

Tardivo, G. (2008) "L'evoluzione degli studi sul knowledge management," *Sinergie*, no. 76.

Tardivo, G., N. Miglietta, R. Schiesari and E. Battisti (2013) "Il sistema finanziario locale come fattore di competitività e sviluppo delle imprese. L'esperienza della Banca d'Alba," *Sinergie Referred Conference Proceeding*, pp. 177–92.

Thomas, L. C., D. B. Edelman and L. N. Crook (2002) "Credit scoring and tts applications," Society for Industrial and Applied Mathematics, Philadelphia.

Tirole, J. (2010) *The Theory of Corporate Finance* (Princeton University Press).

Treacy, W. F. and M. Carey (2000) "Credit risk rating systems at large us banks," *Journal of Banking & Finance*, special issue, vol. 24, nos. 1–2.

Tutino, F. (2005) *La performance delle banche* (Bancaria Editrice, Milan).

Tutino, F., G. Birindelli, and P. Ferretti (2011) *Basilea 3. Gli impatti sulle banche* (Egea).

Udell, G. F. (2008) "What's in a relationship? The case of commercial lending," *Business Horizons*, vol. 51, pp. 93–103.

Ughetto, E. (2007) *Industrial Districts and Financial Constraints to Innovation* (Mimeo).

Valentinov, V. (2004) "Toward a social capital theory of cooperative organization," *Journal of Cooperative Studies*, vol. 37, no. 3.

Vargas, A. and R. M. Vaca Acosta (2009) "Il ruolo della Pubblica Amministrazione spagnola nella promozione della responsabilità sociale d'impresa," *Sinergie*, 27, 80, pp. 45–61.

Velo, D. (2003) "La responsabilità dell'impresa nel mercato globale," *Sinergie*, 60.

Velo, D. (2009) "Etica ed impresa: una prospettiva storica dei rapporti tra Stato e mercato," *Sinergie*, 27, 80, pp. 95-108.

Vicari, S. (1992) "Risorse e funzionamento d'impresa," *Finanza Marketing e Produzione*, no. 3.

Vicari, S. (1998) *La creatività dell'impresa* (Milan: Etas Libri).

Vicari, S. (2008) "Conoscenza e impresa," *Sinergie*, no. 76, pp. 43–66.

Vicari, S., P. Cillo and G. Verona (2005) "Capacità creativa e innovazione," *Sinergie*, no. 67.

Volberda, H. W. and A.Y. Lewin (2003) "Co-evolutionary dynamics within and between firms: From evolution to co-evolution," *Journal of Management Studies*, vol. 40, no. 8, pp. 2111–36.

Williamson, O. E. (1964) *The economics of discretionary behavior: magerial objectives in a theory of the firm* (Upper Saddle River, NJ: Prentice Hall).

Williamson, O. E. (1988) "Corporate finance and corporate governance," *The Journal of Finance*, vol. 43, no. 3.

Yang, X. and L. Casali (2009) "In search of the missing link: an analysis of government influence in CSR," *Sinergie*, no. 27, pp. 31–44.

Zappa, G. (1956) *Le produzioni nell'economia delle imprese* (Giuffrè).

Zattoni, A. (2006) *Assetti proprietari e corporate governance* (Milan: Egea).
Zazzaro, A. (1997) "Regional banking system, credit allocation and regional economic development," *Economie Appliquée*, vol. 50, no. 1.
Zazzaro, A. (1998) "L'articolazione territoriale del sistema bancario: aspetti teorici e alcune evidenze empiriche per la Campania," *Moneta e Credito,* vol. 51, p. 203.
Zazzaro, A. (2004) "Assetti proprietari delle banche e attività economica: possiamo affidarci a Coase?," *Analisi Giuridica dell'Economia*, vol. 3, no. 1, pp. 11–30.
Zoppini, A. (2006) "Incontro con il prof. Henry Hansman su "La proprietà dell'impresa cooperativa," Centro Studi LEGACOOP, Rome.

Index

Printed and bound by CPI Group (UK) Ltd, Croydon, CR0 4YY